PLATO
Theaetetus and *Sophist*

CAMBRIDGE TEXTS IN THE
HISTORY OF PHILOSOPHY

Series Editors

KARL AMERIKS
Professor of Philosophy, University of Notre Dame

DESMOND M. CLARKE
Emeritus Professor of Philosophy, University College Cork

The main objective of Cambridge Texts in the History of Philosophy is to expand the range, variety, and quality of texts in the history of philosophy which are available in English. The series includes texts by familiar names (such as Descartes and Kant) and also by less well-known authors. Wherever possible, texts are published in complete and unabridged form, and translations are specially commissioned for the series. Each volume contains a critical introduction together with a guide to further reading and any necessary glossaries and textual apparatus. The volumes are designed for student use at undergraduate and postgraduate level, and will be of interest not only to students of philosophy but also to a wider audience of readers in the history of science, the history of theology, and the history of ideas.

For a list of titles published in the series, please see end of book.

PLATO

Theaetetus *and* Sophist

EDITED BY
CHRISTOPHER ROWE
University of Durham

CAMBRIDGE
UNIVERSITY PRESS

CAMBRIDGE
UNIVERSITY PRESS

University Printing House, Cambridge CB2 8BS, United Kingdom

Cambridge University Press is part of the University of Cambridge.

It furthers the University's mission by disseminating knowledge in the pursuit of education, learning and research at the highest international levels of excellence.

www.cambridge.org
Information on this title: www.cambridge.org/9781107697027

© Christopher Rowe 2015

First published 2015

Printed in the United Kingdom by Clays, St Ives plc

A catalogue record for this publication is available from the British Library

Library of Congress Cataloging-in-Publication Data
Plato.
[Dialogues. Selections. English]
Theaetetus and Sophist / Plato ; edited and translated by Christopher Rowe.
pages cm. – (Cambridge texts in the history of philosophy)
Includes bibliographical references and index.
ISBN 978-1-107-01483-1 (Hardback) – ISBN 978-1-107-69702-7 (Paperback)
1. Plato. Theaetetus. 2. Plato. Sophist. I. Rowe, C. J. II. Plato. Theaetetus. English.
III. Plato. Sophist. English. IV. Title.
B358.R69 2015
184–dc23 2015020180

ISBN 978-1-107-01483-1 Hardback
ISBN 978-1-107-69702-7 Paperback

Contents

Acknowledgements

My thanks, first, to Hilary Gaskin, for her willingness to wait another whole year for a volume that was originally promised for delivery in December 2013, and for keeping me as firmly as she could within the limits imposed by the general design and intentions of the series. The series editor, Desmond Clarke, provided useful comments on the style of two early drafts. Debra Nails, Frisbee Sheffield, Verity Harte, and in the later stages Matt Duncombe gave help of various kinds. But Terry Penner and Heather Rowe were the true midwives for a project the first origins of which, in retrospect, can be traced back to Cambridge in the 1960s, and the lectures of J. R. Bambrough and A. L. Peck.

Introduction

The *Theaetetus* and the *Sophist* are two of the Platonic dialogues most widely read by philosophers, and they have been read in a variety of different ways, in antiquity as much as in the modern period, and during the centuries in between. Modern discussions of the two dialogues tend to concentrate on specific passages and problems, not always with sufficient attention to the contexts within which those passages and problems occur. The present introduction is constructed on the basis of the evident fact that the two dialogues are written as wholes, and also as a *single* whole, or part of one (see Section 1), and therefore deserve to be read as such. The purpose of the following pages is to help readers find their way through the arguments of the two dialogues from end to end, offering a preliminary way[1] past at least some of the many obstacles – whether problems isolated, or indeed constructed, by modern critics, or other problems of a more mundane sort – that may serve to obstruct an attempt at a continuous reading of two admittedly complex works.

1 A trilogy (or a quartet?)

The *Theaetetus* and *Sophist* form part of a single Platonic project. This is formally signalled by the fact that the end of the *Theaetetus* looks forward

---

[1] There exists a vast body of secondary literature on the *Theaetetus* and the *Sophist*, and the interpretation of both dialogues is controversial. What follows tends to favour one particular interpretation (namely the translator's), for which in the short space available only the outlines of a justification can be given.

to the beginning of the *Sophist*, and the latter correspondingly looks back to the former, the two dialogues supposedly being the record[2] of conversations taking place on successive days with two main characters, Socrates and Theodorus, present throughout. In fact, the project extends beyond these two to a third, *Statesman*, and *Sophist* can be taken as promising a fourth, *Philosopher*, although if Plato ever genuinely planned a quartet, he did not complete it.

What is this project about? *Theaetetus*, *Sophist*, and *Statesman* may each broadly be described as concerned with 'giving an account' of something (whatever an 'account' may turn out to be): of what knowledge is, of what a 'sophist' is, and of what it is to be a statesman. If *Philosopher* had been written, it would, presumably, have done the same for the philosopher. All of these four things, namely knowledge (*epistêmê*, sometimes interchangeable with 'wisdom', *sophia*), the sophist, the statesman (or 'political expert', *politikos*), and the philosopher, are intimately bound up with each other. The philosopher, according to his very name (*philo-sophos*), is a seeker after the wisdom or knowledge that the 'sophist', by virtue of *his* name,[3] appears as claiming already to possess; and the 'statesman' or political expert, for his part, will surely need the same thing – wisdom or knowledge, as Socrates in Plato's *Republic* argues passionately and at great length.

So what exactly is it to be wise, to possess knowledge? Or is there even such a thing as knowledge in the first place? The first main part of the *Theaetetus*, occupying not far short of two-thirds of the whole, is largely devoted to the refutation of an account of knowledge that would make truth relative and leave no room for philosophy, reserving any available space exclusively for one sort of expert: one who happens to label himself a sophist (Protagoras, allegedly the author-in-chief of the account in question). On this account of knowledge, there will be no such thing as falsehood; and this is a topic to which *Sophist* then ultimately returns, as a condition of establishing its final conclusion, namely that sophistry as properly understood deals in just this – falsehood. But the protagonists of the *Sophist* have to work hard to reach that conclusion; as hard, indeed, as the protagonists of the *Theaetetus*

---

[2] *Theaetetus* is actually set up in its opening two pages as something recorded and written down as a book by the Socratic Euclides of Megara; nothing is said about the authorship of its sequel.

[3] *Sophistês*: practitioner or purveyor of *sophia*, depending on one's point of view.

have to work for whatever results *they* achieve, and the issues that the actors in both dialogues have to deal with extend far beyond those of truth and falsehood: for example, to the question about what is to count as real, or as Plato puts it, what is to count among *ta onta*, 'the things that are'.

In the process, they engage in conversation not only with each other, but with most of Socrates' and Plato's best-known philosophical predecessors, and probably also, more covertly, with some of Plato's contemporaries. What has emerged by the end of the *Sophist* is, in effect, a reasoned defence of a particular way of looking at the world (the broadest features of which will be sketched in the following two paragraphs), which we may reasonably take to be that of Plato and his Socrates: a defence that treats their opponents entirely seriously, is sometimes prepared to reach compromises with them, and takes very little for granted. For example, if the *Sophist* treats 'sophist' as a disputed term, Socrates makes clear that 'philosopher' is so too (216d[4]), and, most remarkably, the dialogue goes on not only to suggest some similarities – however misleading these may be – between the sophist and Socrates himself, but to take issue with what looks like one extreme reading of Plato's own position, attributed to the 'friends' or supporters 'of the forms' (see Section 2).

In the third part of the trilogy, *Statesman*, there is a rather more assertive tone, less openness to the views of others. The idea that statesmanship, properly understood, might be anything other than knowledge-based is given hardly any space at all. What dominates is the portrait of an impracticable, perfect statesmanship, and the roughest of sketches of a slightly more practicable ideal constitution, by comparison with which all existing constitutions are openly declared 'states of faction' (*stasiôteiai*) rather than constitutions (*politeiai*), while all actual statesmen are called 'the greatest imitators and magicians [and] the greatest sophists among sophists' (*Statesman* 303c). In a way, then, it does no great harm to take the *Theaetetus* and the *Sophist* in isolation from the *Statesman*, as the present volume does, insofar as the latter is already putting to use results obtained in the former two, and is less

---

[4] For this form of reference to Plato's text, see Note on text and translation.

fundamental than they are (unless, that is, for political theory, or for the philosophy of law).

Separating *Theaetetus* and *Sophist* from *Statesman*, however, does have the unfortunate consequence of obscuring one of the central purposes of the whole project: namely to show us the way to living a better life. The *Statesman* offers the Platonic alternative to the Protagorean vision of human life and organization criticized in the *Theaetetus*. 'Whatever sorts of things seem to each city to be just and fine,' Protagoras says, as reconstructed by Socrates (*Theaetetus* 167c), 'these I claim are so for that city, for so long as it thinks them so.' He may also claim to be able to make cities, and individuals, think sounder or healthier thoughts (whatever 'sounder' and 'healthier' might be), but his basic position is that he will work in and with individuals and institutions as they are. There could scarcely be a starker contrast with the *Statesman*, which suggests nothing less than starting all over again from scratch, under the guidance of reason and philosophy.

2 *Theaetetus*, *Sophist* and *Republic* (1): 'forms' and 'kinds'

'Forms' – in Greek, *eidê* (*eidos* in the singular), or *ideai* – play a central role not only in *Republic*, but in other works that were apparently written prior to *Theaetetus* and *Sophist*: *Symposium*, *Phaedo*, *Phaedrus*. 'Forms' are entities such as 'the equal itself', 'justice itself', 'beauty itself', or 'the good itself', which are offered in these dialogues as the real referents of the terms 'equal', 'just', 'beautiful', or 'good', or whichever it may be. According to many modern interpreters, such entities are notably absent from the *Theaetetus* and *Sophist*, being introduced in the *Sophist* only in the context of a discussion of extreme views of how to understand reality, which include the view held by the 'friends of the forms' (246b–252a), and – such interpreters claim – not at all in the *Theaetetus*. If this were true, it would represent a significant volte-face. The 'form [*eidos*] of the good' plays a particularly prominent role in the *Republic*: Socrates there trumpets it as the most important of all the objects a philosopher seeks to know; it is 'even beyond being, superior to it in dignity and in power' (*Republic* VI, 509b), the very key to understanding how we should run our societies and our lives. If this latter topic is as important for *Theaetetus* and *Sophist* as Section 1 has suggested, then we might well expect to find this 'form', 'the good itself', playing the same role in them as in the *Republic*. But according to what is probably now the standard modern interpretation, at least in the Anglophone world, there is hardly a whisper of it in either work. How could this be? Has Plato perhaps undergone a change of mind, so that he no longer believes in the sorts of things he previously had his Socrates announce with such evident passion?

The answer is surely no. 'Forms' are central to *Theaetetus* and *Sophist*. At any rate, both dialogues, and particularly the latter, are full of talk about things called *eidê* (or by whatever term may be used interchangeably with *eidê*),[5] and we are given plenty of reason for supposing that the reference is to exactly the same sort of entities in *Theaetetus* and *Sophist* as it was in *Republic*, or *Phaedo*, or *Phaedrus*. There is, first, that single acknowledged reference to 'forms' in the *Sophist*, in the shape of a criticism of the 'friends of the forms' for proposing to say that their forms are the only things that are (246a–248a), and to treat everything else as perpetually in a process of coming-into-being, never being. These forms of theirs, like the forms Socrates talked about in the *Republic*, are intelligible and bodiless, and 'remain forever exactly as they are'. But there is no indication that *eidê* as they appear in the *Sophist* outside this passage, or indeed in the *Theaetetus*, are to be treated any differently. Again, *Theaetetus* can describe its task as understanding 'what the thing, knowledge, might be in itself' (146e), and 'the thing, knowledge, in itself' sounds not unlike the sort of description usually attaching to 'forms'; it would be an odd way of beginning a discussion that was designed to do away with them.

Those who suppose forms to be absent from the two dialogues tend to translate *eidos* and related terms (like *genos*) not as 'form', but (e.g.) as 'kind', and treat them as referring to something like classes and sub-classes, or Aristotelian genera and species. There are what may look like strong grounds for such an interpretation, especially in the way the *Sophist* approaches its topic: that is, by repeatedly taking an overarching 'kind' (i.e., *genos*, or *eidos*), and dividing it up into sub-'kinds'; or in the way the argument typically progresses by reference to things in the ordinary world, no matter, apparently, whether these are 'kinds' or individuals. But none of this by itself indicates an interest in an analysis into classes, or sets, or anything of the sort. Relationships between

---

[5] See Note on text and translation.

'kinds', and between 'kinds' and particulars, are typically represented as a matter of 'sharing in', which is the same metaphor that *Republic*, *Phaedo* and other dialogues use for the relationship between particulars and forms, and which Socrates in the *Phaedo* treats as interchangeable with either the 'presence' of the form in the particular, or the particular's 'associating with' the form (*Phaedo* 100d, with 101c). The *genê* and *eidê* being talked about in *Sophist* and *Theaetetus* are *somethings*, entities in themselves – 'forms', which can be shared in by or be present in other *genê* or *eidê*, and especially by and in individuals in space and time, but in themselves are still 'somehow graspable by the mind and without body', and 'remain forever exactly as they are' (i.e., neither do they change, nor do they perish with the particulars that 'share in' them: cf. *Phaedo* 103a).

Theaetetus and *Sophist* represent not a change of mind on Plato's part, but a change of emphasis. The stress in *Republic* and *Phaedo* is on the difference it makes to focus on things in themselves (forms), as the philosopher does, rather than on the ordinary world as it appears to perception, even while both these dialogues acknowledge that it is the ordinary perceptible world from which even the philosopher has to begin. How, after all, would we ever be motivated to think about anything in the first place *except* by the things around us? The 'theory of recollection', advanced in *Phaedo* and elsewhere, provides a mechanism whereby the process can start: we begin to see things *as* beautiful or ugly, equal or unequal, thanks to the awakening of knowledge acquired before birth. The two new dialogues, but especially *Sophist*, focus more on forms as 'shared in' by, or 'present' in, particulars, and on the 'associations', or 'mixing', between forms, both in themselves and in their involvement with particulars. The perspective of *Republic* and *Phaedo* still surfaces, as in the following passage from the *Theaetetus* (part of a purple 'digression' comparing the ideal philosopher – the 'leader of the philosophical chorus' – with the lawyer in court):

> only [the philosopher's] body is truly located in the city and resides in it, because his mind, having concluded that all [the things that concern others] are worth little or nothing, rejects them and flies off in all directions ... using every sinew to search out every nature among the things that are, taking each thing as a whole, not lowering itself to any of the things close by.
>
> (173e–174a)

But the whole context of the passage strongly suggests that this Socrates of Plato's, who is giving this description, does not regard himself as such a 'leader of philosophy'. He may be involved in 'searching out every nature[6] among the things that are, taking each as a whole', rather than concerning himself with particulars, 'things close by'. But if he is the same old familiar, Platonic Socrates, he is firmly located in the city, both body *and* soul. Indeed, according to his defence in the *Apology*, his philosophical questioning is chiefly for the city's sake; and in the *Theaetetus* itself he begins by announcing his fondness for his fellow-citizens (143d). Perhaps the visitor from Elea – who takes over the role of main speaker in *Sophist* and *Statesman* – is different (away from his city, and not even given a name). But if so, he has come down from the clouds for the occasion, since he quite evidently shares Socrates' interest in the practical outcomes of his discussions.

3 *Theaetetus*, *Sophist* and *Republic* (2): knowledge and its objects

Real knowledge, for Plato, is only of 'forms'. What this amounts to is the claim, first, that we only know a thing when we know what it is, in and by itself, and second, that there *is* such a thing (whatever it may be: goodness, justice, fire . . .) in itself, apart from anything that shares in it. The first of these two claims is made by Plato's Socrates in the course of a long argument (with the 'lovers of sights and sounds', a.k.a. ordinary people) in *Republic* v, 474b–480a; forms as such are probably only introduced later in the dialogue. The second claim is made by Timaeus, presumably on Plato's behalf, in *Timaeus* 51d (to paraphrase: 'I cast my vote for saying that if intellect [= knowledge], and true belief are two separate kinds of things, then there are things, forms, that are imperceptible to the senses and graspable only by intellect').

But this only tells us what knowledge is of, not what knowledge is – that is, it does not tell us what it actually is to *know* something as opposed to having some other sort of cognitive relationship to it. Socrates' discussion with Theaetetus in the *Theaetetus* actually begins with Socrates rebuking his younger interlocutor for suggesting that he can say what knowledge is by giving a list of its objects. It would, then, be strange if it

---

[6] For this use of 'nature', see Note on text and translation.

turned out that giving an account of real knowledge, which is what they are trying to understand, amounted, after all, to no more than specifying its objects. In any case, if the only things we can (really) know are things that are beyond the reach of the senses, only accessible to the mind, it becomes more, not less, urgent for Plato to say how such access is to be gained. Answering that question ought, surely, to be the absolute and first priority for someone so evidently committed, as is his Socrates, to the importance of discovering the truth about things.

Some of the dialogues may suggest that knowing forms involves a sort of direct contact, a mental variety of seeing or touching. But if forms themselves are outside time and space, that appears to make real knowledge less rather than more accessible: something to be hoped for in an after-life, or dreamed of as some kind of out-of-body experience in this life (as perhaps in the passage cited from the *Theaetetus* in Section 2), but in fact out of our reach while we are alive and apparently most in need of it. Given the practical nature of much of Plato's concern, as illustrated by dialogues like *Republic* and *Statesman*, it would seem extraordinary if he had left matters there. The trilogy *Theaetetus-Sophist-Statesman* may be seen as part of his attempt to fill that crucial gap, and say how it may be possible to acquire knowledge of the most important subjects.

True, *Theaetetus* appears to end in impasse. The argument has shown that knowledge cannot be perception, and neither can it be true belief; and then the third candidate, true belief with an account, is also found wanting. But as Section 1 has indicated, the discussion does not end with the *Theaetetus*. If the *Theaetetus* is taken on its own, then no conclusion about knowledge is reached. But *Sophist* does reach conclusions, not only about the sophist, but about how to understand false belief, and the *Statesman*, too, successfully concludes its treatment of the statesman. Nor are these conclusions subject to any sort of explicit qualification. We are thus left with a situation in which the attempt to say directly what knowledge is apparently runs into the sand, but two attempts to say directly what *other* things are – that is, in *Sophist* and *Statesman* respectively – appear to succeed splendidly.

This contrast between the apparent failure of *Theaetetus* and the success of *Sophist* and *Statesman* may be explained in different ways. Perhaps it is just that knowledge is a more difficult subject to take on. That is certainly true, at least to go by the continuing inability of philosophers over twenty-four centuries to agree on what it is. (The last

account proposed and seemingly rejected in *Theaetetus*, true belief plus
'an account', looks strikingly like a strong modern candidate, justified
true belief; but we should not be too quick to assume that Plato would
have thought of 'justification', or of truth, or of belief, in the sorts of
ways that we do.) Perhaps the switch of main speakers, from Socrates
in *Theaetetus* to the anonymous Eleatic in *Sophist* and *Statesman*, has
something to do with the matter. But the fact remains that both the two
latter dialogues reach results that at least appear to claim to add something to our understanding – our knowledge – of the way things are.
Neither dialogue tells us what the thing, knowledge, actually is; but quite
evidently the failure to answer that question has no tendency to suggest
to anyone involved that they should stop inquiring into anything else
until that first question is answered.

What *Sophist* offers us, like *Statesman* after it, is a demonstration of
how we can progress towards knowledge. And what makes that progress
possible is, as it must inevitably be, the gradual construction of an
account of the thing being investigated – not an account belonging
to any of the three varieties of 'account' considered and rejected in
the *Theaetetus*, but one of an altogether more interesting and sophisticated sort (on which, see Section 7 below). In which case, it seems,
that last account of knowledge from the *Theaetetus* lives on. Socrates
may behave at the end of the dialogue as if he and Theaetetus have
managed to kill it off. But that, it turns out, is not the case. To go by
the evidence of the *Sophist* and its sequel, knowing what a thing is will
after all include giving an account – a very particular sort of account – of
that thing.

4 *Theaetetus*, *Sophist* and *Republic* (3): knowledge and belief

But what of the other elements of that last account, 'true' and 'belief'?
Truth, presumably, must be included along with the account; knowledge
could hardly involve any old account, however sophisticated, regardless
of its truth. 'Belief', however, may be more problematic (as it may be to
know how it can be true). Knowledge, in Plato, is frequently treated as
a state of mind that *contrasts* with belief. From this perspective, belief
may precede knowledge, but will be a cognitive state distinct from
knowledge; it becomes, turns into, knowledge – as the *Meno* puts it,
by being 'bound down by the working out of the reason' (*Meno* 98a).

It has often been held, and is still held by many, that Plato thought belief, like knowledge, had its own special objects. (The term here is *doxa*, often also translated as 'opinion', sometimes as 'judgement': see Note on text and translation.) More specifically, Plato is held to have thought that knowledge is exclusively of forms, belief exclusively of particulars, so that just as there is no knowledge, or real knowledge, of particulars, so there are no beliefs about forms. The chief justification for this interpretation is purportedly discovered in those passages from the *Republic* and the *Timaeus* referred to at the beginning of Section 3 above (*Republic* V, 474b–480a; *Timaeus* 51d), particularly in the first, which includes the plain statement – agreed to by both Socrates and his interlocutor – that, subject to certain conditions, it is impossible to know and believe the same things (478a–b).

This looks, on the face of it, like an open-and-shut case. Or, more strictly, it would look like that if it were not for (a) the fact that Socrates will go on in Book VI of the *Republic* to describe his own beliefs (*doxai*) about the form of the good, (b) the fact that in Plato generally belief can be about anything (as the *Theaetetus* confirms), and (c) the conditions attached to the statement in question,[7] one or more of which will hold, if at all, only in the particular context in which the statement at issue is being made – that is, one in which Socrates is trying to persuade non-philosophers that their grasp of beauty is a matter of belief (merely), not of knowledge. In short, the passage does not show what it is supposed to show, and neither does its counterpart in the *Timaeus*. The real upshot of the *Republic* passage is not that knowledge and belief have distinct sets of objects, 'forms', and particulars respectively, but rather that knowledge of anything is not to be got from particulars, only from recognizing and investigating things in themselves; and that particulars can give us no more than beliefs about those things. The *Timaeus* passage, for its part, confirms what is implied but not shown by the *Republic* argument, namely that 'forms' are what make knowledge possible, while adding the new information that particulars can give us *true* belief; not only that, Timaeus tells us, but everyone has a share in it. (Thus everyone,

---

[7] 'It's impossible,' [Glaucon] said, 'given what we've agreed; if it's true (1) that different capacities are naturally for different things, (2) that both of the two things in question, belief and knowledge, are capacities, and (3) that they're different capacities, it follows that there's no room for what's known to be the same as what's believed.'

it seems, will have access of some sort to truth: presumably in virtue of their access to particulars, and because these latter 'share in' what things are 'in themselves'; even ordinary, non-philosophical people must have some basic ability to generalize across particular cases. None of this is incompatible with the *Republic* passage, though to have made it explicit there would have got seriously in the way of the argument being made in that particular context, namely that the 'lovers of sights and sounds' – who turn out to be people in general – have *mere* belief, not knowledge.)

Given this reading of *Republic* and *Timaeus*,[8] they constitute no reason for excluding belief from figuring in Plato's account of knowledge, in *Theaetetus*, *Sophist*, or anywhere else. This is a matter of some importance. If we had reasons, independently of these latter two dialogues, for excluding belief from the account of knowledge, then the second and third accounts proposed in *Theaetetus* – true belief, then true belief plus an account – would have to be regarded as doomed from the start, like the first (knowledge = perception): no-hopers, not more or less plausible candidates that come to be rejected in the face of the specific arguments Socrates and Theaetetus raise against them. If, on the other hand, there is no such external reason preventing us from supposing that belief and knowledge can coexist, as it were, then both the second and the third of the proposed accounts may be taken at face value – that is, as serious answers to the problem of knowledge – even if one or both turn out to be judged unsatisfactory, and one of them almost immediately (most of the discussion of true belief actually being taken up with the problem of *false* belief). With the first of these two alternatives, the whole 'inquiry' into knowledge was always a set-up, its intentions ultimately negative (as is surely the case with knowledge = perception); with the second, it is more like a genuine inquiry, undertaken with positive intent, albeit an inquiry whose eventual outcomes will presumably be known in advance to the author, if not to the participants.

Which of the two alternatives is correct cannot finally be settled here. It should be noticed, however, that belief, *doxa*, is introduced into the argument of the *Theaetetus* well before the second and third accounts of

---

[8] Which will be particularly controversial. Many interpreters have had, and still have, a great deal invested in the idea that Plato posits distinct and exclusive sets of objects for knowledge and belief. But there is a clear case for abandoning the idea; and *Theaetetus* and *Sophist* themselves strengthen that case.

knowledge, and in a way that makes it a central and apparently even indispensable aspect of knowing. The relevant part of the argument, completing the refutation of the first account of knowledge (knowledge = perception), is summed up in the following exchange:

> SOCRATES:... our aim in starting this conversation wasn't at all to find out what knowledge was not; it was to find out what it is. Still, at least we have advanced far enough to know not to look for it in perception at all, but rather under whatever name we're to use to describe the soul when it's occupied with the things that are, itself by itself.
>
> THEAETETUS: Yes, and the name we give it, I think, Socrates, is forming and having beliefs.
>
> SOCRATES: Yes, my friend, you think correctly.
>
> (*Theaetetus* 187a)

'Forming and having beliefs' translates the single Greek word *doxazein*, the verb corresponding to *doxa*. Thus Socrates appears perfectly content, here in the *Theaetetus*, to put thinking in general under the heading of *doxa*; and not only that, the kind of thinking – by the soul on its own – that has just been treated as a requirement of attaining being, truth, and knowledge. Perception, it has been established, cannot aspire to this, reduced as it has been to bare, unthinking sensation. Perception grasps white now, or hot now, but not whiteness or heat, and certainly not the being of either (that they are, or what they are); neither, then, can it grasp the truth of anything, or *know* anything at all. By contrast, *doxa* – whether we render this as 'belief', 'opinion', or 'judgement', or just 'thinking', or 'calculation'[9] – can do all of these things. And having failed with perception, Theaetetus will now duly offer 'true belief' as his next candidate (as he says, knowledge cannot be any and every belief, given that there can be false beliefs). Plainly, far from there being a contrast between belief and knowledge in this context, believing is, here in the *Theaetetus* at least, a part of knowing. And this is significant, because there is nothing *here* that would be affected by the failure of either the next candidate for the title of knowledge, true belief, nor the last, true belief plus an account; whatever knowledge may be, we cannot access it without thought, or calculation, or 'belief'.

---

[9] 'Forming and having beliefs', above, as a translation of *doxazein*, is an attempt at a compromise between these alternatives, while maintaining 'belief' as the standard rendering of *doxa*. See Note on text and translation.

But then the question can be raised again: is it so certain that this last candidate fails? If we consider *Theaetetus* in isolation, perhaps it does fail, though with the proviso that the failure may only be for want of a serviceable model of 'account' (not because of its reference to belief), and another model might have saved it. On the other hand, if we consider *Theaetetus* along with *Sophist*, as the evidence suggests that we should, then Plato will be admitting that the list of ways of 'giving an account' that Socrates and Theaetetus considered actually *was* incomplete, and he will be opening the way for us to suppose that the search for knowledge has made real progress – enough progress, indeed, for the discussion to move on from a theoretical discussion of knowledge to a practical demonstration, in the shape of the treatment of the sophist, of what it might be like to add to our store of it.

5 'Dialectic'

Theaetetus and *Sophist* are both written illustrations of 'dialectic',[10] philosophical conversation. Dialectic proceeds mainly by way of question and answer, founded – at least ideally – on collaboration between the interlocutors; and written 'dialectic', written 'dialogues', reproduce the same collaborative process. Or, more strictly, they *pretend* to reproduce it (pretend quite literally, in the case of the *Theaetetus*, through the fiction of Euclides' authorship). Any actual conversation, even involving philosophers, is clearly capable of being unpredictable, uneven, shapeless, and unproductive – features that are of more interest to novelists than to a philosophical author, or at any rate one like Plato. Plato's dialogues may take unexpected turns; they may vary enormously in style and tone; and they may even appear to be unproductive. But shapeless they are not. They are, rather, products of the most careful design.

An important part of that design is that the author, Plato, should be as little visible as possible. Strictly speaking, he is not there at all. He never appears, and is referred to only twice (once, in the *Phaedo*, as absent). Maybe, then, we should leave him out of the equation, and just let the dialogues speak for themselves. This is how some literary interpreters of Plato in fact do operate, as in a way do those philosophical interpreters

---

[10] In Greek, *dialektikē* (*sc. technē*): 'the art of conversation'.

who content themselves with analysing and commenting on the arguments without too much reference to their context within a particular dialogue or within the corpus as a whole. But Plato's dialogues are not just imagined, isolated snatches of conversation between Socrates (or whoever it may be) and various interlocutors, like Xenophon's *Memoirs of Socrates* – vignettes of the great man bundled together with a minimum of organization. Each of Plato's dialogues belongs to a larger whole, whether this is constituted by a particular cluster or sequence of dialogues, as with *Theaetetus* and *Sophist*, or by Plato's works in general, or by both. The first type of case, which is relatively rare, will have been illustrated well enough by preceding sections of this Introduction. As for the second, here, too, the interconnections between the various and supposedly self-standing parts of the whole are so obvious that no interpretation of any individual part – that is, of any individual dialogue in the corpus – can usefully ignore them; although the fact that neither the connections themselves nor their implications are usually spelled out explicitly makes understanding them difficult and controversial, and is indeed the chief reason why there has always been, and no doubt always will be, so little agreement among even the most informed readers of Plato as to what exactly he stands for.

At the macroscopic level, then, there is shape to Plato, but dimly or at any rate differently discerned. At the microscopic level of the individual dialogue (or group of dialogues), on the other hand, the shape is more readily visible. Every dialogue has a more or less well-defined *structure* – and in this it begins to show its real differences from any actual conversation. Even teachers planning a discussion with students cannot arrange that their interlocutors will offer a particular intervention at a particular time, in order for the conversation to go in this direction rather than that, as Plato can; they may well try to influence the outcomes by making their own interventions, but this is an entirely different matter. In Plato's dialogues, the interlocutors are as much under his control as are the main speakers. He not only dictates the destination, but the route to that destination. This is not of course to suggest that the written dialogue has nothing in common with what it claims to imitate. A fictional conversation, however rigged, still has the capacity to draw the reader in, as a real conversation may draw in the bystander, and that is no doubt one of the chief motivations for Plato's use of the dialogue form. He wants to avoid 'talking like a book', as his Socrates accuses Protagoras of doing in the

Protagoras (328d–329a), instead allowing his readers to march in step with the actual partners in the dialogue as they move the conversation forward. But this underlines how *un*like a live conversation the written Platonic dialogue actually is; if anything, it is the virtual 'conversation' between Plato and his reader that approximates more nearly to the real thing, insofar as the reader has the freedom of response that real conversations presuppose and that the interlocutors in the dialogues universally and necessarily lack.

The structures of *Theaetetus* and *Sophist* themselves will be sketched below (see 'Short summaries of *Theaetetus* and *Sophist*'), but in the meantime it may be useful to list some general features of the organization of the Platonic dialogue. There is, first, the choice of characters – typically, Socrates plus one other, but sometimes, in the later dialogues, Socrates will cede his place as questioner, and sometimes there will be more than one respondent. Insofar as dialectic, in its Platonic form, evidently derives from the practice of the original Socrates, the presence of Socrates or a substitute will in a way be a basic requirement; the choice of respondent or respondents will often be determined by the subject matter, but failing that it will typically be someone younger than the main speaker, a feature that simultaneously reflects the implicit hierarchical relationship between questioner and respondent, and the archetypal image of Socrates in conversation with the youth of Athens with which that relationship begins. Second, the argument will, broadly speaking, be linear. It may veer off course, or digress, or loop back on itself: still, it will always maintain a forward momentum. A third typical feature of the Platonic dialogue, and for present purposes the most important, is a corollary of the second: the forward momentum of the argument tends to be maintained by having each successive stage build on what has gone before – having it not merely take off from the preceding stage, but actually use its results, positive as well as negative, as the basis on which to construct the next part of the argument.

A concrete example, from the *Theaetetus* (one that will already be partly familiar): perception – as reduced to immediate sensations – fails as an answer to the question about what knowledge is because it has no access to being or truth; for such access, we need *doxa*, (roughly translated as) 'belief'. So what about *doxa* as a candidate? Obviously not *doxa* on its own, because *doxa* may be false as well as true; true *doxa*, then. But now true *doxa* too proves inadequate. What about adding 'together with an account'? But the line of argument may also be seen as extending both further back and further forward: further back, given that *doxa* will need to be combined with perception, and further forward, given what was proposed in Sections 1–4 above about the relationship between *Sophist* (and *Statesman*) and *Theaetetus*, and that *Sophist* may actually build on the supposedly failed final account of the *Theaetetus*.

This third feature might be summed up by saying that Platonic dialogues tend to work cumulatively. Or if this is too large a generalization to make without rehearsing the evidence, the proposal is that in any case *Theaetetus* and *Sophist* can be seen to work in this way: that is, by a sort of accumulation, so that by the end of the process, despite setbacks along the way, not only is there an account of knowledge on the table, but an account (as we can see, reading back) of some depth.

6 The *dramatis personae* of *Theaetetus* and *Sophist*

Such an interpretation, as applied to the *Theaetetus*, is virtually the converse of one of the oldest and best known of interpretations of the dialogue (advanced by the so-called 'New Academy' in the centuries after Plato's death), which takes it as evidence that Plato is sceptical about any possibility of knowledge. This latter interpretation is hard to square with many aspects of the *Theaetetus*, and particularly with many of the things that are said in the context of the refutation of Protagorean relativism in the first part. It does gain some traction from Socrates' description of himself, in *Theaetetus* 149a–151d, as a midwife who can assist with the birth of others' ideas, and nurture them or kill them off as appropriate, but is barren of ideas himself. But this need be no more than a variant of his normal stance, as announced in Plato's *Apology* and exhibited in a number of short dialogues like *Charmides*, *Euthyphro*, or *Lysis*: as someone who knows nothing of substance, except for one thing, namely that he knows nothing. Not only does he know nothing, but he claims (this, too, is in the *Apology*) to discover only ignorance in others too,[11] and his conversations as Plato 'records' them not infrequently end in impasse, as they do in the last three dialogues named, and as *Theaetetus* does. At the same time, even in such cases, Plato's Socrates

---

[11] He refers at *Theaetetus* 149a to his reputed ability to reduce people to perplexity.

plainly shows himself a person of strong convictions, and in other dialogues, like *Phaedo* and, especially, *Republic*, he appears perfectly ready to put forward positive proposals of his own, even while steadfastly avoiding any suggestion that he possesses anything beyond beliefs; these he will typically represent as the outcomes of arguments, and as conclusions to be held on to for so long as those arguments stay unrefuted.

Here, in *Theaetetus*, the subject is that very thing that he says matters more than anything, for any human being, and yet claims not to possess: knowledge. It thus seems particularly appropriate that *this* conversation should end in at least apparent impasse, and that all three proposals about what knowledge is should come from Theaetetus, not from him. What would *Socrates* know about knowledge, of all things? All he can do is what he always does, act as midwife, and see to Theaetetus' offspring. If it happens that any of these shows promise, then that is none of Socrates' doing; the idea was conceived by someone else, not by him. But such a strategy on Plato's part is not only dramatically appropriate. He does not deploy it merely in order to preserve Socrates' role as a know-nothing (*Theaetetus* 179b). Nor, surely, is it intended as ironic. We might be tempted, especially if we have read the *Republic*, to take Socrates' comparison of himself as midwife as at worst a sham, at best disingenuous, but this would be a mistake. Granted, it may be more than a little overdone. Socrates is, in general, very much in charge, as he always is; for example, it is certainly not Theaetetus who creates the complex picture of Protagoreanism as the kernel of his proposal that knowledge is perception. But there is a point of substantial importance behind the midwife image, namely that whether or not some particular thesis – whether Theaetetus', about knowledge, or anybody else's about anything – is able to survive or proves not to be viable has nothing to do with any special insight or knowledge Socrates has into the subject. If it survives and flourishes, that is because it deserves to do so. Socrates is the divinely appointed midwife-critic, or, to put it more prosaically, the representative of an impersonal reason ('is what is before us true, or is it not?').

It is this critical role of Socrates' that characterizes the *Theaetetus* as a whole, and in a way explains its ending: what could fit better than to have Socrates still worrying away at whatever the argument (or Theaetetus) may have thrown up, however promising it might appear to be? (Isn't that just what Socrates is supposed to do?) The *Sophist* includes a large critical component, but overall it is more openly and directly construct-ive, not only ending with a positive conclusion, but reaching it via a series of moves all instigated and systematically carried through by the main speaker. This is plainly not a role for the midwife of the *Theaetetus*. Instead Plato gives it to a nameless visitor, who is identified only as originating from Elea in southern Italy – the birthplace of the philoso-pher Parmenides, who, by the dramatic date of the *Sophist* (shortly before Socrates' trial and execution), was long since dead, but who is nevertheless an important presence in the dialogue, as he is in the *Theaetetus*. The visitor is introduced merely as a philosopher and 'a friend of the followers of Parmenides and Zeno', and presumably, since neither we nor those present learn much more about him than that, either in *Sophist* or in *Statesman* (in which he again leads the discussion), that is enough to explain Plato's choice of him to lead this next stage of the conversation. The fulsome way in which Socrates treats him when he is introduced may suggest that we are supposed to think of him as further on, philosophically, than Socrates is; certainly he is well placed, through his Eleatic connections, to mount the major amplification, or revision, of Parmenides' position[12] that turns out to be key to the final account of the sophist. He certainly assumes a degree of authority, regarding question-and-answer as easier than monologue, 'provided one's partner causes no trouble and is easily led' (*Sophist* 217d). The sentiment immediately differentiates him from the Socrates of *Theaete-tus*; but it is entirely in keeping with the greater directness of the *Sophist* as a whole.

The Visitor, in fact, chooses as his interlocutor the boy Theaetetus, who showed few signs of being 'easily led' when paired with Socrates in *Theaetetus*; he actually made a fair bit of the running. But the Visitor in *Sophist* gives him little opportunity to do so, and Theaetetus is happy to go along. Nor is there any reason for him not to go along, insofar as the *Sophist* as a whole, like the *Statesman* after it, reads like something of a tour de force: a demonstration of philosophical expertise that turns even apparent missteps into lessons in method. In the *Statesman*, Theaetetus will be replaced by a friend of the same age (see *Sophist* 218b) who happens to share Socrates' name, just as Theaetetus shares Socrates'

---

[12] The Visitor wants it to be clear that he is no 'parricide': see 241d.

looks; is it being suggested that the older Socrates, too, is one of those being led by the Eleatic Visitor?

Theaetetus is an outstanding pupil of the mathematician Theodorus, a native of Cyrene currently staying in Athens. Theodorus is Socrates' friend and the original partner in the main conversation in *Theaetetus*, before Theaetetus arrives on the scene; he is the one who arranges to meet Socrates the next day, when the sophist is discussed, and the one who introduces the Eleatic Visitor. He is, then, a major player, and indeed for a considerable part of the *Theaetetus* it is he and not Theaetetus who responds to Socrates' questions: the part, that is, which is mainly concerned with the discussion and refutation of the relativist Protagoras' views. Socrates refers to him as Protagoras' friend several times, and Theodorus accepts the description; but Socrates also once refers to Protagoras as Theodorus' teacher (179a), and to Theodorus as the guardian of Protagoras' legacy (164e–165a). Theodorus thus appears as something of a contradiction. His expertise as a mathematician is emphasized, and provides an immediate, and apparently secure, example of knowledge. Indeed that might in itself be a good enough reason for his inclusion in the cast list. Yet there he is, defending the views of someone who systematically rejects the very possibility of any expertise except in one small area (which apparently does not include mathematics).

No one in the dialogue points to the contradiction, and maybe Theodorus is simply ensuring that an old friend gets a decent hearing. But there may be more to it. Cyrene was the birthplace of the Socratic Aristippus, who was known for his extreme views on pleasure, but who also became the founding figure of a group, later labelled as 'the Cyrenaics', who reportedly developed an epistemology that looks closely related both to Protagorean relativism and to the kind of theory to which Socrates reduces this in the *Theaetetus*. 'The Cyrenaics' are reported as holding that our immediate affections or sensations are knowable, but what causes those affections is not: we can know, for example, that we are becoming hot, but we can say nothing for certain about what is making us hot (except that it, whatever it is, is making us hot). It is by no means certain that such ideas were already current in Cyrene at the time of writing of *Theaetetus*. But it is at any rate worth noting that (a) a version of them is worked out in *Theaetetus*; (b) Cyrene is the only place we know of (apart from *Theaetetus*) where such ideas were developed;

(c) the main conversation in the dialogue starts with a reference to Cyrene, and with Socrates saying that he would have asked 'whether there were any young people in Cyrene interested in geometry or philosophy of some kind' had he not been more interested in the state of the intellectual health of young Athenians (143d); and (d) the link between Cyrenaic and Protagorean ideas was acknowledged even in antiquity. It may even be that we should label Cyrenaic epistemology as the new Protagoreanism. According to this story, Theodorus will be defending Protagoras not merely out of friendship, but out of loyalty to the intellectual tradition of his native city and its new take on his friend's ideas.

This is, of course, all highly speculative, and the *Theaetetus* can for the most part be read quite satisfactorily without it. It may nonetheless serve as a useful reminder that reading any part of Plato in context is not just a matter of linking one part of his oeuvre to others, but also of understanding the wider intellectual and philosophical environment within which he was writing, during the years following Socrates' death. For dramatic reasons, the philosophical rivals with whom Socrates explicitly engages must all belong to the past: Parmenides and Zeno, Heraclitus, Empedocles, Protagoras. But philosophy did not stop with these great figures, or with unnamed others (the atomists, for example, whom Plato refuses ever to name, though they are in all probability often on his mind: for example, at *Sophist* 246a–b); nor is it plausible to suppose that Plato, of all people, wrote without attention to what had gone on, philosophically, in the time between him and them, or to what was going on as he wrote. And as it happens, in both *Theaetetus* and *Sophist*, the focus is ultimately not so much on individual philosophical figures as on the types of theory and the ways of thinking that they represent. If it is difficult for us to identify specific contemporary references, it is as well to be aware of their likely presence in both dialogues, not least since Plato repeatedly signals as much, whether by representing the *Theaetetus* as written by Euclides, who reputedly had his own 'school' of philosophy at Megara; whether by making *Theaetetus* and *Sophist* a sort of memorial to Theaetetus (who is dying as Euclides introduces 'his' book);[13] or by

---

[13] Theaetetus' death is datable either to 369 BCE or, more probably, to 391 BCE. This, incidentally, will fix the dramatic date of Euclides' authorship (or give it a *terminus post quem*: see 146a), but not the date of Plato's own.

wheeling in an anonymous Eleatic, 'friend of the followers of Parmenides and Zeno', to give a new perspective on Parmenides. (Or are we, perhaps, to take the visitor's anonymity as a sign that the new perspective owes more to Plato than to anyone now in Elea?)

There is probably one further identifiable reference to contemporary philosophical developments in the last part of *Theaetetus*. Theaetetus attributes his third and final proposal about knowledge (knowledge is true belief plus an account) to someone else, whom he has heard proposing to treat knowable things as things of which a reasoned account can be given, unknowables as unaccountable (201c–d). He cannot spell this out, but Socrates can: he proposes to 'swap with you, a dream for a dream. ... I thought I was hearing certain people saying' that the primary elements of things could only be named, and nothing else could be said about them, so that they were 'unaccountable'; of things composed out of these, by contrast, an account could be given – by weaving together the names of their component elements. Now it happens that Aristotle[14] attributes a theory rather like the one just inadequately summarized to another, older Socratic for whom Plato evidently had little more love than he did for Aristippus: Antisthenes.[15] Socrates' reference to 'swapping ... a dream for a dream' could be understood as a covert acknowledgement by Plato that actually neither Theaetetus nor Socrates could have heard of the theory, which is still in the future. This is important for the interpretation of this final part of the dialogue, for the three interpretations of 'account' that Socrates considers and rejects are introduced as the ones the author of the theory in question 'intended "account" to signify for us' (206c), and indeed the second is precisely the one we would expect to go with the theory (a listing of components). We cannot be certain, of course, that Plato is alluding to Antisthenes, or indeed that he is not inventing the whole theory for himself; but the fact is that, as he presents it, what is refuted is strictly not the proposal itself, that knowledge is true belief plus an account, so much as someone else's version of that proposal.

[14] *Metaphysics* 1024b26–1025a1.
[15] Another possible reference to Antisthenes is in *Sophist* 251b–c. For the source material on Antisthenes and other Socratics, in English translation, see George Boys-Stones and Christopher Rowe (eds), *The Circle of Socrates: Readings in the First Generation Socratics* (Hackett, 2013).

7 Questions of method: 'collection' and 'division'

> Now I am myself, Phaedrus [says Socrates in Plato's *Phaedrus*], a lover of these divisions and collections, so that I may be able both to speak and to think; and if I find anyone else that I think has the natural capacity to look to one and to many, I pursue him 'in his footsteps, behind him, as if he were a god'. And the name I give those who can do this – whether it's the right one or not, god knows, but at any rate up till now I have called them 'experts in dialectic'.[16]

'Collecting' and 'dividing' seems to be what the 'godlike' Eleatic Visitor in the *Sophist* does. For the purpose of his account of the sophist, he generally starts by taking a larger kind or form that seems to include the one he is looking for, and then he splits this up until he gets to the right one (the final account being, roughly speaking, the sum of all the parts that have not been discarded in the process). This seems to suggest two things: (1) that arriving at the larger kind is 'collecting', the splitting up 'dividing'; and (2) that 'collection' has to precede 'division'. Neither (1) nor (2), however, is a necessary part of the method; and both limit rather than add to our understanding of what is going on in the *Sophist* (see 224c, 251d, and 267b, where 'collecting' is explicitly referred to). Whatever the *Phaedrus* intends by its ('these') 'divisions and collections', the ability to 'divide' and 'collect' in the *Sophist* surely refers to something much richer: namely the general ability to trace the relationships among kinds or forms, and therefore also the relationships among the particular, individual things that share in them, insofar as they do. The aim is a better understanding of all the similarities and differences between 'the things that are', whether forms or spatio-temporal particulars. Thus the discussion of the sophist claims to tell us both about how sophistry itself relates to – is like, and is different from – other things, taken in themselves, and what actual, flesh-and-blood sophists are. This is more than just giving a distinguishing mark[17] of sophistry, and sophists; it amounts to being able to locate them in relation to everything else, seeing them both together with all the things they relate to, and

---

[16] *Phaedrus* 266b–c; compare *Sophist* 253d–254a.
[17] I.e., the third of the interpretations of 'giving an account' discussed in *Theaetetus*.

as distinct from them and from other things.[18] The discussion of the 'greatest kinds' that lies at the heart of the *Sophist* is itself, as the Visitor makes clear (253b–e), an illustration of this process – and a much more fundamental illustration than the discussion of the sophist it helps bring to a successful conclusion.

---

[18] Or in the language of the *Phaedrus*: 'perceiving [things] together ... [and] being able to cut [them] up again, kind by kind, according to the natural joints, and not ... like an inexpert butcher' (*Phaedrus* 265d).

Chronology

BCE

c. 515	Parmenides born
c. 490	Protagoras born
469	Socrates born
424/3	Plato born
c. 415	Theaetetus born
c. 420	Protagoras dies
c. 409?	Plato meets Socrates
399	Trial and execution of Socrates
390s–380s	Plato probably writes the first and largest group of his dialogues (as measured, primarily, by style), including some of those usually described as 'middle': *Cratylus, Phaedo, Symposium*)
391 (or 369?)	Theaetetus dies
c. 380s	Plato founds the Academy at Athens
380s–370s	Plato probably writes the second group of dialogues: *Parmenides, Phaedrus, Republic, Theaetetus*
360s–340s	Plato probably writes the third group of dialogues: *Sophist, Statesman, Philebus, Timaeus-Critias, Laws* (known to be his last work)
348/7	Plato dies

Short summaries of *Theaetetus* and *Sophist*

Theaetetus

160e–165e say the same thing?), and Theaetetus' first offspring has been born.

Now it is Socrates' task, as midwife, to see if it deserves to survive; he raises a series of objections.

165e–168c Theodorus begins to enter the discussion. A series of more superficial objections prompt a spirited and important defence, imagined as spoken by Protagoras himself.

168c–171c Theodorus is finally induced to substitute for the boy Theaetetus. Socrates presses home his attack: if Protagoras says that what appears to everybody is true (by the 'measure' theory), and everybody thinks his theory false, must he not concede that it is false?

171c–172b Where the theory is likely to be accepted by people in general, and where it simply cannot work: namely in relation to what is beneficial, for individual or city.

172b–177c Digression: the contrast between the time available to the philosopher and having to speak against the water-clock in court; the philosopher's perspective on ordinary, accepted goods, and the true perspective on the philosopher.

177c–179d So, again, the theory will not work in the case of the good, or beneficial, and especially what is going to be beneficial. But might it work at least with immediate perceptual experiences? Could 'knowledge is perception' itself work, after all?

179d–183b The answer is an emphatic no. The theory of perception, built on flux, is seen to lead nowhere.

183b–184b The discussion of the 'measure' theory, and of Protagoras, are also completed (and Theodorus bows out). Socrates declines to deal with the monists – like Parmenides – in the way he has with the fluxers.

184b–187a Knowledge as perception is finally rejected; knowing involves something more – namely reasoning about our perceptual experiences; summed up as thinking, or belief (*doxa*).

187a–c Theaetetus' next proposal: knowledge is true belief.

187c–e But what about false belief: how can that come about?

188a–d A first puzzle about false belief, based on the assumption that in every case we either know a thing or we don't know it.

188d–189b	A second puzzle, based on the distinction between being and not-being, i.e., what is and what is not.
189b–191a	A third puzzle: perhaps false belief is a matter of thinking one thing to be another thing. But how on earth could that come about?
191a–196c	One solution proposed (this time by Socrates) and found inadequate: the soul as a block of wax.
196c–200d	A second solution (the soul as aviary) is also found inadequate; the problem of false belief is abandoned.
200d–201c	Refutation of knowledge as true belief.
201c–206c	Theaetetus' third and final proposal: knowledge is true belief plus an account – or so he has heard someone saying. Socrates has heard it too, spelled out in the form of a sophisticated theory, which he proceeds to refute.
206c–210a	Three ways the author of the theory might have meant us to understand 'account', all of which are rejected.
210a–d	None of Theaetetus' three answers to the question about knowledge is acceptable. Socrates goes off on business connected with his trial, but proposes to meet with Theodorus again in the morning.

Sophist

216a–218b	The Visitor from Elea, and the subject of the dialogue, are introduced; Theaetetus is enlisted again as interlocutor.
218b–221c	A model for the investigation of the sophist: the angler.
221c–223b	With an account of the angler safely accomplished, the Visitor and Theaetetus turn to the sophist – who turns out to belong to the same family as the angler, that of the hunter. But the sophist is a different sort of hunter from the angler. First account of the sophist, as a fee-earning hunter of human beings.
223c–224d	Second account: the sophist as importer-exporter of lessons in excellence or virtue.
224d–e	Third and fourth accounts: the sophist as retailer, also selling lessons in excellence, then as selling such lessons as produced by himself.

224d–226a	Fifth account: the sophist as someone making money from competitive speaking.
226b–231b	Sixth account: the sophist is a sort of expert in cleansing souls of the beliefs that stop them learning – or is he? The Visitor hesitates to call this sort of expert a sophist, though there is a resemblance between the two, like that between a dog and a wolf.
231c–e	Retrospect: the six accounts listed.
232a–235a	Clearly we have not yet got to 'the one feature [of him] from which all the things he's learned to do in fact derive' (232a). The Visitor proposes to take up one of his aspects: the sophist as expert in competitive speaking. Such experts seem to claim to be able to deal with any subject whatever, and amazingly, they manage to persuade the young that they can. So they appear wise, but actually their 'knowledge' is only *doxastikê* (i.e., based on belief (233c)); they are magicians, producers of imitations (235a).
235a–237b	Image-making divided: there is likeness-making, and there is 'apparition'-making (i.e., the making of what are only seeming likenesses). The sophist ought to represent the second kind, but what is this seeming as opposed to being, and saying or thinking what is false? Saying or thinking what is not? But Parmenides surely ruled that out?
237b–239c	Puzzles about 'what is not'.
239c–243c	So how are we going to make good the claim that the sophist deals in illusory images? An illusory image 'really is not', but really is a likeness: somehow, strangely, what is not and what is appear woven together. What is not is, after all, in a way (240d). Parmenides gave an incomplete account of what is, as have Heraclitus, Empedocles, and everybody else; there is as much of a puzzle about being as there is about not being.
243c–249d	The Visitor embarks on a discussion of this 'form', or 'kind', 'what is', by starting with the One of Parmenides: is its being separate from its oneness?, and then moving on to the quarrel between those who reduce everything to body and those who, like the 'friends of forms', regard anything bodily not as being, but as 'a sort of coming into being'.

A compromise is proposed, according to which anything is if it has the capacity to act or be acted upon, which will allow both forms and what changes to count as being.

249d–254b Rest, change, and being will be three different forms. And forms in general will mix with each other – or rather, some will, some will not. Clearly we are going to need an expert to say which is which, and whether there are some running through them all to allow them to mix, or to divide off from each other: the expert in dialectic, the philosopher.

254b–260a In the present context, discussion will be restricted to what is (or being), rest, and change, along with what turn out to be the other two of the greatest kinds or forms, sameness and difference. They all are, they are all the same as themselves, and different from each other: that is, they are not each other, or any number of other things. The result is that what is not, too, is a form, and is, as much as being is (so long as one excludes what is not in any way at all, which – as Parmenides rightly said – is not thinkable or sayable at all). So now we need not fear being attacked for saying we can think and say what is not; to say we cannot is infantile, and would make thought and speech impossible.

260a–268d The Visitor proposes an analysis of true and false thought, or belief, and speech; he then goes back to the division of image-making, and puts the sophist firmly in the 'apparition-/seeming-likeness-making' kind. The way is now open for a final account of the sophist, as a particular sort of expert – the Visitor specifies precisely which sort – in imitation.

Further reading

The whole of Plato in translation is conveniently collected together in *Plato, Complete Works*, edited by John Cooper (Hackett, 1997). *Theaetetus* in this volume is translated by M. J. Levett (revised by Myles Burnyeat), *Sophist* by Nicholas White; *Statesman*, the third in the trilogy to which *Theaetetus* and *Sophist* belong, is translated by Christopher Rowe – who has also translated three of the Platonic dialogues most often referred to in the Introduction and the footnotes to the translations in the present volume (*Phaedrus*, Penguin, 2005; *Phaedo*, in *The Last Days of Socrates*, Penguin, 2010; and *Republic*, Penguin, 2012). *Theaetetus* and *Sophist* also appear together in F. M. Cornford, *Plato's Theory of Knowledge: the Theaetetus and the Sophist* (The Liberal Arts Press, Inc., 1957), which includes a running commentary; another is the Loeb: *Plato*, vol. VII, *Theaetetus, Sophist*, translated by Harold North Fowler (Harvard University Press, 1921), which, like all Loeb editions, includes a facing Greek text.

The Levett translation of the *Theaetetus*, first published in 1928, in its revised form appeared originally in *The Theaetetus of Plato* (Hackett, 1990), accompanied by a seminal introduction of 250 pages by Myles Burnyeat. John McDowell's *Plato, Theaetetus*, in the Clarendon Plato series (Clarendon Press, 1973), includes a very detailed philosophical commentary; the translation was reissued separately, and almost unchanged, with introduction and notes by Lesley Brown (Oxford World's Classics), in 2014. David Bostock's *Plato's Theaetetus* (Clarendon Press, 1991) offers 'a sustained philosophical analysis and critique' of the dialogue. David Sedley's *The Midwife of Platonism: Text and Subtext in Plato's Theaetetus* (Oxford University Press, 2004) is an interpretation that also brings clarity to many aspects of the argument of the dialogue. Timothy Chappell's *Reading Plato's Theaetetus* (Academia Verlag, 2004) resembles Cornford's *Plato's Theory of Knowledge* in design, with sections of text preceded by summary and followed by philosophical comment. For the *Sophist*, there are commentaries by R. S. Bluck, *Plato's Sophist: A Commentary* (edited by Gordon Neal, Manchester University Press, 1975), and by L. M. de Rijk, *Plato's Sophist: A Philosophical Commentary* (North Holland Publishing Co., 1986). Paolo Crivelli's *Plato's Account of Falsehood: A Study of the Sophist* (Cambridge University Press, 2012) is a systematic examination of one important part of the *Sophist*.

Most of the secondary literature on both dialogues takes the form of articles and book chapters, which are easily accessed from the bibliographies in the volumes listed above. It tends to concentrate into a multitude of different daisy-chains, each more or less loosely related to a given context or passage in Plato's text; entering each of these chains in its later stages will give access to the earlier links. The best entry-points, in traditional print form, are currently Sedley 2004 for the *Theaetetus*, and Crivelli 2012 for the *Sophist*; or Mary Louise Gill's *Philosophos: Plato's Missing Dialogue* (Oxford University Press, 2012) for either. But most readers will probably use the internet route. The *Stanford Encyclopaedia of Philosophy* gives immediate – and free – access, for example, to Richard Kraut's 'Plato' (revised in 2013), Timothy Chappell's 'Plato on Knowledge in the *Theaetetus*' (also revised in 2013), and Mary Louise Gill on 'Method and Metaphysics in Plato's *Sophist* and *Statesman*' (2009); while *Oxford Handbooks Online*, offers (at a price) 'The Platonic Corpus' by Terry Irwin, 'Methodologies for Reading Plato' by Christopher Rowe, 'Plato's Ways of Writing' by M. M. McCabe, 'Plato's Philosophy of Language' by Paolo Crivelli, 'Plato's Metaphysics' by Verity Harte, and 'Plato's Epistemology' by Christopher Taylor. All of these online articles include bibliographies.

The above is restricted to work in English. There is a wealth of literature available in other languages. Two examples that will give a taste of the often very different approach to the *Theaetetus* and *Sophist* (and to Plato in general) employed by scholars working on the European continent are Denis O'Brien, *Le non-être: Deux études sur le Sophiste de Platon* (Academia Verlag, 1995), and Monique Dixsaut, *Platon et la question de la pensée* (Vrin, 2000).

Note on the text and translation

In common with all modern editions and translations, the present volume identifies particular passages by using the page numbers and page sections in the 'Stephanus' edition of Plato's text (Stephanus being the Latin name of the sixteenth-century editor and publisher Henri Estienne). *Theaetetus* occupied pages 142–210, *Sophist* pages 216–68, of the first volume of this edition, and each page was typically divided into five sections marked 'a' to 'e'; hence *Theaetetus*, for example, begins at '142a' and ends at '210d'.

The text of the *Theaetetus* and the *Sophist* that forms the basis of the present translation is that printed in the revised Oxford Classical Text of Plato: *Platonis opera*, volume 1, edited by E. A. Duke, W. F. Hicken, W. S. M. Nicoll, D. B. Robinson, and J. C. G. Strachan (Clarendon Press, 1995: hereafter 'the OCT'). In some places, however, the translation deviates from the new Oxford text: occasionally in the case of the *Theaetetus*, rather more often in that of the *Sophist*. Such deviations are indicated briefly in the footnotes to the translation, and justified as necessary in the 'Further notes on the text' at the end of this volume; changes to punctuation are not normally noted. An asterisk attached to a footnote indicates additional comments on a particular passage in the 'Further notes on the text'.

The translation aims to combine readability – that is, an English that reads as such – with accuracy (including a sense of the varying tone of the original). There are, however, some points at which accuracy has to take precedence over readability. These occur most often when the interlocutors are involved in building up a detailed argument, and a certain awkwardness is necessitated by the demands of clarity. But there are also three special cases that should be noted, two of which have already been signalled in the Introduction.

1. *Genos, eidos*, and related terms (see Introduction, Section 2). Plato often uses different terms for the same things, and so in this case: *eidos*, *genos*, and *idea* (itself from the same root as *eidos*) are all used interchangeably of the 'form' of whatever it may be – both in *Theaetetus* and *Sophist*, but quite demonstrably in the latter (see, e.g., 253d–e). The term *phulon* ('tribe': 'phylum' in Latin/English) is occasionally used in what is much the same role, as, slightly more often, is 'nature', *phusis*. In the translation, 'kind' always indicates the use of *genos* (which is also Greek for 'kin', 'family'), while 'form' always represents *eidos* or *idea*, 'tribe' *phulon*, and 'nature' *phusis*. This policy is partly in recognition of Plato's love of *variatio* (in some contexts usefully avoiding a pile of occurrences of the same word), but partly also for the sake of neutrality; the latter being an especially important consideration here, given the reluctance of many interpreters to find Platonic forms in *Theaetetus* and *Sophist* at all (except in the 'friends of the forms' passage, 246b–252a). Of the five terms, the last, 'nature', fits most easily into English sentences, especially when followed by a genitive, as in 'the nature of the beautiful'; it is also semantically the most transparent, if 'the nature of the beautiful' is translatable into something like 'the real nature of beauty'. The 'form of the beautiful', or even 'of beauty' is both awkward and opaque, the 'kind of knowledge' still more so. The translator may mitigate the awkwardness, by writing 'the form, beauty', or 'the kind, knowledge'; but the inescapable fact is that the Greek is here using technical or semi-technical language that cannot be properly conveyed in English without circumlocution and/or distortion.

2. *Doxa* (see Introduction, Section 4). 'Belief' is probably the least bad option for rendering this central term, and is consistently used in the following translations – except in a few cases, as indicated, where it fits particularly badly.

3. Probably the greatest problem for the translator lies in rendering the Greek verb *einai*, 'to be'. The third person singular of *einai*, namely *esti*, can appear to function in what many philosophers have been used to separating out as four distinct ways: as the 'is' of predication ('*x* is *F*'), as the 'is' of identity ('*x* is *x*'), as 'is' as in 'God is' (i.e., exists), and as 'is (*sc.* the case)', the 'veridical' use. From such a perspective, the manner in which Greek philosophical writers employ the verb may appear singularly neglectful, insofar as they generally fail to indicate which of these uses is in play in a

particular instance. Take the Protagorean dictum, that a human being is the 'measure' of everything, both 'of the things that are, that they are, and of the things that are not, that they are not' (*Theaetetus* 152a). It turns out, as we follow Socrates' exposition, that it is hard to say in which, exactly, of the four ways of using 'are' Protagoras is employing it (or rather, *esti*): it could be in three, even four of them. Plato's own phrase 'the things that are' (*ta onta = ha esti*) has a similar elasticity, from the same perspective; for example, if one tries substituting 'exist' for 'are', as it may be tempting sometimes to do in *his* use of the phrase *ta onta*, it turns out to be far too limiting. This and other similar problems mean that the translation has to stick to 'are', and 'is', despite the fact that it reads oddly in English.

The reader will find numerous occurrences in the following translations of the phrases 'what is' and 'what is not'. Some of these require a separate explanation. 'What is' represents *to on*, which is typically used as the singular of *ta onta* and refers either to some particular thing that is, or generically to anything/everything that is (again, however 'is' is to be understood). But it can also be used in a different way, to refer to *being* itself. The expression *to on* in this case stands for 'what it is to be', just as *to agathon* can stand for 'what it is to be good', or *to kalon* for 'what it is to be beautiful'; and there is a form, *eidos/idea* (or kind, *genos*), of it, just as there is a form of the good, or goodness – that is, it *is* a form, just as the good or goodness is a form. Sometimes in contexts of this sort (as indeed in those of the other sort) the noun *ousia*, 'being', may be substituted for *to on*: being-*ness*, then, here, or the nature of being. (Once again, one needs to avoid the temptation to specify which sort of being, or 'is', is in question: the answer is likely again to be 'more than one sort – if one wants to look at it that way'.) But because Plato mostly chooses to use the same expression, *to on*, as in the other case, it seems best to render it in the same way in both: that is, as 'what is'. This is the policy followed in the present volume, except in a few cases indicated in the footnotes.

'What is not', *to mê on*, in most respects needs to be treated in the same way, *mutatis mutandis*, as 'what is'. The Visitor in the *Sophist*, after a tortuous argument, concludes that it is just as possible to talk about what is not as a form as it is to talk about what is as a form: as 'what is' can stand for 'what it is to be', so 'what is not' can stand for 'what it is, not to be' ('the nature of not-being'). The difference is that here (what we call, as Plato does not) the 'is' of existence is strictly excluded: what is not *at all* is simply *nothing*.

Theaetetus

EUCLIDES: Are you just back from the country, Terpsion – or have you 142a been back some time?

TERPSION: A fair while. Actually I was looking for you, in the market-place, and I was surprised that I couldn't find you there.

EUCLIDES: That's because I wasn't in town.

TERPSION: So where were you? a5

EUCLIDES: I was going down to the harbour, when I met Theaetetus being carried back to Athens from the army camp at Corinth.

TERPSION: Alive or dead?

EUCLIDES: Alive, but only just; he's in a bad way, from some wounds b1 too, but what is really bringing him down is the sickness that has broken out in the army.

TERPSION: Not dysentery, I suppose?

EUCLIDES: Yes, dysentery.

TERPSION: That's quite a man we'd be losing! b5

EUCLIDES: A fine example to us all, Terpsion; only just now I was listening to people showering praises on his conduct in the fighting.

TERPSION: There's nothing strange about that; it would be much more of a surprise if he hadn't shown that sort of quality. But why c1 didn't he think of stopping off here in Megara?

EUCLIDES: He was hurrying to get home – I kept begging him to stay here, and telling him it was for his own good, but he didn't want to. So then I saw him on his way, and as I left him I recalled once again how wonderfully prophetic Socrates had proved to be about him, as about so c5 much else. I think it was just before his death that he encountered Theaetetus, then a young lad. They got together, and by the end of

1

their conversation[1] Socrates was totally in awe of the boy's natural qual-
d1   ities. When I went to Athens he relayed to me the exchange he'd had with
him – and well worth the hearing it was; he said the boy would certainly
become someone to reckon with if he made it to the right age.

TERPSION: That's turned out true enough, it seems. But what was
d5   their discussion like? Could you give a report of it?

EUCLIDES: Zeus, no! Or at any rate not just like that, off the cuff. But
143a   I did make notes at the time, as soon as I got home. Later on I would
go back over it all in a leisurely fashion and write it up, and then every
time I arrived in Athens I would ask Socrates again about anything I'd
not remembered, making the corrections when I got back to Megara.
a5   The result is that I have pretty much the whole discussion written up.

TERPSION: Yes, I've heard you say that before. I've always been
meaning to ask you to show it to me, and putting it off – till this moment.
What's to stop us going through it now? I'm myself quite ready for a
rest, anyway, after my journey from the country.

b1   EUCLIDES: In fact I saw Theaetetus all the way to Erineum,[2] so I'd
not be against a rest myself. Come with me, and the slave will read to
us while we put our feet up.

TERPSION: A good idea.

b5   EUCLIDES: Well, Terpsion, here's the book. I didn't write it out with
Socrates reporting the discussion as he reported it to me, but instead had
him in direct conversation with the people he said were there. These,
c1   he said, were the geometer, Theodorus, and Theaetetus. To avoid the
trouble of writing out the narrative bits between the speeches – like
'And *I* said' or 'And *I* told *him*', whenever Socrates was talking about
himself, or 'He assented', or 'He wouldn't agree' when he was talking
c5   about the respondents – well, I took out all that, and simply had him
conversing directly with them.

TERPSION: And quite reasonably so, Euclides.

EUCLIDES: So, boy, take the book and start.

d1   SOCRATES: If it had been Cyrene I cared about more, Theodorus,
I would be asking you how things were there – whether there were any
young people in Cyrene interested in geometry or philosophy of some

---

[1] Or 'dialogue' (*dialegesthai*/*dialogos*). See Introduction, Section 5.
[2] I.e., most of the way to Athens, and a considerable distance by foot.

sort; as it is, I'm less fond of the people there than I am of people here,   d5
and I'm keener to know which of *our* young people are expected to turn
out respectably. That's just what I try to find out for myself, so far as
I can, and I also ask any others I see the young wanting to spend their
time with. You yourself have no mean following, and justly so; you   e1
deserve it, especially for your geometry. So if you've encountered
anyone worth talking about, I'd be delighted to know.

THEODORUS: Well, Socrates, there is one lad I've met, among your   e5
fellow-citizens, whose quality absolutely demands that I talk and you
hear about him. If he were beautiful, I'd be afraid to be enthusiastic about
him in case anyone should think I was lusting after him. But as it is, and
don't be cross at my saying so, he's not a beauty, but with his snub nose
and bulging eyes he rather resembles you, though both features are less
pronounced in his case than in yours. So I can be straight with you: 144a
among all the people I've ever yet come across – and I've got together
with a good many in my time – I've never known anyone with such
wonderful natural gifts. So incomparably quick at learning, yet exceptionally quiet-tempered, and with a courage, too, that's second to none.   a5
I would not have thought such a combination possible, nor do I see it
occurring in anyone else. Those who are as sharp, quick, and retentive as
he is are generally unstable and short-tempered, rushing around and
shifting about like vessels with no ballast, and more manic than
courageous; the weightier ones are somewhat sluggish in approaching   b1
their studies, and brimming with forgetfulness. This lad approaches
study and inquiry so smoothly, so unerringly, and so effectively – and
with great calm, like the noiseless flow of olive oil from the jar – that one   b5
wonders how someone so young can carry all this off so well.

SOCRATES: That's good news. Which of our citizens is his father?

THEODORUS: I've heard the name, but I can't remember it. No
matter – he's the middle one in this group that's approaching us now.   c1
He and his friends there with him were rubbing themselves down with
oil just now on the track outside; I think they've finished and are coming
over here.[3] See if you recognize him.

SOCRATES: I do. He's the son of Euphronius of Sunium, who was,   c5
yes indeed, very much the sort of man you described the lad as being.

---

[3] We are evidently to picture the conversation taking place in a gymnasium; the boys have been
training on a running track.

He was well respected in many ways, and to cap it all he left very substantial wealth when he died. But I don't know the lad's name.

d1 THEODORUS: His name, Socrates, is Theaetetus; as for his inheritance, I think some of the trustees have ruined it. Despite that he's also amazingly generous with his money, Socrates.

d5 SOCRATES: He sounds like a paragon, this one. Tell him to come and sit here by me.

THEODORUS: I shall. Theaetetus, come over here by Socrates!

SOCRATES: Yes, please do, Theaetetus, so that I can check for myself

e1 what sort of face I have. Theodorus says I have one like yours. But now if each of us had a lyre and Theodorus said both instruments were tuned in a similar way, would we immediately take his word for it, or would we have tried to find out first whether he was speaking as a musical expert?

THEAETETUS: We would have asked that first.

e5 SOCRATES: And we would believe him if we found he was an expert, but if we found he was no musician, we wouldn't trust him?

THEAETETUS: True.

SOCRATES: And in the present case, I imagine, if we've any interest in

145a whether our faces are similar or not, we should ask whether or not he's speaking as an expert in painting.

THEAETETUS: I think we should.

SOCRATES: So is Theodorus an expert painter?

a5 THEAETETUS: Not so far as I know.

SOCRATES: And he's not an expert in geometry either?

THEAETETUS: Oh, he's certainly that, Socrates!

SOCRATES: Is he also expert in astronomy, arithmetic, music, and everything else that goes to make an educated person?

a10 THEAETETUS: I certainly think he is.

SOCRATES: So if he claims that we're similar in some physical respect, whether by way of praising or of criticizing us, it's not worth paying him the slightest attention.

THEAETETUS: Perhaps not.

b1 SOCRATES: But what if he were to praise one of us for the state of our soul – for our goodness and wisdom? Wouldn't the one who heard him praising the other be justifiably keen to check on the object of the praise, and the other to show what he was made of?

b5 THEAETETUS: Certainly, Socrates.

SOCRATES: So see here, my dear Theaetetus: in this case the showing is for you to do, the inquiring for me, because the fact is that however many foreigners or citizens Theodorus may have praised to me, he has never praised anyone as he did you just now.

THEAETETUS: That would be a fine thing, Socrates. But just watch out that he wasn't joking.   b10
     c1

SOCRATES: That's not Theodorus' style. Don't try ducking out of what we agreed, pretending that our friend here was only joking, because otherwise he'll actually be forced to give evidence against you; and no one's going to charge *him* with perjury. Be a man and stick by our agreement.   c5

THEAETETUS: I'll have to, if that's your decision.

SOCRATES: So tell me – I suppose you're learning a bit of geometry from Theodorus?

THEAETETUS: I am.

SOCRATES: And a bit about astronomy, and music, and arithmetic?   d1

THEAETETUS: I'm keen to, anyway.

SOCRATES: I am too, my boy, whether from Theodorus or from anyone else I think has some understanding of such things. All the same, while I get on well enough with these subjects in most respects, there's one thing about them that puzzles me, and I'd like to explore it with you and the others here. Tell me: to learn is to become wiser[4] about the subject one's learning about, isn't it?   d5

THEAETETUS: Obviously.   d10

SOCRATES: And I imagine wise people are wise through wisdom.

THEAETETUS: Yes.

SOCRATES: And this isn't different at all from knowledge?   e1

THEAETETUS: What isn't?

SOCRATES: Wisdom. Aren't people wise about the things they know about?

THEAETETUS: Of course.   e5

SOCRATES: So knowledge and wisdom are the same thing?

THEAETETUS: Yes.

SOCRATES: Well, this is the very thing that I'm puzzled about, and can't get a proper hold on for myself – what knowledge actually is. So can we give an answer? What do all of you say? Which of us will be the first to speak? The one who tries and misses will sit down and be donkey, as children say   146a

---

[4] 'Wiser': i.e., more expert.

when they play ball, and so will the next one who misses, and so on; anyone
a5 who gets through without missing will be king over us and make us answer
any question he wants. – Why the silence? I don't suppose, Theodorus, that
my love of discussion is making me a boor, so keen am I to have us engage
in conversation together, and become friends who talk to one another?

b1 THEODORUS: Boorish is the last thing that would be, Socrates! But
please get one of the lads to answer your question. I'm unused to this
sort of discussion myself, and I'm too old to get used to it either, whereas
b5 it will suit them, and do much more for them than it would for me; youth
truly gives room for improvement in everything. Go on as you started,
and don't let Theaetetus off: question him!

c1 SOCRATES: You hear what Theodorus says, Theaetetus. I don't think
it'll be your wish to disobey him, and it wouldn't be right in any case,
when a wise person gives instructions in such matters, for the younger
not to listen. So take your courage in your hands and tell me: what do
you think knowledge is?

THEAETETUS: I'll have to do it, Socrates, seeing that the two of you
c5 are telling me to. In any case, if I do somehow miss the target, you'll
both set me right.

SOCRATES: Definitely we will – at any rate if we can.

THEAETETUS: Well, I think the things one can learn from Theodorus
d1 are knowledges,[5] that is, geometry and the subjects you just mentioned;
cobbling too, and the skills that belong to other craftsmen – each and
every one of these is nothing other than knowledge.

SOCRATES: That's certainly a brave answer, and a generous one, my
d5 friend: you're handing over a whole collection of things when you were
only asked for one, and a mixed bag instead of something simple.

THEAETETUS: Can I ask why you say that, Socrates?

SOCRATES: It's probably nothing, but I'll tell you what I'm thinking.
When you mention cobbling, you're not talking, are you, about anything
other than knowledge of the making of shoes?

---

[5] Theaetetus here uses the plural of *epistêmê*, 'knowledge'; this is perfectly natural in Greek, because
epistêmê does duty both for knowledge in general and for any form or branch of it. 'Knowledges' is
scarcely English, but to introduce 'forms' or 'branches', or even 'examples', of knowledge here – or
to substitute the singular for the plural – would be unhelpful; Socrates' response to Theaetetus'
proposal, at any rate, in the following lines, will be to take him as identifying knowledge with what are
in fact forms/branches/examples of it, while not recognizing that this is what they are. Knowledge
for Theaetetus, according to his present account, is just geometry, cobbling, carpentry . . .

THEAETETUS: I'm not. d10

SOCRATES: And what about when you talk about carpentering? Are e1
you treating that as anything other than knowledge of the making of
wooden objects?

THEAETETUS: Here too, no.

SOCRATES: So in both cases you're marking out what each is knowledge *of.* e5

THEAETETUS: Yes.

SOCRATES: But what was asked for, Theaetetus, wasn't what things
knowledge is of, or how many knowledges there are; we didn't ask the
question what knowledge is because we wanted to count examples of
knowledge, but because we wanted to know what the thing, knowledge,
might be in itself. Or is there nothing in what I'm saying? e10

THEAETETUS: No, you are absolutely right.

SOCRATES: Now think about the following. Suppose someone put 147a
the same question to us about some everyday thing that's ready to hand:
clay, for example – what is it, actually? Wouldn't we be a laughing
stock if we replied to him 'potter's clay and ovenmaker's clay and
brickmaker's clay'? a5

THEAETETUS: Possibly.

SOCRATES: Because I suppose first of all we'd be expecting the
questioner to understand whenever we said 'clay' in our answer,
whether we add 'figurine-maker's' or refer to any other craftsman who b1
uses clay. Or do you think anyone will understand the name of a thing at
all if he doesn't know what the thing is?

THEAETETUS: Certainly not.

SOCRATES: Then anyone who doesn't know what knowledge is won't
understand what knowledge of shoes is either. b5

THEAETETUS: No, he won't.

SOCRATES: Then anyone who's ignorant of what knowledge is won't
understand what cobbling is, or indeed what any other expertise is.

THEAETETUS: That's so. b10

SOCRATES: Then if someone is asked what knowledge is and he
answers with the name of some expertise or other, the answer is absurd.
He's offering knowledge of something when that wasn't what he was c1
asked for.

THEAETETUS: It seems so.

SOCRATES: And I think we can also say he's taking an awfully long way round when he could be giving a short and everyday answer. In the case
c5 of clay, for example, I suppose he could have answered the question in an easy and simple way by just saying 'Clay will be earth thoroughly mixed with liquid', and leaving out whose clay it is.

THEAETETUS: Now that you put it like that, Socrates, it seems so easy! And actually you may be asking the very sort of question that occurred
d1 to us – me and your namesake Socrates here – just now when we were talking amongst ourselves.

SOCRATES: What sort of question was that, Theaetetus?

THEAETETUS: Theodorus was using diagrams to illustrate a point for
d5 us about powers,[6] in relation to a figure of three square feet and one of five square feet, namely that they are not commensurable in length with a figure of one square foot; and he proceeded in this way case by case until he reached a figure of seventeen square feet, where somehow or other he came to a halt. Well, this sort of thing occurred to us – given that the powers were apparently unlimited in number, we should try to combine
e1 them into one, so that we'd have something to call all these powers.

SOCRATES: And did you find something like that?

THEAETETUS: I think we did. But see what you think.

SOCRATES: Go on.

e5 THEAETETUS: We divided the whole of number into two. Any number that can be produced by multiplying two equal numbers we compared to a square figure, and called it 'square' or 'equal-sided'.

SOCRATES: Good; well done.

THEAETETUS: So then any number between these, namely three, and
148a five, and any other that can't be produced by multiplying equal numbers, but only by multiplying a greater by a less or a less by a greater, and is always contained by a side that's greater and a side that's less – this we
a5 compared to an oblong figure, and called it an 'oblong' number.

SOCRATES: Very fine! And what was your next step?

THEAETETUS: Lines that as sides of a square produce the 'equal-sided'
b1 plane numbers we marked off as 'lengths', and those that produce the

---

[6] Which Theaetetus will shortly attempt to define as 'oblong numbers'. To understand this, we need to recognize at least the following: (a) that the mathematics of the time does without 'irrational' numbers; (b) that it therefore has to deal with what we call the roots of non-square numbers in a special way; (c) that this special way is geometrical in form; but (d) that the whole exercise is not just about numbers, but geometry too.

'oblong' ones as 'powers' – on the grounds that while these are not commensurable in length with the other sort of lines, they *are* commensurable in the plane figures they have the power to produce. And we made another, similar distinction in relation to solids.

SOCRATES: Boys, no one on earth could give a better example! It seems to me there's no danger of perjury on Theodorus' part.   b5

THEAETETUS: And yet, Socrates, I wouldn't be able to answer your question about knowledge in the way I answered about lengths and powers, and I think it's something of that sort that you're looking for. So once again Theodorus does appear to be perjuring himself.   c1

SOCRATES: How so? If it had been your running he was praising, and he said he'd never come across another young runner as good as you, do you think his praise of you would be any less truthful if you happened to finish behind the fastest runner at his best?   c5

THEAETETUS: No, I don't.

SOCRATES: And do you suppose, as I was saying just now, that finding out about knowledge is a small matter? Don't you think it's something for those at the top of their game in every way?

THEAETETUS: Zeus! Yes, I do – it certainly is for people at the very top.

SOCRATES: So be confident about yourself, believe what Theodorus   c10
said about you, and commit yourself completely to getting an account of   d1
knowledge: what, exactly, is it?

THEAETETUS: If commitment is what counts, Socrates, the answer will appear.

SOCRATES: Come on then. You've just given us a good start. Try mimicking your answer about powers: just as there were many of them,   d5
and yet you covered them all with a single form, try now to apply a single account to the many knowledges there are.

THEAETETUS: You can be sure, Socrates, that I've made numerous   e1
attempts to figure it out, on hearing the questions they said you were asking. But the fact is that I can't persuade myself that I've anything adequate to say myself, or that I'm hearing anyone else give the sort of   e5
account that you're insisting on. On the other hand, I can't stop worrying about it either.

SOCRATES: Those are birth-pains, my dear Theaetetus. You're having them because you're not empty-headed, you're pregnant.

THEAETETUS: I don't know, Socrates. I'm just telling you how I feel.   e10

149a SOCRATES: Then – how ridiculous of you! – you've not heard that I'm the son of a midwife? A very fine and muscular one, too: Phaenarete?[7]

THEAETETUS: That much I have heard.

SOCRATES: Haven't you also heard that I practise the same art as she does?

a5 THEAETETUS: Certainly not.

SOCRATES: I can assure you I do. But don't tell on me to everybody else. They don't recognize this skill of mine, my friend, and it's not one of the things they say I do, because they don't know about it; instead they say I'm

a10 very strange, and reduce people to puzzlement. You've heard *that* said of me?

b1 THEAETETUS: I have.

SOCRATES: So shall I tell you the cause?

THEAETETUS: Yes, certainly.

SOCRATES: It'll help you understand what I'm getting at if you think

b5 about the whole situation with midwives. I imagine you know that none of them acts as midwife to others while she is still conceiving and bearing children herself, only when she's no longer capable of doing so.

THEAETETUS: Yes, I do.

b10 SOCRATES: Well, they say Artemis was the cause of this, having been allotted childbirth as her province when she was herself childless. Not

c1 that she actually assigned midwifery to the barren, because human nature lacks the strength to acquire skill in things where it has no experience; rather she gave the function to women now too old to give birth, as recognition of their similarity to herself.

THEAETETUS: That's likely enough.

c5 SOCRATES: And isn't it also likely, indeed inevitable, that it should also be midwives more than anyone who can tell whether a woman is pregnant or not?

THEAETETUS: It certainly is.

SOCRATES: And what's more, it's the midwife who by applying homely

d1 drugs and singing incantations is able to bring on birth-pains, and to make them gentler if she wishes; she will even bring about the birth when women are in difficulties, or else she will cause a miscarriage in the early stages,[8] if it seems right.

---

[7] The name can be read as/sounds like 'revealer of excellence/virtue/goodness' (*phainein* + *aretê*).

[8] Two words in the text here (*neon on*) are marked as irredeemably corrupt by the editors of the OCT.*

THEAETETUS: That's right.

SOCRATES: And have you noticed yet another characteristic of mid- d5
wives? They're the most skilful of matchmakers, because of their versa-
tility at telling which woman should marry which man in order to
produce the best children possible.

THEAETETUS: That's complete news to me.

SOCRATES: Well, I can tell you that they pride themselves more on this d10
than on their skill at cutting the umbilical cord. Ask yourself: telling e1
what sort of soil is suitable for sowing each particular plant – does that
seem to you to be a part of the same expertise as tending and harvesting
the crops, or of a different one?

THEAETETUS: No, part of the same one. e5

SOCRATES: But when it comes to sowing in a woman, you think, my
friend, do you, that the sowing and the harvesting belong to different arts?

THEAETETUS: No, that's not at all likely.

SOCRATES: No, it isn't. But because there's also that other way of 150a
bringing men and women together, the inappropriate, skill-free one we
call procuring, midwives avoid matchmaking too, to protect their august
status, because they're afraid that if they practise matchmaking they'll be
charged with procuring; though in fact it's pretty well only those who are a5
true midwives who can actually make the right matches.

THEAETETUS: Apparently.

SOCRATES: Well, that's how much midwives do; but it's still not as
much as *I* have to do. Women don't sometimes give birth to phantoms, b1
sometimes to true children, with no easy way of telling them apart. If
they did that too, it would be the greatest and finest task of the midwife
to judge which was true and which not, don't you think?

THEAETETUS: I do. b5

SOCRATES: Now my own art of midwifery has all the same features as
theirs, but with the difference that I act as midwife to men, not women,
and it's their souls I oversee giving birth and not their bodies. And the
greatest aspect of my skill is that it enables me to test this way and that c1
whether the mind of a young person is giving birth to a phantom and a
falsehood or something fruitful and true. Yet I do have this much in
common with midwives, that I am unproductive myself – unproductive,
that is, of wisdom. Many people have complained about me that c5
I put questions to everybody else without declaring my own view on
anything, because I've nothing wise to contribute; and that is true

enough. The cause of it is this, namely that the god[9] compels me to act as midwife while forbidding me to procreate anything myself. I am, then,

d1 not at all wise myself, nor has any discovery that could be called wise been born as offspring of *my* soul.

But those who associate with me are a different matter. Some at first appear quite hopelessly ignorant, but as we continue being together,

d5 there they are, all of them – all, that is, whom the god permits – making the most amazing progress, in their own eyes and everybody else's; and this, quite plainly, without their ever having learned a single thing from me, just by their having discovered and brought to birth lots of fine things from within themselves. The actual delivery of their off-

e1 spring, though, *is* the god's responsibility and mine. This is clear from the fact that many people who were ignorant of the situation and looked down on my role, giving all the credit to themselves, went off earlier than they should have done, either of their own accord or on the advice of others; then, having gone off, they not only caused the miscarriage of

e5 what was left, by getting into bad company, but even neglected and lost the offspring of theirs that I'd already delivered, because they preferred falsehoods and phantoms to the truth of things, and ended

151a up looking stupid both to themselves and to everybody else. One of these has turned out to be Aristides, son of Lysimachus,[10] but there are lots and lots of others. When they come back, begging for my company again and prepared to do anything to get it, in some cases the divine sign that comes to me stops me being with them, in others it allows it, and

a5 then they resume their progress. Those who get together with me have something else in common with women in childbirth: they suffer birth-pains, and a sense of helplessness fills them, night and day – much more,

b1 indeed, than a woman, and my expertise is able both to awaken and put a stop to the pain. That's how it is with these people. But for some, Theaetetus, who don't seem to me pregnant in one way or other, I act as a perfectly well-meaning matchmaker, recognizing that they have no

b5 need of me; and I'm quite good enough at guessing whose company they

---

9 Plato's Socrates frequently refers to 'the god', as here, without specification; he may have one particular god in mind (Apollo, as in the *Phaedo*), but in Plato generally 'god' can serve as a collective noun, used interchangeably with 'gods'.

10 A young man whose education Plato's Socrates discusses in the *Laches*; perhaps this is an authorial cross-reference.

might benefit from – many of them I've passed on to Prodicus,[11] many to other founts of oracular wisdom.

If you're wondering, dearest boy, why I've described all this for you at such length, it's because I suspect that you're suffering birth-pains from something you're carrying inside you; you think so yourself.[12] So treat me as the son of a midwife who has some midwife's skills of his own, and be ready to answer as you can any questions I ask of you. If at any point I think, on examination, that something you've said really is a phantom, not a true child of yours, and I take it from you and dispose of it, don't go wild like a mother over her first baby. You'd be amazed, my friend, how many people get cross with me – cross enough even to sink their teeth into me, when I take some bit of nonsense away from them. They don't imagine that I'm doing it out of good will, so far are they from understanding that no god is ever guilty of ill will towards human beings, and no more do I do anything of this sort out of ill will either: for me it is simply not permissible to accept what is false and hide away the true.

So then, Theaetetus, go back to the beginning and try again to tell me: just what is knowledge? Whatever you do, don't say it's beyond you; god willing, and if you have the courage, it won't be.

THEAETETUS: Well, Socrates, with you cheering on like that it would be a disgrace for anyone not to make every effort he can to say what he has to say. So here's what I think: if a person knows something, he is perceiving the thing he knows; the way it appears now, knowledge is nothing other than perception.

SOCRATES: That's a good, straight answer, my boy; just the sort of way one should express oneself. But now come on, let's jointly examine what you've said, and see whether in fact it's fruitful or a bag of wind. Perception, you say, is knowledge?

THEAETETUS: Yes.

SOCRATES: Well, that's very probably no bad account to give of knowledge; it's the one Protagoras[13] too used to give. In a somewhat different way, he said this very same thing. His claim, I think, is that the 'measure of all things' is a human being, 'of the things that are, that they

---

[11] A 'sophist' who is portrayed in Plato's *Protagoras* as specializing in nice verbal distinctions.
[12] See 148e: Theaetetus put it differently, but Socrates' diagnosis was the same.
[13] See Introduction, Section 1.

are, and of the things that are not, that they are not.' I imagine you've read it?

a5   THEAETETUS: Indeed I have, many times.

SOCRATES: Well, isn't he saying something like this, that as each and every thing appears to me, so it is for me, and again, as they appear to you, so they are for you – you and I both being human beings?

THEAETETUS: Yes, that is what he's saying.

b1   SOCRATES: And it's a reasonable assumption that a wise man won't be talking rubbish. So let's follow out what he's saying. Isn't it the case sometimes that when there's a wind blowing, even though it's the same wind, one of us will be cold and another won't? And one will be slightly cold, another very cold?

THEAETETUS: Yes, very much so.

b5   SOCRATES: So in such cases are we going to say that the wind, taken itself by itself, is cold, or that it's not cold? Or shall we accept Protagoras' line that it's cold for the person who is shivering, and not for the person who isn't?

THEAETETUS: It seems we will.

b10   SOCRATES: And this is also how it appears to each of them?

THEAETETUS: Yes.

SOCRATES: But now 'appearing' here is a matter of someone's perceiving?

THEAETETUS: Yes, it is.

c1   SOCRATES: A thing's appearing to someone, then, is the same as his perceiving it, in the case of hot things and of everything like that. For[14] how each of us perceives a thing is likely also to be how it is for each of us.

THEAETETUS: It seems so.

c5   SOCRATES: As befits knowledge, then, perception is always of what is, and never plays us false.

THEAETETUS: It appears so.

SOCRATES: By the three Graces! So has Protagoras turned out to be even wiser than we thought? Has he given us this as a riddle for the

c10 common riff-raff, while revealing the truth[15] to his disciples in secret?

d1   THEAETETUS: Why on earth do you say that, Socrates?

---

[14] Reading *gar*, which the OCT reads, but reluctantly.*
[15] There is probably punning here: *Truth* will have been the title of the book of Protagoras' that Theaetetus says he has read and re-read (152a); see 161c.

SOCRATES: I'll tell you a theory that certainly ought not to be written off. It's to the effect that actually nothing is just one thing, itself by itself, and that you cannot refer to a thing correctly by any description whatever. If you call something big, it will appear as small as well, and   d5
if you call it heavy, it will appear as light too; and similarly with everything, just because – so the theory says – nothing is one, whether a one something or a one any sort of thing. If we say, of anything, that it is, we're wrong, because in fact all things are in a process of coming to be through motion, and change in general, and mixture with each other; nothing ever is, it's always *coming* to be. On this account of things we   e1
may take it that all the wise in succession, apart from Parmenides, are agreed: not just Protagoras, but Heraclitus[16] and Empedocles, and among the poets, the top representatives of both genres, Epicharmus   e5
for comedy and, for tragedy, Homer, who in composing the line 'Ocean, begetter of the gods, and Tethys their mother'[17] made everything the offspring of flux and change. Or don't you think that's what he's saying?

THEAETETUS: I do.   e10

SOCRATES: Who then could still dispute the theory and not make   153a
himself a laughing stock, up against so powerful an army, with Homer himself as its general?

THEAETETUS: It wouldn't be easy, Socrates.

SOCRATES: No, Theaetetus, it wouldn't, since in fact there is evidence   a5
enough for saying that being, or what seems to be such, and coming to be are produced by change, while rest produces not-being and passing away. Heat or fire, after all, the very thing that generates and controls everything else,[18] is itself generated from motion and friction, and both of these are changes. These are what generate fire, are they not?   a10

THEAETETUS: Indeed they are.   b1

SOCRATES: And what's more, every kind of living creature[19] springs from these same things.

---

[16] Heraclitus, notorious for the slogan 'everything flows', is actually the only one of those named who can be said for certain to be much interested in the theory Socrates is outlining; but precision is not his priority in the present context; see next note.

[17] The same line appears twice in the *Iliad* (14.201 and 302). It has only a superficial connection with what Socrates proposes to get from it, as he will virtually admit later on (see 180c–d).

[18] Especially (or even only) in Heraclitus' account of things (see n.16 above).

[19] This is the first occurrence of the term 'kind' in the *Theaetetus* (see Introduction, Section 2). The Greek has 'the kind of/belonging to living creatures' (*to . . . tôn zôiôn genos*), which is presumably the sum of its sub-kinds.

THEAETETUS: Of course.

b5 SOCRATES: And what about the condition of our bodies? Isn't that destroyed by rest and idleness, and generally preserved by exercises, that is, by change?

THEAETETUS: Yes.

SOCRATES: And the condition in our soul – isn't it by study and
b10 practice, themselves changes, that it acquires learning of different sorts, and is preserved and improved, whereas lack of activity, when there is
c1 no practice or study, means that it not only fails to learn anything but forgets anything it has learned before?

THEAETETUS: Very much so.

SOCRATES: One of the two, then, namely change, is good for both soul
c5 and body, whereas the other is the opposite?

THEAETETUS: It seems so.

SOCRATES: So then let me go on and draw your attention to what happens when there is an absence of wind, calm, and things like that – how in each case the absence of change rots and destroys things, whereas the other sorts of conditions preserve them. And for my finishing touch,
c10 I'll bring on that golden cord of Homer's. It's the sun he's talking about,
d1 nothing else; what he's pointing out is that so long as the circumference and the sun are moving and changing, everything is, and is preserved, in both the divine and the human sphere, whereas if they came to a standstill, as if tethered,[20] all things would be destroyed, and we'd have
d5 that famous situation where everything up is down and everything down is up.[21]

THEAETETUS: Yes, Socrates, this does seem to me to demonstrate what you're saying.

SOCRATES: The best way to think of it, my friend, is this. In the case of the eyes, first of all, you shouldn't think of what you call white colour as
d10 some other thing outside your eyes, or within the eyes, and neither
e1 should you assign it some particular location; if you do, it will surely then be fixed and resting, and come to be no longer in the process of coming to be.

[20] As Zeus says he could use a golden cord to bind up and tether everything to Mount Olympus, leaving it hanging in mid-air (Homer, *Iliad* 8.19-27).
[21] Probably another reference to Heraclitus, who was famous for claiming that opposites were somehow identical – as the road up is the same as the road down.

THEAETETUS: How should I think of it, then?

SOCRATES: Let's follow out what we were saying just now, and posit nothing that is just one thing, itself by itself. That way we'll find that black or white or any colour you like must have been generated from the eyes' meeting the relevant motion, and what we actually call colour in each case won't be either what is doing the striking or what is being struck, but rather something that has come to be in between the two, peculiar to each. Or would you prefer to insist that as each colour appears to you, so it appears to a dog or whatever other living creature too?

e5

154a

THEAETETUS: Zeus! No, I would not.

a5

SOCRATES: What about another human being? Does the way anything appears to someone else match the way it appears to you? Are you sure about that? Aren't you much surer that it won't even appear the same to you, because you yourself won't ever be the same as yourself?

THEAETETUS: That does seem the more likely to me.

SOCRATES: Well, if the things we measure ourselves against or touch were large or white or hot, they wouldn't ever have become something different simply through meeting something else, without undergoing any change in themselves; and similarly if it was what was doing the measuring against or touching that was large or whatever it might be, that couldn't have become different without anything having happened to it, just as a result of something else's having approached it or had something happen to *it*. Though as matters stand, my friend, we're all too readily forced into saying amazingly ridiculous things, as we'd be told by Protagoras and anyone who sets out to say the same things as he does.

b1

b5

THEAETETUS: What are you saying? What sorts of ridiculous things?

b10

SOCRATES: One small example and you'll know exactly what I have in mind. Take six dice. If you put four next to them, we say the six are more than the four, in fact half as many again; if you put twelve next to them, we say the six are fewer, in fact half as many, and I imagine we won't put up with anyone saying otherwise in either case. Or perhaps you will?

c1

c5

THEAETETUS: I certainly won't.

SOCRATES: So what if Protagoras or anyone else asks you 'Theaetetus, is it possible for a thing to become bigger or more in number in any way other than by being increased?' How will you answer?

17

d1 THEAETETUS: Well, Socrates, if I say what I think in relation to the present question, I'll reply that it isn't possible; but if I answer in relation to the previous question, in order to guard against contradicting myself I'll say I think it is possible.

SOCRATES: A brilliant answer, by Hera! Well done, my friend! But evidently, if you reply 'Yes, it is possible', we'll have a situation like the
d5 one in Euripides: we'll find that you've a tongue that's safe from being challenged, but a mind that is not.[22]

THEAETETUS: True.

SOCRATES: Now if the two of us were wise and clever people who had already examined all the contents of our minds, we'd have more than enough time available to try each other out; we'd have been
e1 rushing like sophists into the sorts of battles sophists have, using arguments as weapons to beat each other's arguments down. But as it is, we're not experts like them, and what we'll want to do first is to look at the things we're thinking and see how they relate to each other –
e5 whether they chime together, or whether there is complete disharmony between them.

THEAETETUS: That's quite certainly what I'd want to do.

SOCRATES: And the same goes for me. In that case, since we're in
155a no hurry, should we not go back and ask again – without getting cross about it, just doing a proper job of examining ourselves – what we're to make of these things that seem apparent to us?[23] The first of these, I think we'll say, as we go through them, is that nothing will ever become
a5 greater or smaller, whether in size or in number, so long as it is equal to itself. Right?

THEAETETUS: Yes.

SOCRATES: And second, that if a thing had nothing either added to it or taken away from it, it never grows or shrinks but is always equal.
a10 THEAETETUS: Yes, surely.
b1 SOCRATES: Isn't there a third thing that seems apparent, too: that it's impossible for a thing to be, later on, what it was not before, and for it to be this without having become it or becoming it?[24]

---

[22] Cf. Euripides, *Hippolytus* 612: 'It was my tongue that swore; my mind remains unsworn.'
[23] I.e., these things that appear to us (to be true); 'the things we're thinking', as Socrates just called them.
[24] Omitting *alla* in this much debated sentence, apparently with Proclus.*

THEAETETUS: This certainly seems something we need to look at again.

SOCRATES: These three things we've agreed on really are, I think, battling with themselves in our souls when we talk about what happens with the dice, or when we claim that I, being the age I am, without having grown or the opposite, will be within the same year now bigger, now smaller than your adolescent self, not because my size has been reduced at all but because yours has increased. In this case I actually am, later on, what I was not before, without having become so; for it's impossible for anything to *have* become something without its coming to be that thing, and I could never become smaller without my losing any size. And there are myriads upon myriads of other examples where the same is true, that is, if we're going to admit the cases mentioned. You follow me, I think, Theaetetus; at any rate you seem to me familiar enough with the sort of thing I'm referring to.

THEAETETUS: Yes, Socrates, and I perpetually wonder – by the gods I do! – how to make sense of it all; sometimes just looking at it makes me literally quite dizzy.

SOCRATES: My friend, it appears Theodorus' guess about your nature wasn't far wrong. This wondering of yours is very much the mark of a philosopher – philosophy starts nowhere else but with wondering, and the man who made Iris the offspring of Thaumas wasn't far off with his genealogy.[25] But let me ask: do you now understand why the things in question are as they are, from what we're claiming our friend Protagoras says – or are you not yet grasping it?

THEAETETUS: I don't think I am, yet.

SOCRATES: So I'll be doing you a favour if I help you sniff out the hidden truth in the mind of a famous man, or rather, of a number of famous men?[26]

THEAETETUS: You certainly will – a very big favour.

SOCRATES: Then take a look round and make sure none of the uninitiated is listening in on us. The people I have in mind[27] are those that think there is nothing in the world except what they can grasp firmly in their hands, and refuse to accept an action or a coming into being, or anything that can't be seen, as part of what is.

b5

c1

c5

c10

d1

d5

d10

e1

e5

---

[25] See Hesiod, *Theogony* 265. *Thaumas* is the personification of wonder or amazement; Iris is messenger of the gods as well as the rainbow.

[26] See n.28.   [27] The atomists, perhaps?

THEAETETUS: What an obstinate and thick-skinned sort of person
156a you're describing, Socrates!

SOCRATES: Yes, my boy, because they're quite entirely without culti-
vation. But others are much more subtle, and it's their mysteries I'm
going to tell you about.[28] Their starting point, on which hangs every-
a5 thing we were talking about just now, was that everything was change
and that there was nothing besides change; and of change there were two
forms, each unlimited in plurality but with different powers, one to act,
the other to be acted upon. From the coming together of these two
motions, and the friction of one against the other, offspring come into
b1 being – unlimited numbers of them, but twins in every case, one twin
being what is perceived, the other a perception, emerging simultaneously
with what is perceived and being generated along with it. Well, for the
perceptions we possess names such as seeing, hearing, smelling, cooling
b5 down, or burning up, ones we call pleasures and pains, too, desires and
fears, and others besides – an unlimited number that lack names as well
as a huge range that are named. As for the kind of thing that is perceived,
c1 it shares its birth with the perception, so that colours of all different
varieties come to be with different seeings, sounds similarly with hear-
ings, and the other sorts of things perceived with the other sorts of
perceptions, kindred births in every case. So, Theaetetus, what is this
c5 story telling us, in relation to what we were saying before? Do you see?

THEAETETUS: Not entirely, Socrates.

SOCRATES: Well, see if we can somehow round the story off. What it's
trying to tell us is that all these things are changing, as we're saying, but
that there is a quickness and a slowness in their changing. All of it that is
c10 slow changes in the same place and in relation to neighbouring things,
d1 and that's how it gives birth, but the change relating to its offspring is

---

[28] These 'mysteries' seem to be the same as 'hidden truth' just mentioned, at 155d–e, as being 'in
the mind of a famous man', i.e., Protagoras. They will amount to a development of the theory of
flux, which was attributed at 152e to 'all the wise in succession' apart from Parmenides, including
Empedocles, Epicharmus, and Homer, as well as Heraclitus (actually the main 'fluxer'); logic
then suggests that these are the other famous men referred to in 155d. In this case, the 'hidden
truth' (another pun on the title of Protagoras' book?), and the 'mysteries', will be hidden and
secret not least because their supposed authors had never heard of them; after all, most of them
were not even fluxers in the first place. Nor, strictly speaking, was Protagoras: Socrates brings in
the theory of flux, and the theory he is now going to introduce, in order to give the Protagorean
idea of the individual as 'measure' (152a), as interpreted in terms of the equation knowledge =
perception, the sort of underpinning he thinks will give it the best chance of working (cf. 157c–d,
160d–e, 183a).

of the other sort, and that's why they are quicker[29] – for they move from place to place, and that is what their change consists in, namely locomotion. So when something commensurate with an eye has come into the neighbourhood of an eye, together the eye and it generate both whiteness and a perception twinned with whiteness – two things that would never   d5
have come to be if either the eye or the other thing had approached anything else. Sight then moves between them from the eyes, whiteness   e1
from the co-producer of the colour, and now – hey presto! – the eye is full of sight; now it *sees*, having become, certainly not sight, rather a seeing eye, and what has co-generated the colour has been filled full of   e5
whiteness, having become for its part not whiteness but white, whether a white piece of wood or a white stone or whatever thing happened to have become coloured with this sort of colour. And so with everything – hard, hot, or anything else, we're to understand it in the same way: nothing is, itself by itself, as we were saying before; rather, it is in coming   157a
together with each other that all things and all sorts of things come to be, from their changing. In fact it's not possible, they say, to get a stable fix, in the one case, even on which of them is doing the acting and which is being acted upon, for neither is there anything acting before it comes   a5
together with what is acted on, nor anything being acted on before it comes together with what is acting; and what does the acting when together with one thing turns out to be what is acted on when together with something else. The consequence of all this, according to the theory, is that nothing – as we were saying at the beginning – is just one thing, itself by itself, but instead is always coming to be in relation to   b1
something. The verb 'is' must be removed from every context, even though we ourselves have been forced to use it many times over even just now, out of habit and lack of knowledge. In fact, according to these wise people's theory, we shouldn't consent to using 'something', or 'somebody's', or 'mine', or 'this', or 'that', or any other name that brings   b5
things to a standstill. Instead our utterances should conform to nature and have things 'coming to be', 'being made', 'passing away' and 'altering', since if anyone ever uses language that brings something to a stop, he lays himself wide open to challenge. The rule applies to talk both about the individual case and about many collected together – the

---

[29] The translation here attempts to convey the sense of a supplement suggested by an editor to fill an evident lacuna in the transmitted text (immediately before 'and that's why they are quicker').*

c1 sort of collection for which people posit entities like human being, and
rock, and so on with each living creature and form. – So, Theaetetus, do
you like the look of all this? Is it appetizing enough for you to try it out?

THEAETETUS: For myself, I'm not sure, Socrates, and actually I can't
c5 make out where you stand on it, either – whether you're saying it
because you agree with it, or in order to test me.

SOCRATES: You're forgetting, my friend, that I myself neither know
anything of such things nor claim to know anything of them; none of
them is my offspring. I'm acting as midwife to you, and that's why I sing
d1 my incantations, setting out dishes from this and that wise person for
you to taste until I can help bring what *you* think out into the light. Once
I've done that, then I'll look and see whether it will prove a bag of wind
or something fruitful. Keep your spirits up, and bear with me, telling me
d5 in a good, forthright way whatever appears to you in relation to the
things I ask you about.

THEAETETUS: Ask away, then.

SOCRATES: So tell me again whether you're attracted by the proposal
that neither good, nor beautiful, nor any of the things that were on our
list just now *is* at all, but is rather always in a process of *coming to be*.
d10 THEAETETUS: When I hear you setting out the theory like this, to me
it appears so wonderfully reasonable that we should take things to be just
as you've set them out.

e1 SOCRATES: Then let us not leave out any aspect of it that still remains
to be filled in. What is missing is anything about dreams and diseases,
especially madness, and all the things that one is said to mis-hear or mis-
see, or mis-perceive in some other way. In all these cases, as I'm sure you
e5 know, the theory we've just been describing is generally thought[30] to be
158a found lacking, on the basis that quite plainly we find false perceptions
turning up in them: far from things being as they appear to each person,
it's rather the reverse, and nothing is as it appears to be.

THEAETETUS: That's very true, Socrates.

a5 SOCRATES: So then, my boy, what argument is left for someone who
posits that perception is knowledge, and that what appears to each
person also *is*, for the person to whom it appears?[31]

---

[30] Evidence, perhaps, that the theory in question is not just an invention of Plato's (see Introduction, Section 6)?
[31] See 151d–152a.

THEAETETUS: I really am hesitant, Socrates, about admitting that I don't know what to say, because you've only just told me off for saying it. Though I'd truly be unable to dispute that a madman believes what is b1 false when he thinks he's a god, or that a dreamer believes falsely when he thinks he's got wings, and in his sleep imagines that he's flying.

SOCRATES: So you have no notion, either, of the sort of dispute there b5 is about these cases, and especially about sleeping and being awake?

THEAETETUS: What sort of dispute is that?

SOCRATES: One that I think you've often heard, when people ask what evidence one could show if asked now, offhand, at this very moment, b10 whether we're asleep and dreaming everything we're thinking, or whether c1 we're awake and really talking to each other, not dreaming it.

THEAETETUS: Yes, Socrates, it certainly is hard to see what evidence one should point to. Each and every feature of either state is mirrored, as it were, in the other. There's nothing to stop us believing in our sleep, too, that we're having the same conversation with each other that we've c5 been having here and now; and indeed when we're dreaming and thinking we're describing dreams, the resemblance between this experience and the other is uncanny.

SOCRATES: So you can see that getting a dispute started here isn't difficult, given that it's disputed even whether we're awake or asleep. d1 Indeed, since the time we are asleep is equal to the time we are awake, and in either case our soul contends that whatever we currently believe is absolutely and completely true, it follows that we spend an equal amount of time claiming that one set of things is so and an equal amount claiming d5 that the other is, advancing both claims with similar confidence.

THEAETETUS: Yes, you're quite right.

SOCRATES: So won't the same argument apply in cases of illness and madness, except in relation to time, since in them it is not equal?

THEAETETUS: Right. d10

SOCRATES: So is what is true really going to be determined by the length or shortness of time?

THEAETETUS: That would be quite absurd, in all sorts of ways. e1

SOCRATES: Can you offer any other evidence to show clearly which of these beliefs are true?

THEAETETUS: I don't think I can.

SOCRATES: Then I shall tell you the sorts of things that would be said e5 on the subject by those who lay it down that what seems to someone at any moment is true for the person to whom it seems so. I think their exposition would begin with this question: 'Theaetetus, if something is entirely different from something else, it can't, can it, somehow have the same power as the other thing? You're not to suppose, by the way, that

e10 the thing in question is in one way the same, in another different; it's wholly different.'

159a THEAETETUS: Well, it's impossible for it to have any feature in common with the other thing, whether by way of a power or in any respect whatever, when it's completely different.

SOCRATES: So mustn't one concede that such a thing is also unlike the other?

a5 THEAETETUS: I think so.

SOCRATES: Suppose, in that case, that a thing is coming to be like or unlike something, whether that something is itself or another thing: will we say that when it's becoming like, it's coming to be the same, and when it's becoming unlike, it's coming to be different?

THEAETETUS: Necessarily so.

a10 SOCRATES: Weren't we saying earlier that there were large, in fact unlimited, numbers of things that act upon other things, and similarly with things acted upon?

THEAETETUS: Yes.

SOCRATES: And also, that when one thing is mixed with another, and then another, it won't generate the same things, but different things?

b1 THEAETETUS: Yes, certainly.

SOCRATES: So now let's apply the same rationale to me and you and everything else. Take Socrates healthy and then Socrates sick: shall we

b5 say the one item is like or unlike the other?

THEAETETUS: The sick Socrates – you're taking this as a whole, and similarly the other thing, the healthy Socrates?

SOCRATES: You've taken the point beautifully; that's exactly what I'm doing.

THEAETETUS: Then the answer is: unlike.

b10 SOCRATES: And different too, insofar as it's unlike.

THEAETETUS: It must be.

c1 SOCRATES: And similarly, you'll claim, with Socrates sleeping or in any of the situations we were talking about just now?

THEAETETUS: I shall.

SOCRATES: Then won't it surely be the case that when any of the things whose nature it is to act on other things comes across Socrates healthy, it will interact with me as one thing, and when it comes across Socrates sick, with me as a different thing? c5

THEAETETUS: It certainly must.

SOCRATES: And in either case both I, the one acted on, and the thing that's doing the acting will generate different things?

THEAETETUS: Of course. c10

SOCRATES: Now when I drink wine and I'm healthy, it appears to me pleasantly sweet?

THEAETETUS: Yes.

SOCRATES: And that, from what we agreed before, is because what is c15 acting and what is being acted on, both being simultaneously in locomo- d1 tion, have generated both sweetness and a perception: the perception, being from what is acted on, has rendered the tongue perceiving, while from the wine, the sweetness moving around it has made it both be and appear sweet to the healthy tongue. d5

THEAETETUS: Yes, that's certainly in line with what was agreed between us before.

SOCRATES: And when it[32] comes across Socrates sick, first of all it must truly not be the same person it's confronting – right? After all, it's d10 encountering something we've agreed is unlike.

THEAETETUS: Yes.

SOCRATES: So to spell it out again, Socrates in this condition plus the e1 drinking of the wine have generated different things: perception of bitterness around the tongue, and bitterness coming to be and moving around the wine, so that it, the wine, comes to be not bitterness, but bitter, while I come to be perceiving, not perception. e5

THEAETETUS: Quite so.

SOCRATES: And I shall never come to be perceiving in this way in relation to anything else, since a perception of something else is another perception, and makes the person perceiving of another sort, in fact 160a another person; nor will what is acting on me ever at any time generate the same thing and come to be as it is now by coming together with something else, since having generated something else from something else it will itself come to be different.

---

[32] I.e., whatever it is that is doing the acting in this case.

a5 THEAETETUS: That's right.

SOCRATES: And neither will I come to be like this for myself, nor it like that for itself.

THEAETETUS: No.

SOCRATES: But I must inevitably come to be perceiving something,
a10 when I come to be perceiving, because it's impossible for me to come to
b1 be perceiving but perceiving nothing; and in turn it must come to be for someone, when it becomes sweet or bitter or anything of that sort, because it's impossible for something to have come to be sweet and yet have come to be sweet for nobody.

THEAETETUS: That's certainly so.

b5 SOCRATES: So all that is left, I think, is that I and it, whether we are or whether we come to be, are or come to be for each other, since necessity binds what each of us is[33] with what the other is and not with anything else, or even with ourselves. That we are bound to each other really is the only possibility left. So whether someone uses the word 'is' about something or talks about it as coming into being, he'll need to say that it is
b10 or is coming into being *for*, or *of*, or *relatively to* someone or something. He
c1 mustn't allow himself or anyone else to talk of a thing as being or coming to be itself by itself – or so the theory we've been describing indicates.

THEAETETUS: That's certainly so, Socrates.

SOCRATES: So given that what is acting on me is for me and nobody
c5 else, it's also I who perceive it, and nobody else?

THEAETETUS: It must be.

SOCRATES: In that case my perceptions are true for me, because they are of what is for me, personally, in every case; and I am judge, in Protagorean mode, both of the things that are for me, that they are, and of the things that are not for me, that they are not.[34]

c10 THEAETETUS: It seems so.

d1 SOCRATES: So if there is no falsehood in me, no stumbling in my thought about the things that are or come to be, how can I not *know* the very things of which I am perceiver?

THEAETETUS: There's no way you can fail to know them.

d5 SOCRATES: In that case it was quite right for you to say that knowledge was nothing else but perception. Everything has come together – the

[33] Or our 'being' (*ousia*).
[34] This is basically Protagoras' dictum as quoted at 152a, but with the addition of 'for me'.

view of Homer and Heraclitus and the whole of that sort of tribe, that all things change like rivers;[35] that idea of Protagoras, too, wisest of all, that the measure of all things is a human being; and now Theaetetus' proposal, to the effect that if these things are so, perception turns out to be knowledge. How about it, Theaetetus? Shall we claim this as your newborn baby, as it were, delivered by me as midwife? Or what do you want to say? $\quad$ eɪ

THEAETETUS: It's as you say, Socrates; I can't deny it. $\quad$ e5

SOCRATES: This, then, it seems, is what we've finally brought to birth after so much trouble, whatever it may actually be worth. Now that the birth's over, instead of running around the hearth with the baby we must do things properly, and run our argument around the baby in a circle, to make sure what's taking shape isn't fooling us and pretending to be worth bringing up, when it's actually a bag of wind and falsehood. Or $\quad$ 161a what do you think? Do you think your offspring should be brought up anyway, and not disposed of? Or will you put up with seeing it put to the test, and not be too angry if someone robs you of your first-born?

THEODORUS: Theaetetus will put up with it, Socrates – he's not at all $\quad$ a5 the ill-tempered sort. But by the gods, come on! Say why things *aren't* like this!

SOCRATES: You're simply a glutton for debate, Theodorus! It's good of you to suppose that I'm some sort of sack of arguments, and can easily pull one out to say that on the other hand, no, these things aren't so. $\quad$ bɪ You don't notice what's happening. The arguments never emerge from my side; they always come from my partner in discussion, and I have no more knowledge than the little required to get an argument from someone else who *is* wise and to receive it in a measured way – as I'll be $\quad$ b5 trying to get one from Theaetetus now, and not trying to say something on my own account.

THEODORUS: The way you put it is better, Socrates. Go on and do as you say.

SOCRATES: So do you know, Theodorus, what I wonder at in your friend Protagoras? $\quad$ bɪo

THEODORUS: What's that? $\quad$ cɪ

SOCRATES: I'm happy enough with other aspects of his claim, that things are what they seem to be to each individual. But I do wonder at

---

[35] Or so, again, *Heraclitus* said ('all things flow/are in flux', as he is frequently reported as saying).

c5   the way he begins. Why didn't he open his *Truth* by saying 'The measure of all things is a pig', or 'a baboon', or choosing some still stranger sort of thing that possesses the capacity to perceive? That way he could have begun addressing us with magnificent and total contempt, by demonstrating that while we were busy revering him like a god for

d1   his wisdom, when it came to knowing things he was actually no better than a tadpole, let alone any other human being. What else are we to say, Theodorus? If whatever belief each person comes to through perception is going to be true for him, and no one is going to be a better judge of what has happened to someone else than that someone himself, nor

d5   will anyone be better placed to judge whether what another person believes is correct or false – if, that is to say, as has been repeated many times, each and every person is going to believe what he believes, by himself, on his own, and all of his beliefs are going to be correct and true, then how on earth, my friend, can it be that Protagoras is wise?

e1   How can anyone be justified in supposing him qualified to teach others, for large fees, and the rest of us more ignorant than him, so that we need to go to him to be taught? How so, when we are each the measure of our own wisdom for ourselves? How can we avoid conclud-ing that *that* idea was mere demagoguery on Protagoras' part? I say

e5   nothing about my side of things, and how ridiculous it makes *me*, if his theory is correct – me and my art of midwifery, presumably along with all this business of philosophical conversation. Examining the things that appear to and are believed by one another, and trying to refute

162a   them, when each person's appearances and beliefs are correct – isn't this just an inordinately drawn-out piece of tomfoolery, if Protagoras' 'truth' is true, and isn't simply making fun of us from the oracular recesses of his book?

    THEODORUS: The man was a friend, Socrates, as you said yourself

a5   just now. So I wouldn't want Protagoras to be refuted because of concessions I'd made on his behalf; nor again would I resist you by going against my own beliefs. So take it up with Theaetetus again; the way he was following your lead just now appeared altogether very appropriate.

b1   SOCRATES: If you went to Sparta, Theodorus, and visited the wrest-ling schools, would you think to watch other people naked, some of them inferior specimens, and not take your turn to strip off and show them what shape you were in?

28

THEODORUS: Well, what do you think – if I could persuade them to let   b5
me choose? Just as now I imagine I'll persuade you people to let me
watch, not drag my stiff joints off to the gymnasium. The bout should be
with the younger and more supple among us.

SOCRATES: Well, Theodorus, I'm happy if you are, as people say who   b10
like their proverbs. Back it is to the wise Theaetetus, then. So start by   c1
telling me, Theaetetus, about the things we were saying just now: does it
not make you wonder, that you're suddenly going to find yourself every
bit as good, when it comes to wisdom, as any human – or even any god?   c5
Or do you think the Protagorean measure applies any less to gods than it
does to human beings?

THEAETETUS: Zeus! I certainly don't. And to answer your question, it
really does make me wonder. When we were discussing the manner of
their claim, that what seems to each individual also is for the individual   d1
thinking it, it appeared completely fine to me; but now all of a sudden it's
quite the opposite.

SOCRATES: That's your youth, my dear boy, making you quick to
listen to crowd-pleasing talk and to allow it to take you in. The response
to this objection from Protagoras, or from anyone who speaks for   d5
him, will be 'You people, young and old, you sit there merely playing
to the crowd! Not only do you try to bring gods into it, when   e1
I specifically omit to say, whether in person or in writing, either that
they are or that they are not,[36] but when you say how strange, if no
human being is going to be any wiser than the next sheep or goat, then
you're just saying what ordinary people would accept if you told it to   e5
them. You mention nothing whatever by way of compelling proof;
instead you rely on what merely looks likely. If Theodorus or some
other geometer tried doing geometry like that, they wouldn't be worth a
single moment's attention.' So you and Theodorus had better look and
see whether you're going to be content to accept statements, on questions of such great importance, that rely on mere plausibility and   163a
likelihoods.

THEAETETUS: It wouldn't be right, Socrates; neither you nor we
would say it was.

---

[36] Diogenes Laertius, *Lives of the Philosophers* IX.51, reports Protagoras as saying 'About the gods,
I am incapable of knowing either that they are or that they are not; for many are the things that
prevent my knowing, both obscurity and the shortness of the life of a human being.'

SOCRATES: Then it seems we must take a different line in our inquiry. That's what you and Theodorus are saying.

THEAETETUS: Yes, definitely a different line.

SOCRATES: So here's a way we might consider whether knowledge and perception are after all the same thing, or different – I suppose that was the point of our discussion all along, wasn't it? That's how we came to stir up all these weird subjects?

THEAETETUS: It certainly was.

SOCRATES: Well now, are we going to accept that when we perceive anything by seeing or hearing, we also know it at the same time? For example, are we going to say that before we've learned their language, we don't hear non-Greeks speak, or that we both hear and know what they're saying? Again, if we don't know our letters, will we claim that we're not seeing them when we look at them, or insist that we do know them, if indeed we're seeing them?

THEAETETUS: What we'll say we know, Socrates, is exactly what we see and hear of them: the shape and the colour, we'll say, we both see and know in the case of the letters, while in the other case we both hear, and at the same time know, the high or low pitch of the voices. But as for what schoolmasters or interpreters teach about them, we'll say we don't perceive that by seeing or hearing it and we don't know it either.

SOCRATES: Very well done, Theaetetus, and it's not worth disputing the point with you, if you're to progress. But watch out for this new objection that's looming, and think how we're to fend it off.

THEAETETUS: What sort of objection?

SOCRATES: The sort where someone asks 'Suppose someone has come to know something, and suppose he still has a memory of this same thing, which he's preserving: at the time he remembers it, is it possible for him not to know the very thing he remembers?' It seems I'm using too many words, when all I want to ask is whether someone who has learned something doesn't know it when he remembers it.

THEAETETUS: How could he not know it, Socrates? What you're saying would be monstrous!

SOCRATES: So perhaps I'm being crazy? But look here. Aren't you saying that seeing is perceiving, and that sight is perception?

THEAETETUS: I am.

SOCRATES: So, according to what you were saying just now, the person who has seen something has come to know the thing he has seen? e1

THEAETETUS: Yes.

SOCRATES: And what about memory? You do say there is such a thing?

THEAETETUS: Yes. e5

SOCRATES: And is memory of nothing, or of something?

THEAETETUS: Of something, I imagine.

SOCRATES: Of things that a person has learned and things that he has perceived – those sorts of things?

THEAETETUS: Obviously.

SOCRATES: And I suppose a person sometimes remembers what he has seen? e10

THEAETETUS: He does.

SOCRATES: Even when he's shut his eyes? Or has he forgotten once he's done that?

THEAETETUS: That would be a strange thing to say, Socrates!

SOCRATES: And yet it's something we'll have to say if we're going to save our proposal; if we don't, it's dead and buried. 164a

THEAETETUS: Zeus! That's what I'm suspecting too, but I'm not entirely clear why. Explain it to me.

SOCRATES: The point is that according to what we're saying, the person seeing has come to know the thing he's come to be seeing, given our agreement that sight – that is, perception – and knowledge are the same thing. a5

THEAETETUS: Certainly.

SOCRATES: But if the person who has come to be seeing, and thus to know the thing he was seeing, now shuts his eyes, he remembers the thing but isn't seeing it. Right? a10

THEAETETUS: Yes.

SOCRATES: But 'isn't seeing' is 'doesn't know', if seeing is also knowing. b1

THEAETETUS: True.

SOCRATES: It follows, in that case, given that he's not seeing it, that a person doesn't know, even while he still remembers, what he came to know. Which is just the result we said would be monstrous. b5

THEAETETUS: Very true.

SOCRATES: Something impossible, then, appears to follow if one claims knowledge and perception to be the same thing.

31

b10   THEAETETUS: It looks like it.

SOCRATES: In that case we need to say that the two things are different from each other.

THEAETETUS: Very likely.

c1   SOCRATES: What, then, *will* knowledge be? It seems we'll have to begin our account again from the beginning. – But hold on, Theaetetus! What on earth are we thinking of?

THEAETETUS: In what respect?

c5   SOCRATES: We appear to me to be behaving like a badly bred fighting cock, leaping away from the thesis we're opposing and crowing before we've won.

THEAETETUS: How so?

SOCRATES: It looks as though we've reached agreement between us in the way antilogicians do,[37] content if we defeat the thesis somehow by
c10 basing ourselves on issues of mere verbal consistency. We're not in it for
d1 the sake of winning, we say, in the way those clever fellows are, we're *philosophers* – not noticing that we're actually doing the same as they do.

THEAETETUS: I don't yet understand your point.

d5   SOCRATES: I'll try to show what my thinking is about it all. Our question was whether someone who has learned something and remembers it won't know it. By showing that the person seeing and then shutting his eyes was remembering and not seeing, we showed that he didn't know even while he was actually remembering; and this we said was impossible. And so the Protagorean story met its end, and your
d10 story, about knowledge and perception being the same thing, went with it.

e1   THEAETETUS: It appears so.

SOCRATES: I don't think, my friend, that it would have met its end at all, if only the father of the first of the two stories were alive – he would find plenty to say in its defence. But as things are, it's an orphan, and we're trampling over it. Not even the guardians Protagoras left
e5 behind him are willing to come to its aid, one of whom is Theodorus here. But come on, for the sake of justice we'll risk helping it out ourselves.

---

[37] An expert in 'antilogic' would typically claim to be able in one way or another to lead a respondent who starts with one position, on anything whatever, into asserting the opposite of that position.

THEODORUS: You see, Socrates, I'm not the one looking after Protagoras' legacy; that's more Callias, son of Hipponicus.[38] We on our side somehow headed rather quickly away from abstract arguments, to geometry. All the same we'll be grateful if you will come to the orphan's aid. 165a

SOCRATES: You're right, Theodorus. So see what you think of my attempt to help out, for what it's worth. The fact is that we might find ourselves making even stranger concessions than we did just now, if we don't pay attention to the words we use, and the way we're mostly used to asserting and denying things. Shall I tell you how it might happen – or should I be telling Theaetetus? a5

THEAETETUS: You should tell us both, but let the younger of us answer the questions, because he'll make less of a spectacle of himself when he trips up. b1

SOCRATES: Well, here is the strangest question. I think it goes something like this: is it possible for the same person to know something and yet not know this thing he knows?

THEODORUS: So what shall we answer, Theaetetus? b5

THEAETETUS: That it's pretty much impossible, I think.

SOCRATES: Not so, or at least not if you're going to assume that seeing is knowing. If you are, how will you deal with a question you can't escape – one that will leave you 'trapped in a well', as people say: what if some forthright individual claps his hand over one of your eyes and asks if you see his cloak with the covered eye? c1

THEAETETUS: I imagine I'll say that I don't see it with this one, but I do with the other.

SOCRATES: So you're seeing and not seeing the same thing at the same time?

THEAETETUS: I am, yes, in a way. c5

SOCRATES: 'That', he'll say, 'isn't at all what I'm after; my question wasn't about how, just *whether* what you know you also don't know. And as things stand, you're plainly seeing what you're not seeing; since you've actually admitted that seeing is knowing, and that not seeing is not knowing, you can work out for yourself where this leaves you.' c10

---

[38] A wealthy patron of intellectuals; the main conversation in Plato's *Protagoras*, with Protagoras and Socrates as protagonists, takes place in his house.

d1 THEAETETUS: Yes, I can – saying the opposite of what I proposed before.

SOCRATES: Indeed, my wonderful friend, and probably more of the same would have happened to you, if someone went on to ask you if it's possible to know things now sharply, now dimly, or know them from
d5 close up but not from a distance, or know a lot or just a little bit about the same thing. There are tens of thousands of such questions you would be ambushed with in discussion by some fee-earning expert in skirmishing, as soon as you proposed that knowledge and perception were the same thing. Sallying into hearing and smelling and all sorts of perceptions like
e1 that, he would keep challenging you and not let up until he'd bound you hand and foot with wonder at his much-envied wisdom; at which point, having made you his prisoner and tied you up once and for all, he would ransom you for whatever sum you decided on between you. – So, you
e5 may ask, what answers will Protagoras give in support of his offspring? Should we try to say?

THEAETETUS: We certainly should.

166a SOCRATES: He'll say all the things we are saying in his defence, and then I imagine he'll come to close quarters with us and say contemptuously. 'Good for Socrates! Didn't he do well, bullying some little boy by asking him if it was possible for the same person both to remember and not to know the same thing at the same time – and then, when the boy
a5 said no because he was frightened and couldn't see what was coming, using the discussion to make *me* a laughing stock! That's just lazy of you, Socrates. This is the way it is: when you use your method of questioning to examine something I have said, I am the one that is refuted if the person questioned slips up by giving the very sorts of answers I would
b1 give; but if his answers are not the sort I would give, the refutation is of him, not of me.

'To begin with, do you think anyone is going to concede to you that when we have a present memory of things that have happened to us, this is the same sort of experience as the one we had originally, if we're no longer experiencing the things in question? Far from it.[39] Or, con-
b5 versely, that anyone will hesitate to concede that it's possible for the same person to know and not know the same thing? Or, if he's too

---

[39] In other words, why do you suppose that I (Protagoras) cannot construct an account of a present memory consistent with the one I've given of perception?

frightened to make that concession, do you think he'll ever grant you that someone who is becoming unlike is the same person he was before becoming unlike, or indeed even that he's some*one*, and not a plurality of individuals coming into being – an unlimited plurality at that, if things are going on becoming unlike? Certainly not, if we're going to have to watch out for people pouncing on our use of words. Be more adventurous, my good man,' Protagoras will say, 'and direct your attack at what I'm actually saying. Refute me, if you can, by showing that the perceptions that come to be for each one of us are not peculiar to that individual, or that, if they are peculiar to him, it does not follow at all that what appears to him comes to be – or is, if we have to call it that – for that person alone, that is, the one to whom it appears. By talking about pigs, or baboons, you not only behave like a pig yourself, you persuade the audience to do the same towards my writings, and that's not right.

'I say the truth is as I have written it: each one of us is the measure both of the things that are and of the things that are not, but people differ ten thousand times over from each other, for the very reason that different things are for, and appear to, different people. I am far from denying that there is such a thing as wisdom, or that an individual can be wise; but the only individual I do call wise is the one who effects change in the person to whom bad things appear, and for whom they are, and brings it about that good things both appear to him and are for him.

'I ask you again – don't attack what I'm saying merely for the way I say it. But let me explain yet more clearly what I *am* saying. Recall the sort of example we used before: how what the sick person eats both appears and is bitter to him, whereas the opposite is and appears to the healthy person. What is required in this case is not to make one or the other of them wiser, which is ruled out in any case; nor is it to call the ill one ignorant for having the beliefs he has, the healthy one wise for having different ones. What is needed is to change the one to the other state, because one of them is better. In education, similarly, the aim must be to effect change from the worse of two states to the better; the difference is that the medical doctor brings about the change with drugs, whereas the sophist[40] does so with words. Nobody ever made anyone with false

c1

c5

d1

d5

e1

e5
167a

a5

---

[40] I.e., a professional purveyor of wisdom (*sophia*); as 'Protagoras' himself has now set things up, only he or someone like him will qualify.

beliefs about anything go on to have true ones; for it's impossible for anyone to believe either things that are not, or things that go against what he is currently experiencing, which is in every case true. What I think *can* be done is to make someone who has a soul in unsound condition, and believes things akin to that condition, come to believe different and sound things with a soul in correspondingly sound condition – things, that is, appearances, that some people, out of inexperience, call true, whereas I myself don't call them in any way truer than the others, but simply better. And, my dear Socrates, so far from reducing wise people to frogs, I call them doctors if they deal with human bodies, farmers if they deal with plants; for I claim that farmers too produce sound and healthy perceptions and truths[41] in plants, when some aspect of them is sickly, in place of unsound perceptions, and that wise and good public speakers are those that make sound things seem to cities to be just in place of unsound ones. Because whatever sorts of things seem to each city to be just and fine, these I claim are so for that city, for so long as it thinks them so; but the wise person in each case makes sound things be for and seem to the citizens instead of things that are unsound. The same argument applies to the sophist too: it is his ability to educate his pupils in this way that makes him both wise and worth a great deal of money to those he has educated.

'That is how it can be *both* that some people are wiser than others *and* that no one has false beliefs about anything, so that whether you like it or not, you too have to put up with being the measure; the conjunction of the two things preserves that thesis of mine. If you are able to dispute this, starting at the beginning, then do so by setting out the opposing case – or if you prefer to use questioning, do it that way; one shouldn't run away from questioning either, and indeed any sensible person should encourage it more than anything. But I ask one thing of you: make sure that you don't treat me unjustly in your questions. It is quite unreasonable for someone who claims to care about goodness to persist in behaving unjustly in discussion. The sort of injustice I have in mind is when one fails to separate two different things, namely having one's say in a spirit of competition, and doing so as part of a conversation.[42]

---

[41] Reading *alêtheias* (accusative plural) in place of the manuscripts' *alêtheis*.*
[42] I.e., presumably, a thoughtful or philosophical one; a proper dialogue (the term Protagoras uses is *dialegesthai*).

Competing is a matter of playing about and trying to trip the other person up as much as possible, whereas in conversation one is in earnest, and helps put the respondent back on his feet, pointing out to him only those slip-ups that he is responsible for himself or has been misled into 168a by the company he's been with previously. If you do keep the two things apart, people who spend time with you will blame themselves for their own confusion and puzzlement, not you. You they'll follow and love, while reserving their hatred for themselves, fleeing from their own a5 company into philosophy, in order to become different people and be rid of the people they were before. But if you do the opposite of this, as most do, then you'll get the opposite result, and instead of making your companions into philosophers you'll make them hate the whole idea b1 when they become older. So as I said before, if you take my advice you'll approach what we're saying with kindly intent and not in a hostile or aggressive manner; you'll settle down with us and genuinely examine what it is that we're saying when we assert that everything is changing, b5 and that things are for each, individual and city, what they seem to each to be. And you'll use *that* as the basis for considering whether knowledge and perception are the same thing or different; not, as you were doing just now, the conventional use of words and names, which people c1 generally drag in somehow or other and create all sorts of puzzles for one another in doing so.'

I present this, Theodorus, as my contribution towards helping your friend out. Small it may be, but so are my resources; it's the best I can do. If only he were alive, he'd have mounted a more magnificent defence c5 for his own offspring.

THEODORUS: You're joking, Socrates. You've defended the man with a quite youthful vigour!

SOCRATES: Good of you to say so, my friend. Tell me – did you perhaps notice how when he was speaking just now Protagoras criticized us for addressing our arguments to a little boy,[43] and competing against d1 his case by using the boy's fears? And how he wrote off what we said as an amusing trifle, while extolling this 'measure of all things' of his, and telling us to take his position seriously?

THEODORUS: I could hardly fail to notice it, Socrates. d5

---

[43] 166a.

37

SOCRATES: So do you think we should do as he says?

THEODORUS: Very much so.

SOCRATES: Well, you can see that all here are 'little boys' except you. So if we are going to do what the man says, it's the two of us that will

e1 have to 'take his position seriously' by doing the questioning and answering between ourselves. Then at least he won't be able to complain that we treated examining his position like a game with adolescents.

THEODORUS: What are you saying? Won't Theaetetus be better at

e5 following the investigation of a thesis than any number of us who have big beards?

SOCRATES: Certainly no better than *you*, Theodorus. There's no reason why I should be making every effort to support your dead

169a friend while you make none at all. Be a good man and follow for a little while – up until the point when we know whether it's you after all that should be the measure when it comes to geometrical figures, or whether everyone is just as much an authority as you are on astronomy and the

a5 other subjects in which you are said to excel.

THEODORUS: It isn't easy, Socrates, for anyone sitting beside you to avoid giving an account of himself. It was crazy of me to pretend just now that you would allow me not to strip off, and wouldn't use compul-

b1 sion as the Spartans do; in fact I think you're more like Sciron.[44] The Spartans give an option, either to leave or strip, but you seem to me rather to be playing the scene Antaeus-style[45] – if anyone comes near you, you don't let him go until you've forced him to strip and wrestle with you in discussion.

b5 SOCRATES: Yes, that's a first-rate analogy for my affliction, Theodorus. But I'm harder to shake off than Sciron or Antaeus. I've come across tens of thousands of powerful speakers in my time, veritable Heracleses and Theseuses, and they've given me a thoroughly good

c1 thrashing, but even so I'm still no more likely to stand back, so extraordinarily deep is the passion in me for working out on these subjects. So no, don't you begrudge me a bout with you, either; it'll do you good as well as me.

c5 THEODORUS: I won't resist any more. Lead on as you will. I shall have to put up with it anyway, whatever fate you spin for me with your

---

[44] A legendary brigand, proverbial for his combination of viciousness and cunning.

[45] Another legendary figure, who wrestled any passer-by to death.

questioning. But I'll not be able to offer myself to you beyond what you've proposed.

SOCRATES: Even that far will suffice. And please do watch out that we don't use some childish sort of strategy in the discussion and not notice   d1
it. We don't want anyone reproaching us for that again.

THEODORUS: I'll certainly try, so far as I can.

SOCRATES: So let's first attack the same point we were attacking before, and see whether we were right or not to be upset at Protagoras'   d5
theory for making each individual self-sufficient in wisdom, and whether he was right or not in agreeing with us that some individuals were in fact superior to others, that is, in relation to what is better or worse, so that these individuals *were* wise. Right?

THEODORUS: Yes.

SOCRATES: Well, if he were here to make the concession for himself,   d10
instead of our making it for him, to help him out, there wouldn't be any   e1
need for us to take up the point again and confirm it; but as things are, someone might declare us to be lacking the authority to make the concession for him. So it's better for us to reach a clearer agreement on this particular point, because it makes no small difference whether it   e5
is so or not.

THEODORUS: That is true.

SOCRATES: Then let's not get the concession through others but from   170a
what he himself says, in the shortest possible way.

THEODORUS: How?

SOCRATES: Like this. I think he says that what seems to each individual also is for that person?

THEODORUS: Indeed he does.   a5

SOCRATES: Well then, Protagoras, we too are saying what seems to a human being,[46] or rather what seems to all human beings, and we claim that there is no one who doesn't think that in some respects he is wiser than others and in other respects others are wiser than him. That certainly holds at times of greatest danger: whether we're on military   a10
campaigns, we're ill, or we're in a storm at sea, we treat whoever is in charge like a god, looking to him to save us through his superiority in   b1

---

[46] Or 'what a human being believes' (Socrates is using the term *doxa*); but what Socrates says here appears designed to pick up 'what seems', *to dokoun*, in what he last said – a person's 'beliefs' being, *inter alia*, the things that seem (true) to him or her.

precisely this respect, that he *knows*. And practically every area of human life is full of people looking for those who will teach them or otherwise take charge, whether of themselves, of other animals, or of productive

b5 activities; full too of others who think they're up to teaching and to taking charge. Is it possible to avoid the conclusion that in all these cases human beings themselves think there is wisdom and ignorance among them?

THEODORUS: No.

b10 SOCRATES: And they think wisdom is true thought, ignorance false belief?

c1 THEODORUS: Of course.

SOCRATES: So how, Protagoras, shall we deal with this outcome? Are we to say that what human beings believe is in every case true, or that it

c5 is in some cases true, in others false? It looks as if it follows either way that their beliefs are not always true, but sometimes true, sometimes false. For think, Theodorus: would Protagoras and his supporters, or would you, really be prepared to maintain that no one ever thinks that someone else is ignorant and has false beliefs?

THEODORUS: It's hard to credit, Socrates.

d1 SOCRATES: And yet that's the predicament this thesis, that a human being is the measure of all things, necessarily finds itself in.

THEODORUS: How so?

SOCRATES: Suppose you have made a judgement about something

d5 privately to yourself, and you then declare your belief to me: granted that on Protagoras' thesis it will be true for you, will it not be possible for the rest of us to be our own judges of your judgement? Or do we always judge your beliefs to be true? Don't tens of thousands of people resist you every time with their own opposite beliefs, and suppose your judgements and thoughts to be false?

e1 THEODORUS: Zeus! Yes, Socrates, 'countless tens of thousands', to quote Homer,[47] who give me the sort of trouble human beings do.

SOCRATES: What then? Do you want us to say that you find yourself

e5 on such occasions believing things that are true for you yourself, but false for tens of thousands of others?

THEODORUS: It seems that must be so, at least from what we've said.

---

[47] *Odyssey* 16.121, of the numbers of enemies Odysseus faces on his return home.

SOCRATES: And how about for Protagoras himself?[48] Mustn't it be the case that if not even he thought human beings were the measure, and neither did most people (as in fact they don't), this *Truth* he's written isn't the truth for anybody at all? And if he did think it himself, and the generality of people do not, you'll recognise that, first, it's more the case that it's not the truth than that it is, by the same proportion as those to whom it doesn't seem to be so outnumber those to whom it does.

171a

THEODORUS: Inevitably, given that it is going to be so or not so according to individuals' particular beliefs.

a5

SOCRATES: Yes, and there is this second, quite exquisite consequence: on the one hand, in relation to his own thinking, I suppose Protagoras agrees that the thinking of those holding opposite beliefs, by virtue of which they consider *his* thinking false, is in fact true, since he concedes that everyone believes things that are.[49]

THEODORUS: Certainly.

a10

SOCRATES: Will he then concede that his own thinking is false, if he admits that the thinking of those who consider his to be false is true?

b1

THEODORUS: He can't avoid it.

SOCRATES: But they, on the other hand, do not concede that *their* view is false?

b5

THEODORUS: They do not.

SOCRATES: And he for his part concedes that this belief too is true, to judge by what he has written.

THEODORUS: Apparently.

SOCRATES: It follows, then, that Protagoras' view will be disputed from all sides, starting from Protagoras – or rather *he* will be agreeing with it, as soon as he concedes to someone taking the opposite view to his own that this person in this moment believes what is true. And[50] Protagoras himself will concede on his own behalf that neither a dog nor any random human being is the measure in relation to anything whatever if he hasn't learned it. Isn't that so?

b10

c1

---

[48] This seems to pick up the question at 170c. Socrates has just established that Theodorus is not 'prepared to maintain that no one ever thinks someone else is ignorant and has false beliefs'; now he asks whether Protagoras would be.

[49] 'Believes things that are' (*ta onta doxazein*): another way of putting the by now standard formula 'what seems to each person (to be) also is for that person'; it picks up Protagoras' claim at 167a that 'it's impossible for anyone to believe either things that are not, or things that go against what he is currently experiencing, which is in every case true.'

[50] Deleting the comma before *tote* and inserting a full stop after it (after Sedley).

THEODORUS: It is.

c5 SOCRATES: So, since it's disputed by everybody, Protagoras' *Truth* will be true for nobody; not for anybody else, and not even for him.

THEODORUS: We're pushing my friend too hard, Socrates.

c10 SOCRATES: But I have to say, my friend, it isn't clear that what we're saying is breaking any rules.[51] In any case the likelihood is that being

d1 older than us, the man really is wiser than we are. If he could suddenly poke his head up from the ground just there in front of us, as far as the neck, I've no doubt he'd find me out many times over for talking nonsense, and you for agreeing to my nonsense; then he'd sink back down again and be gone before we knew it. But we must just make the

d5 best of ourselves as we are, I suppose, and simply say what seems to us in each case. And in fact, in the present case, surely we'll say that anybody and everybody would agree at least to this much, that one person can be wiser or more ignorant than another?

THEODORUS: It certainly seems so to me.

SOCRATES: And do you also think the position we're discussing holds

e1 up best in the way we ourselves sketched it when we were coming to Protagoras' aid, namely that most things are for each individual as they seem to him – hot, dry, sweet, everything of that type; but that if it was going to concede at all that there were things in which one person is

e5 superior to another in certain things, it would want to say that not every female or child, or indeed animal, is competent to recognize what is conducive to its own health, and to heal itself, and that if there is indeed any context in which one person is superior to another, it's here?

THEODORUS: That's how it seems to me.

172a SOCRATES: And similarly in the political sphere, in relation to what is fine or shameful, just or unjust, or pious or not: whatever a city thinks about these, and lays down as the norm for herself, that, according to the thesis, will also in truth *be* fine, shameful, and so on for each city, and in

a5 such matters no individual will be any wiser than another, nor any city wiser than another; but when it comes to laying down what is advantageous or not for herself, that is where, if anywhere, one adviser will again be superior to another, and one city's decisions superior to another's, in

b1 relation to their truth. It would be simply too much for the thesis to

---

[51] An admission that the last objection to Protagoras might be somewhat *ad hominem*?

claim that anything a city thought was advantageous to herself and laid down as such would with absolute certainty turn out to be so. But with the things I'm talking about, the just and the unjust, the pious and the impious, it is different – people are happy to maintain that none of them is a thing in nature with its own being;[52] what seems just, pious, or whatever to people collectively comes to be true at the moment it seems so to them and for as long a time as it seems so. Even those who don't go all the way with Protagoras' view hold something like this sort of view of wisdom. – Just look, Theodorus, we discuss one thesis, and then another one comes along, bigger than the last!

THEODORUS: We have the time for it, don't we, Socrates?

SOCRATES: Evidently. I've frequently thought to myself on other occasions, my friend, and I'm thinking it now, how unsurprising it is that those who have spent a lot of time on things like philosophy appear such buffoons when they go and speak in a court of law.

THEODORUS: Why exactly do you say that?

SOCRATES: Take people who have knocked around since their youth in the courts and other such places, and compare them with those brought up on philosophy and activities like that: it's pretty much like comparing the upbringing of slaves to that of free men.

THEODORUS: How so?

SOCRATES: Because the latter sort always have the thing you mentioned – time. They say what they want to say at their leisure, with nothing to disturb them: they can swap the thesis before them for another one if they like the look of it, just as we are now already happily taking on our third in succession; and it doesn't matter to them whether they use many words or only a few, so long as they hit the target – what *is*.[53] The other sort, by contrast, never have time when they speak, because the flow of the water in the clock always hurries them on; nor can they ever talk about whatever they want, because the opposing speaker is always there standing over them, forcing them to stay within the limits of the affidavit he keeps reading out. Their speeches are always about a fellow-slave, addressed to a slave-master sitting there with some penalty or other in his hand. The contests are never without a clear purpose, always about the matter before them, and frequently the race is

b5

c1

c5

d1

d5

e1

e5

---

[52] I.e., (at least) a thing in its own right.   [53] 'What is' (*to on*): see Note on text and translation.

173a   even a matter of life and death. As a result of all this they become intense and driven, knowing how both to flatter the slave-master and to creep into his good graces, and they are stunted and warped in their souls. Slavery since youth has prevented them from growing straight and true

a5   like free men, forcing them into crooked dealings by heaping great dangers and fears upon souls still tender. Unable to bear the weight of these in the company of justice and truth, they turn at once to falsehood and paying each other back, injustice for injustice; constantly bent and

b1   broken as they are, they end up passing from adolescence to maturity with nothing sound in their heads, and grown clever and wise – as they suppose. So much for them, Theodorus; do you want us to describe the

b5   members of our own chorus before we go back to our discussion, or shall we leave them to one side? As we said just now, we're free to change the subject of discussion, but we shouldn't overdo it.

    THEODORUS: Certainly not, Socrates; we should describe our sort of

c1   people first. You got it absolutely right when you said that, as members of our sort of chorus, we are not slaves of our discussions; it's our discussions that are our slaves, as it were, each one of them waiting around to be completed when *we* decide. There are no jurymen to stand

c5   over us, no spectators to find fault with us and order us about as they do poets in the theatre.

    SOCRATES: So we're to do it, it seems, since you think we should. And let's talk about the leaders of our chorus; why would anyone want to discuss people who do philosophy badly? The leaders, I imagine, first of

d1   all haven't known since they were children how to get to the market-place, or where to find a law court, a council chamber, or any other of the city's public meeting places. Laws and decrees, spoken or written down, our chorus leaders neither see nor hear. Political clubs scrambling after

d5   office; parties; dinners; revelling with pipe girls: not even in their dreams does it occur to them to join in. If someone in the city is born well or badly, or something bad has come down to someone from his ancestors, male or female, our chorus leader knows less about it than about the proverbial number of pitchers-full there are in the sea. And he doesn't

e1   even know that he doesn't know any of this. It isn't even that he's standing back from it for the sake of a good reputation; rather it's that it is only his body that is truly located in the city and resides in it, because his mind, having concluded that all these things are worth little

e5   or nothing, rejects them and flies off in all directions, both 'to the deeps

of the earth', as Pindar says, and measuring its surfaces, tracking the
stars 'in the heights of heaven' too, and using every sinew to search out
every nature among the things that are, taking each thing as a whole, not
lowering itself to any of the things close by.[54] 174a

THEODORUS: How so, Socrates?

SOCRATES: It's like when Thales fell into a well while doing astronomy, Theodorus, and looking up at the stars; they say a witty and a5
charming Thracian slave girl joked that he was so eager to know about
the things in the heavens that he omitted to notice what was in front of
him, right by his feet. The same joke can be used against anyone who b1
spends his time in philosophy, because such a person really does fail
to notice not just what his neighbour is doing, right next to him, but
practically even whether he's a human being or some other sort of
creature; what he looks for, and takes pains to track down, is what a b5
human being is, and what it is a part of a nature of that sort, as distinct
from others, to do and have done to it. I think you see what I'm getting
at, Theodorus, don't you?

THEODORUS: Yes, I do, and what you say is true.

SOCRATES: That, my friend, is why, as I was saying at the beginning,
someone like this makes a laughing stock of himself, whether he's dealing c1
with someone in private or in public, as soon as he is forced, in a law
court or somewhere else, to hold a conversation about things by his
feet or before his very eyes. It isn't just Thracian girls that laugh at him;
it's the mass of people in general, as he falls into wells and all sorts of c5
puzzlement because of his inexperience. The unseemliness of it all is
extraordinary, and makes him seem a fool. When it comes to insults, he
has none of his own to offer against anyone – not being practised in
finding fault, he recognizes none in anybody; so, having nothing to say, d1
he appears ridiculous. If others are boasting and expecting praise, he
openly laughs at them, and it's genuine, not fake laughter, which they
take as a sign of craziness. When he hears an encomium for a tyrant or
a king, it sounds to him like a herdsman of some sort, a swineherd, d5
a shepherd, or perhaps a cowherd being called happy for the quantity
of milk he gets from his cows; only in his eyes they have a more ill-
tempered and treacherous animal to herd and milk – one that it takes all

---

[54] On this passage, see the final paragraph of Section 2 of the Introduction to this volume.

e1 their time to handle, so that inevitably somebody like that becomes no
less boorish and uneducated than ordinary herdsmen, only with a city
wall surrounding them instead of a mountain sheep pen. Again, when he
hears ten thousand *plethra*[55] or even more being spoken of as an aston-
e5 ishing amount of land to own, it seems to him a quite tiny amount to
speak of, accustomed as he is to gazing upon the whole earth. When
people hymn family connections, counting someone as noble if he has
seven generations of wealthy ancestors to boast of, it seems to him to be
175a what only thoroughly dim and short-sighted people would praise; he
puts it down to a lack of education and an inability on their part to keep
their gaze fixed always on the whole, or to work it out that each and every
person has had countless tens of thousands of ancestors and forebears,
among which there will have been rich and poor and kings and slaves,
a5 non-Greek and Greek – many times ten thousand of each for anybody
you care to name. When people pride themselves on a list of forebears
going back twenty-five generations, and trace their line back to Heracles,
son of Amphitryon, it appears to him a strangely petty sort of counting,
b1 and he laughs to think that they can't rise far enough above the vanity of
their mindless souls to work out that it will have been a matter of pure
chance what sort of person Amphitryon's own twenty-fifth ancestor was,
and the twenty-fifth before that. It's in all these cases, I'm saying, that
b5 the generality of people ridicule him for his behaviour, sometimes for his
supposed arrogance, sometimes for not knowing what is just in front of
him and being puzzled by everything.

THEODORUS: That's exactly what happens, Socrates.

SOCRATES: But what, my friend, if he himself manages to drag
c1 someone upwards, and finds him willing to move away from perpetually
having to ask 'How have I wronged you?' or 'How have you wronged
me?' to inquiring into justice itself, and injustice – what each of the two
things is, and how they differ from everything else or from one another;
or from a question like 'Whether happiness is being king', or again
c5 'Whether happiness is having a little gold',[56] to an inquiry about king-
ship, and about human happiness and misery in general, asking what
sorts of thing they are and in what way it befits human nature to acquire

---

[55] A *plethron*, as a measure of area, is roughly 10,000 square feet/1,000 square metres/a tenth of a
hectare.
[56] Perhaps a quotation, from an unknown source.*

the one and avoid the other? When that stunted, driven soul, so good in   d1
court, has to give an account of all *these* subjects, the tables are turned;
dizzily suspended on high, and looking down from the skies, the
unfamiliarity of his situation bewilders and puzzles him, and his stam-
mering responses make him a laughing stock, not to Thracian slave girls,   d5
or to anyone similarly uneducated, because they don't notice such
things, but to anyone who has been brought up in the opposite way to
a slave.

These are the modes of our two types, Theodorus. One is that of
someone who has been truly brought up in freedom, without constraints   e1
on his time – you call him a philosopher; someone who counts it no
reproach to seem a simple-minded good-for-nothing when he finds
himself asked to perform slave-like tasks, like tying up the bedclothes
when he knows nothing about bed-tying, or flavouring a sauce, or
making flattering speeches. The other mode is that of someone who is   e5
keen and sharp at doing everything of that sort, but doesn't know how to
strike up an elegant tune like a free man, let alone how to tune his words
correctly in celebrating a life fit for the gods, and for human beings if   176a
they are to be happy.

THEODORUS: If only you could persuade everyone of what you're
saying, Socrates, as you persuade me, peace would be more widespread
among men, and bad things less so.

SOCRATES: But it's not possible, Theodorus, for bad things to be   a5
abolished – because there is necessarily always something opposite to
good – nor can they ever find a place among the gods; but around mortal
nature, and this region of ours, they always circle, of necessity. That is
why one must try to escape from here to there as quickly as possible.
Escape is becoming as like god as one can, and becoming like god is   b1
acquiring justice and piety along with wisdom. But I tell you, my good
friend, it is not at all easy to persuade someone that the reasons most
people give as to why one should avoid badness and pursue goodness,
namely so as not to be thought bad but be thought good, are actually the   b5
wrong reasons. This is just the rubbish that the proverbial old wives talk,
or so it appears to me. The truth, let's say, is like this: god is in no case
and in no way unjust, but as just as it is possible to be, and nothing is   c1
more like him than whichever one of us succeeds in becoming as just as
can possibly be. It is here that we see whether a man is truly clever or an
unmanly good-for-nothing; understanding this is what constitutes true

c5 wisdom and goodness, while not understanding it is patent ignorance and badness, and all other sorts of seeming cleverness and wisdom are either vulgar, as among those wielding political power, or in the case of

d1 craftsmen merely mechanical. Thus if someone behaves unjustly and says and does impious things, it is best by far not to attribute to him a cleverness driven by lack of scruple, since people revel in such a reproach; they hear it as telling them that they are not examples of futility, useless burdens on the earth, but men with the qualities neces-

d5 sary for surviving in the city. So we must tell them the truth, which is that they are all the more the sort of people they do not think they are for the fact that they do not think it; for they do not know the penalty for injustice, and that is the last thing one should be ignorant about. It is not what they think it is – flogging, execution and the like, which they

e1 sometimes escape altogether even when they do behave unjustly; it's a penalty that it's impossible to escape.

THEODORUS: What is *that*?

SOCRATES: In the nature of things there are two models available to us, my friend, one divine and most happy, one godless and most miserable;

e5 but these people fail to see that this is so, and through foolishness and an

177a utter lack of intelligence they fail to notice how through their unjust actions they make themselves like the second model and unlike the first. And for that they pay the penalty of living the life that resembles the model they follow. But if we tell them that unless they rid themselves of

a5 their cleverness, that other region, pure of all that is bad, will not receive them even when they are dead, and meanwhile here they will always have an existence that reproduces their own selves, bad people keeping the company of things that are bad – if we tell them that, they will respond exactly like the clever, unscrupulous characters they are, and hear it as coming from imbeciles of some sort.

THEODORUS: They certainly will, Socrates.

b1 SOCRATES: I can tell you, my friend, I know. Not that they are totally unaffected, though: when in private conversation they have to give and receive an account[57] of the things they are so critical of others for discussing, then so long as they're prepared to be like men and put up with it for long enough, not run away like cowards, it's strange, I tell you,

---

[57] A standard Socratic-Platonic expression for dialectical discussion.

how they end up not being happy with what they're saying, and how that b5
rhetorical know-how of theirs somehow dries up and leaves them looking
no better than children. – Well, now we should stop talking about this
subject, since it is really a digression; if we don't, more and more will c1
flood in and drown out our original argument. If you agree, we'll go back
to what we were saying before.

THEODORUS: To me, Socrates, these sorts of things aren't at all
unpleasant to listen to; for someone of my age it's easier to follow. Still,
let's go back, if that's your decision. c5

SOCRATES: Well, the following is roughly where we were in our
argument, isn't it? We were discussing those who talk about being as
motion, and who claim that what seems to anyone at any time also is for
the one to whom it seems. We were saying that they will happily
maintain their position in other cases, and not least on questions of
justice – so that by their account whatever a city decides on and lays d1
down as just *is*, incontrovertibly, just for the city that has laid it down as
such, and for as long as she continues to do so; but no one, we said, will
be brave enough to go on to make the same claim in relation to what is
good, and brazenly insist that whatever a city lays down as beneficial for
herself, because it thinks it so, is actually beneficial for as long as she so d5
lays it down. Someone might of course talk as if it were like that, and use
the name 'beneficial', but that, I imagine, would be just to make fun of
what we're saying. Am I right?

THEODORUS: Yes, certainly.

SOCRATES: So let him not use the name, but rather look at the thing e1
being named.

THEODORUS: Indeed.

SOCRATES: In fact whatever a city calls it, it is surely what *is* beneficial
that she is aiming at when she makes her laws, and she makes every one e5
as beneficial for herself as she can, within the limits of her thinking and
of what that allows her to achieve. Or will she have some other goal in
view when making her laws?

THEODORUS: Certainly not. 178a

SOCRATES: So do cities always succeed in hitting the mark, or does
every city often make mistakes too?

THEODORUS: I think myself they also make mistakes.

SOCRATES: Well now, everyone would be still readier to accept all of a5
this if one tried asking about the whole form to which the beneficial

actually belongs; and among other things, I imagine, it relates to time that is going to be. Whenever we make laws for ourselves, we frame our
a10 laws on the basis that they will be beneficial in future time; and the right thing to call this will be what is 'going to be'.

b1 THEODORUS: Yes, certainly.

SOCRATES: So come on, let's put this question to Protagoras, and to anyone else who says the same things as he does. '"A human being is the measure of all things", as you people say, Protagoras – of white things,
b5 heavy things, light things, of everything whatever like that: having the means for judging them within himself, when he thinks them to be as he experiences them he is thinking things that are true for him, and that are. Isn't that what you say?'

THEODORUS: It is.

SOCRATES: 'Well, Protagoras,' we'll say, 'does he also have in himself
c1 the means for judging things that are *going* to be? If someone thinks things are going to be like this or that, do they actually turn out that way for the person who thought it? Take hot things. When one person thinks, as a layman, that he's going to get a fever, and that there will
c5 be this hotness in him, while a second person, who is a doctor, thinks the opposite, are we to say that the future will turn out to accord with what the first believes, or the second? Or will it turn out in accordance with what both of them believe, so that for the doctor the patient won't become hot, or fevered, whereas for himself he will become both?'

THEODORUS: That would be quite ridiculous.

SOCRATES: 'And when the question is whether wine is going to be
d1 sweet or dry, I suppose it is what the farmer believes, not the cithara player, that will be decisive?'

THEODORUS: Of course.

SOCRATES: 'Nor again, when it comes to whether something is going
d5 to be out of tune or well-tuned, would a gymnastic trainer have better beliefs than a musical expert as to what will in the event seem well-tuned to the gymnastic trainer himself.'

THEODORUS: Quite so.

SOCRATES: 'Or suppose someone is going to attend a feast, and lacks culinary skills: if the banquet is still being prepared, his judgement about
d10 the pleasure to come will have less authority than the cook's. Let's not
e1 fight it out between us, at this stage, about what is now pleasant to each individual, or has been in the past; our question is about what is *going* to

seem and be for each individual, and whether each is the best judge of that for himself – or whether you, Protagoras, will be better than any layman whatever at predicting at any rate what sorts of speech each of us is going to find persuasive in a law-court.'

THEODORUS: Yes indeed, Socrates, he used to claim vehemently to be superior to anyone else in that!

SOCRATES: Zeus! He certainly did, my friend. Or else no one would ever give large sums of money to talk to him; that is, if he actually tried to persuade the people who came to him that in relation to how things are *going to* be, too, and *going to* seem, neither a seer nor anyone else will be a better judge than a person is for himself.[58]

THEODORUS: Very true.

SOCRATES: Surely, then, legislation anywhere, and the beneficial, both have to do with what is going to be, and everyone would agree that a city that is legislating for herself will necessarily often fail to achieve what is most beneficial.

THEODORUS: Very much so.

SOCRATES: Then our measured response[59] to your teacher will be to say that he cannot avoid conceding both that one person is wiser than another, and that it is that sort of person that is the measure; whereas there is no compulsion, from any point of view whatever, on the know-nothing that I am to become the measure, as just now the argument on his behalf was compelling me to be whether I wanted it or not.

THEODORUS: That, Socrates, seems to me where his argument is most vulnerable, though it is also caught out by the way in which it gives authority to other people's beliefs, when these turned out to treat the things he says as not true at all.

SOCRATES: There are plenty of other ways too, Theodorus, of catching out this sort of claim, that any belief anyone has is true. But if one sticks to what each individual experiences in the immediate present, from which his perceptions and the corresponding beliefs derive, it is harder to convict these of not being true. But perhaps I'm talking nonsense. Maybe they are simply unassailable, and those who claim that they're evident, and so cases of knowledge, are perhaps saying things that are – and Theaetetus here was not off the the mark when he proposed that

e5

179a

a5

a10
b1

b5

c1

c5

d1

---

[58] Retaining *hautôi* at the end of the sentence, and reading *dê* for *mê* after *ei* near the beginning.*
[59] I.e., *this* won't be 'pushing him too hard' (Theodorus' complaint at 171c)?

perception and knowledge were the same thing. So we must get closer up, as we were urged to do by the argument on Protagoras' behalf, and test this idea of being as motion to see whether it rings true or is flawed.

d5 In any event there's no minor battle over it, and there are more than a few combatants.

THEODORUS: It's certainly far from minor, and in fact in Ionia it's growing very considerably. Heraclitus' friends are chorus-leading for this theory for all they are worth.

e1 SOCRATES: All the more reason to examine it, then, my dear Theodorus, and right from the very beginning, just as they themselves lay it out.

THEODORUS: I quite agree. The truth, Socrates, about these Heracli-
e5 tean notions – or Homeric, as you say they are, or even earlier – is that with the people around Ephesus[60] themselves, those of them who profess to be experts, there's no more possibility of a conversation than there is with the raving mad. They're simply as it says in his writings – perpetually in motion, and as for the capacity to stay with a discussion, or a question, and stay still enough to reply and then ask their questions in
180a turn, they have less than none; or rather, even to say 'less than none' is an exaggeration, given the lack even of a vestige of stillness in these people. If someone asks them a question, they pull out a set of riddling
a5 little phrases from their quiver, as it were, and shoot them off; if you try to get hold of an explanation of what they've said, you'll only get hit with another, freshly invented for the occasion. You'll never get to make any progress with any of them – indeed they don't make any progress even with each other, so careful are they to avoid allowing anything to stay
b1 constant either in what they say or in their own souls. They think, it seems to me, that if something stays constant it will be standing still, and this is something that they're totally at war with, and try so far as they can to expel from everywhere.

b5 SOCRATES: Perhaps, Theodorus, you've only seen these people in combat, and not had experience of them when they're at peace; they're not exactly people you spend your time with. But I imagine they do divulge such things at leisure to whichever of their students they want to make resemble themselves.

---

[60] Heraclitus' home city.

THEODORUS: Their *students*? What a wonderful notion! With people like that there is no such thing as one becoming another's student; they just spring up spontaneously from wherever each of them got their inspiration, and each thinks of the next as knowing nothing. So, as I was going to say, you'll never get the account you want from them, whether with their consent or without it. We have to take it all into our own hands and look into it as if it were a geometrical problem.

SOCRATES: Yes, fair enough. Am I right, then, in saying that whereas the ancients who have handed this problem of ours down to us tried to conceal it from ordinary people by using poetry, and saying that the origin of everything else was actually the streams of Oceanus and Tethys (and nothing is at rest), their successors, because they were wiser, have put it on open display – the purpose being that even shoemakers should be able to understand their wisdom when they hear it, so that they would stop thinking, like simpletons, that of the things that are some are at rest while others are changing, and once having realized that everything is in fact changing, would duly honour their teachers? I almost forgot, though, Theodorus, that there are others who have announced the opposite view, as in 'And unchanged shall be the name of the all',[61] and the rest of the things our Melissuses and Parmenideses insist on in opposition to all these people we've been talking about, to the effect that all things are one – a one that is at rest, itself within itself, because it has no place in which to change. So what are we going to do with all this? As we've gone on bit by bit, without noticing it we've been drawn into the middle between the two sides, and if we don't somehow defend ourselves and escape, we'll pay for it, like people in that game in the wrestling schools who find themselves grabbed by both sides and dragged in opposite ways across the line. Well, it seems to me we ought to look at the other group first, the one we started going after: the fluxers, and if they turn out to have something to say, we'll join in with them in dragging ourselves over to their side, and try to get away from the others; but if a better account comes from those who make a stand for the whole, we'll take ourselves off to them, this time away from those who try to make the unchanging change. And if both sides turn out not

c1

c5

d1

d5

e1

e5

181a

a5

b1

---

[61] Reading *hoion akinêton te thelei tôi panti onom'einai*, and treating the (mis)quotation as beginning with *akinêton*. Socrates appears to be thinking of, and misremembering, a pair of lines from Parmenides (fragment 8.37–8).*

to be saying anything that measures up, it will be ridiculous for us to think humble individuals like us have anything to say when we have scrutinized and rejected people as ancient and wise as can be. So b5 consider, Theodorus, whether we gain by advancing into such danger.

THEODORUS: It's surely quite unacceptable, Socrates, for us not to examine what each of the two groups is saying.

c1 SOCRATES: Examine them we must, then, if you're so eager. So now the starting point for our examination seems to me to be about change, and what sort of thing they can possibly be saying when they claim that everything is changing. The sort of question I have in mind is this: are they talking just about one particular form of change, or rather – as it c5 appears to me – about two forms? But don't let this just be about how it seems to me; you need to join in too, so that we can share the suffering, if it should come to that. Tell me this: do you call it change when a thing exchanges one place for another or turns on itself in the same place?

THEODORUS: I do.

SOCRATES: So let this be one form of change. What about the change d1 that occurs when something occupies the same place but grows old, turns black from white, or hard from soft, or undergoes some other alteration: isn't it right to treat this as a second form of change?

THEODORUS: Yes, it must be.

d5 SOCRATES: I'm saying, then, that there are these two forms of change, one of which is alteration, the other motion.

THEODORUS: And you're right.

SOCRATES: So with this distinction made, let's now have a talk with e1 those who claim that everything is changing, and ask them 'Are you claiming that all things are changing in both ways, that is, both moving and undergoing alteration, or that some perhaps are changing in both, others in one way but not the other?'

THEODORUS: Zeus! For myself I don't know what to say; but I think I'd say all in both ways.

e5 SOCRATES: Yes, my friend, or otherwise they'll find things turning out to be both changing and at rest, and it will be no more correct to say that all things are changing than to say they are at rest.

THEODORUS: Very true.

SOCRATES: So given that they must be changing, and that there must 182a be no trace of not changing in any of them, then all of them are always changing with every sort of change.

THEODORUS: Necessarily.

SOCRATES: Now think of the following aspect of their position. We were saying, weren't we, that they talk about hotness or whiteness or whatever it may be as coming about in this sort of way: namely that each of these things is in movement simultaneously with a perception, in between something that is acting and something that is being acted upon, and what is being acted on comes to be, not perception, but something perceiving, while what is doing the acting comes to be, not quality, but something qualified? Well, perhaps 'quality' strikes you as a strange word,[62] and it isn't helping your understanding, either, to have the point put collectively, so here are some individual examples: what is acting comes to be, not hotness or whiteness, but hot and white, and so with everything else – because I imagine you remember that that's how we were putting it before, to the effect that nothing is just one thing, itself by itself, not even what is acting, or what is being acted upon; rather, it's from their both getting together with each other that they generate the perceptions and the things perceived, and some come to be of a certain quality while others come to be perceiving.

THEODORUS: I remember; of course I do.

SOCRATES: Well, let's leave to one side whether we've got these people right or not on other aspects of what they're saying, and keep to the point of our present discussion. Let's ask them 'Everything is changing, and in flux, you're claiming? Right?'

THEODORUS: Yes.

SOCRATES: Is that with both the sorts of change we distinguished? They're both moving and undergoing alteration?

THEODORUS: Of course – if they're going to be completely and utterly changing.

SOCRATES: So if they were only moving, and not altering, I suppose we'd be able to identify the sorts of qualities the things in motion were fluxing with – or how do we put it?

THEODORUS: Like that.

SOCRATES: But this does not stay as it is, either, the fluxing thing fluxing white; it changes too, so that this very thing, whiteness, will be

a5

a10

b1

b5

c1

c5

c10

d1

---

[62] The Greek term Socrates uses here, *poiotês*, is evidently a new coinage ('quality' is its exact etymological counterpart in English, deriving as it does from the Latin *qualitas*, from *qualis = poios*).

itself in flux, and changing into another colour, or else it will be caught
staying as it is. Given that, will it ever be possible to refer to a particular
d5 colour and get its name right?'

THEODORUS: How could it be, Socrates? Or indeed to anything else
like that, if even as one is speaking of anything it is always quietly
slinking off, as it must if it's in flux?

SOCRATES: And what shall we say about perception, of whatever sort –
e1 the sort constituted by seeing, for example, or hearing? Shall we say that
it stays as it is, that is, as seeing or hearing?

THEODORUS: It certainly shouldn't, if everything is to be changing.

SOCRATES: In that case we shouldn't call anything seeing more than
e5 we call it not seeing, or any other sort of perception more that sort of
perception than not that sort, given that everything is changing in every
respect.

THEODORUS: No, we shouldn't.

SOCRATES: And yet perception is knowledge, Theaetetus and I said.

e10 THEODORUS: You did.

SOCRATES: In that case, when asked what knowledge was, we gave
as our answer what was no more knowledge than not knowledge.

183a THEODORUS: You do seem to have done that.

SOCRATES: A fine way this will turn out to be of getting that answer
right, when we were so eager to show that everything is changing just so
a5 it would come out right! What has actually emerged, it seems, is that if
everything is changing, any answer to any question whatever will be
equally correct. It won't matter whether one says 'This is so', or 'This is
not so' – or if you prefer we can substitute 'coming to be' for 'is', so as
not to say things that bring our friends the fluxers to a standstill.

THEODORUS: Correct.

a10 SOCRATES: Yes, Theodorus, except that I said 'so' and 'not so'. We
b1 mustn't use this 'so', even, because the 'so' wouldn't itself be changing,
nor again can we say 'not so', because this isn't a change either; instead
those who support this theory need to establish some other way of
talking, since as things are they have no terms that fit their own
b5 hypothesis – unless perhaps 'not like that either' would suit them best,
applied without limit.

THEODORUS: That way of talking would certainly be most appropriate
for them.

SOCRATES: So we're finished with your friend, Theodorus, and we're not yet conceding to him that every individual is the measure of all things, unless he has some sort of wisdom; nor shall we be going along with saying that knowledge is perception, at any rate on the basis that everything is changing – unless Theaetetus here has something different to say. c1

THEODORUS: This is a wonderful thing to hear from you, Socrates, because now that all this is finished, I too have to be released from the role of respondent, according to our agreement, which was that I should continue until the matter of Protagoras' thesis was settled. c5

THEAETETUS: No, Theodorus; not until Socrates and you have done what you proposed just now, and deal in turn with those who claim that everything is at rest. d1

THEODORUS: At your young age, Theaetetus, are you trying to teach your elders to be unjust and break agreements? Prepare to give Socrates an account of yourself for the rest of the discussion. d5

THEAETETUS: If that's his wish. But I would dearly have liked to hear about the things I mentioned.

THEODORUS: Inviting Socrates to discuss something is like inviting cavalry onto an open plain. So ask away and you'll hear what you want to hear.

SOCRATES: Still, Theodorus, on the subject Theaetetus says he wants discussed, I don't think I'm going to oblige him. d10

THEODORUS: Why on earth not? e1

SOCRATES: Ashamed as I am that I might subject Melissus, and the others who say everything is one and at rest, to vulgar investigation, the shame is less than I feel before one being, Parmenides[63] himself. But Parmenides does appear to me, to use Homer's words,[64] to be someone 'revered in my eyes . . . and dreaded too'. I actually met him, when I was very young and he was a very old man, and he appeared to possess a certain depth that was altogether noble.[65] So my fear is not just that we'll fail to understand what he is saying, and be left much further behind when it comes to grasping what he had in mind in saying it; my greatest fear is that we'll be prevented from examining the question about the e5

184a

---

[63] 'One being, Parmenides': a phrase designed to recall Parmenides' support for the idea that a One (Being) is all there is.
[64] At *Iliad* 3.172.
[65] This is very likely a cross-reference to the meeting between Socrates and Parmenides in Plato's *Parmenides*.

a5 nature of knowledge that has motivated our whole discussion, because of all these theories that keep rushing in on us like disorderly revellers if one lets them – especially the one we're stirring up now, which is of such unimaginable size that to look at it in passing would be to do it less than justice, while an adequate treatment of it will go on and on and drown out the issue about knowledge. Neither of which must happen. Rather

b1 I must use my midwife's art to try to help Theaetetus give birth to what he's conceived on the subject of knowledge.

THEODORUS: Then that's what we must do, if you think so.

SOCRATES: So, Theaetetus, here's a further point I'd like you to think about in relation to what has been said. Your answer was that knowledge

b5 is perception – right?

THEAETETUS: Yes.

SOCRATES: Now suppose someone were to ask you this: 'With what does a person see white and black things, and with what does he hear high and low sounds?' I imagine you'd reply 'With eyes and ears'.

b10 THEAETETUS: I would.

c1 SOCRATES: Going easy on the use of names and expressions, and not pressing people to be precise, is usually no sign of ill-breeding; it's rather the opposite that's lacking in class. But sometimes it is necessary, and

c5 one such moment is now, because I must latch on to one aspect in which your reply is incorrect. Think about it – which is the more correct reply: that what we see with is eyes, or that eyes are things *through which* we see? And ears – are they what we hear with, or are they rather what we hear *through*?

THEAETETUS: Eyes and ears are what we perceive things through, I think, Socrates, rather than what we perceive them with.

d1 SOCRATES: Yes, my boy, because I imagine it would be astonishing to find that there were lots of individual perceptions sitting inside us, as if in wooden horses, and that all these things did not converge in some single form[66] – soul, or whatever we should call it – with which we

d5 perceive everything perceivable through eyes and ears, which would be our instruments,[67] as it were.

---

[66] 'Lots of individual perceptions': as, perhaps, on the Protagorean theory (as reconstructed by Socrates). 'Wooden horses': i.e., what we call 'Trojan' ones. 'Form' (here *idea*): or 'sort of thing', as in colloquial English ('that sort of thing'); a perfectly ordinary, non-technical use of *eidos/idea*.
[67] Or 'organs' (the Greek term used is *organa*).

THEAETETUS: This seems to me more the way it is than what I first said.

SOCRATES: The reason I'm being so precise about this with you is that I want to discover whether there is some one aspect of ourselves, the same in all cases, with which we reach out through the eyes to white and black things, to different sorts of things through the ears, and so on, and whether, if asked, you'll be able to assign all of this sort of thing to the body. But perhaps it's better if you give your own answers rather than have me doing it for you like some busybody. So tell me: do you take each of the things *through* which you perceive hot or hard or light or sweet things to belong to the body? Or perhaps to something else?

THEAETETUS: No, to the body.

SOCRATES: And will you also accept that what you perceive through one capacity it's impossible for you to perceive through another? For example, what you perceive through hearing you can't perceive through sight, and what you perceive through sight you can't perceive through hearing?

THEAETETUS: Of course I will.

SOCRATES: In that case, if you have a thought about both, things seen and things heard, you certainly won't be having a *perception* about both, either through one of the relevant instruments or through the other.

THEAETETUS: No indeed.

SOCRATES: Now when it comes to a sound, or a colour, first of all don't you have this very thought about both of them, that both of them are?

THEAETETUS: I do.

SOCRATES: And that each of them is different from the other, and the same as itself?

THEAETETUS: Of course.

SOCRATES: And that both together are two, and each is one?

THEAETETUS: That too.

SOCRATES: Are you also able to consider whether they are unlike or like one another?

THEAETETUS: Probably.

SOCRATES: Through what, then, do you think all these things about them – given that it's not possible to grasp what is common to them either through hearing or through sight? Here's another bit of evidence relating to what we're saying: if it were possible to examine whether both of them were salty or not, obviously you'll be able to say what you'll

e1

e5

185a

a5

a10

b1

b5

b10
c1

59

examine them with, and this clearly won't be either sight or hearing but something else.

THEAETETUS: Obviously – the capacity that operates through the tongue.

SOCRATES: Beautifully put. And through what does this other capacity
c5 operate, the one that indicates to you what is common, both in every context and in this particular one, namely what you label with 'is' and 'is not', and the other aspects of things we were asking about just now in relation to our examples? What will you assign for all these aspects, as the instruments through which what does the perceiving in us perceives each of them?

c10 THEAETETUS: You're talking about being and not-being, likeness and
d1 unlikeness, same and different, also things being one or having some number; you're clearly asking about even and odd too, and everything that goes along with these. You want to know through which of the parts of the body we could possibly perceive all these things with the soul.

SOCRATES: You're following extraordinarily well, Theaetetus. That's
d5 exactly what my question is.

THEAETETUS: Zeus! I certainly couldn't answer the question, Socrates, except by saying that I don't think there's any such thing in the first place – there's no special instrument in these cases as there is in the
e1 others. Rather, the soul appears to me to investigate the common aspects in relation to everything by and through itself.

SOCRATES: That shows what a beauty you are, Theaetetus, not ugly as
e5 Theodorus said; beautiful words make a speaker beautiful and good.[68] And besides your beauty, you've done me a favour by having saved me a great long discussion, if it already appears to you that the soul investigates some things by and through itself, others through the capacities the body has. This was what I was thinking myself, and I wanted you to be thinking it too.

186a THEAETETUS: It is indeed already apparent to me.

SOCRATES: So to which of the two sets of things do you assign *being*?[69] This is what is most constantly present in all cases.

---

[68] There is something of a pun here: 'beautiful/fine-and-good', *kaloskagathos*, is a standard term of approval in Athenian society, for people we might say were 'of quality' (whatever we – or indeed the Athenians – might have in mind by 'quality').

[69] One of the 'greatest kinds' of the *Sophist* (two more are sameness and difference, introduced in Socrates' next contribution).

THEAETETUS: I myself count it among the things that the soul reaches out to, itself by itself.

SOCRATES: The like, too, and the unlike, the same and the different?

THEAETETUS: Yes.

SOCRATES: What about beautiful and ugly, good and bad?

THEAETETUS: These too, it seems to me, are more than anything things whose being the soul examines in relation to one another, reckoning up in itself past and present in comparison with future.

SOCRATES: Hold it there. It's through touch that it will perceive the hardness of the hard, and similarly the softness of the soft – right?

THEAETETUS: Yes.

SOCRATES: Whereas what our soul tries to judge by itself, going close up to them[70] and comparing them with each other, is their being, namely that they are, their oppositeness to one another, and again the being of their oppositeness?[71]

THEAETETUS: Certainly, yes.

SOCRATES: There will be some things, then, that human beings and animals alike are naturally able to perceive as soon as they are born, namely those things the experience of which extends through the body to the soul; whereas calculations about these, in relation to their being or the benefit they bring, come, to the people to whom they do come, only with difficulty, late on, and after much trouble and education?

THEAETETUS: Yes, quite certainly.

SOCRATES: Now can a person reach truth, if he can't reach even as far as being?

THEAETETUS: Impossible.

SOCRATES: And if he fails to reach the truth of a thing, will he ever have knowledge of that thing?

THEAETETUS: I don't see how he could, Socrates.

SOCRATES: In that case knowledge does not reside in what we directly experience, but rather in our reasoning about those experiences; because in the latter, it seems, it is possible to get a hold on being and truth, whereas in the former it is impossible.

a5

a10

b1

b5

b10

c1

c5

c10

d1

d5

---

[70] I.e., to hardness and softness.
[71] I.e., glossing this as Socrates glosses 'being' in the first case, 'that there is this oppositeness between them'.

61

THEAETETUS: Evidently.

SOCRATES: So are you going to call the two things the same, when there are such great differences between them?

THEAETETUS: There would certainly be no justification for it.

d10 SOCRATES: What name, then, are you assigning to the first – seeing, hearing, smelling, being cold, being hot?

e1 THEAETETUS: I call it perceiving; what else should I call it?

SOCRATES: The whole of it, then, you're calling perception?

THEAETETUS: Necessarily.

SOCRATES: And that's something we're saying has no claim to a hold
e5 on truth, because it can't even grasp being.

THEAETETUS: No indeed.

SOCRATES: So it has no claim to knowledge either.

THEAETETUS: No.

SOCRATES: In that case, Theaetetus, perception and knowledge
e10 couldn't ever be the same thing.

THEAETETUS: Evidently not, Socrates. It has become as clear as it could be, especially now, that knowledge is something other than perception.

187a SOCRATES: But our aim in starting this conversation wasn't at all to find out what knowledge was not; it was to find out what it is. Still, at least we have advanced far enough to know not to look for it in
a5 perception at all, but rather under whatever name we're to use to describe the soul when it's occupied with the things that are, itself by itself.

THEAETETUS: Yes, and the name we give it, I think, Socrates, is forming and having beliefs.[72]

SOCRATES: Yes, my friend, you think correctly. So now go back to the
b1 beginning, wiping from the slate everything you said before, and see if you can see things a bit better, now that you've progressed this far. Say again what knowledge is.

---

[72] 'Forming and having beliefs' translates the single word *doxazein*: the verb has been used before simply of believing something, having a belief (*doxa*), or having something seem (*dokein*) to one, all of which will presumably be included here, along with plain thinking (which will be even more explicitly brought under the umbrella of *doxazein* at 189e–190a). The whole family of terms is sometimes contrasted with those for knowledge and knowing, but clearly not in the present context. If there is such a contrast in the *Theaetetus* at all, it is between knowledge and *true* belief (so, e.g., at 201b–c, or 209a). See Introduction, Section 4.

THEAETETUS: To say that it's any and every belief, Socrates, is impossible, given that there is false belief too; but possibly true belief could be knowledge. So let this be my answer, since if as we go on it appears not to be the right answer, as it presently appears it is,[73] we can try saying something else.

SOCRATES: That's the commitment we need, Theaetetus, not those hesitant answers you were giving at the beginning! If we go on in this way, then one of two things will happen: either we'll find what we've set out to find, or we'll be less inclined to think we know what we don't know at all, and actually that sort of pay-off would be nothing to complain about. So then, what is it that you're now claiming? There being two forms[74] of belief, the one true and the other false, you mark off the true one as knowledge?

THEAETETUS: I do; that is how it appears to me now.

SOCRATES: Well now, is it even now worth picking up that point about belief again –

THEAETETUS: Which point are you talking about?

SOCRATES: It strangely disturbs me, as it has on many other occasions; so much so that I've been completely puzzled, whether thinking about it by myself or with someone else. I just can't say what this thing is that happens with us, and how it comes to happen at all.

THEAETETUS: What sort of thing?

SOCRATES: Someone's believing what is false. I'm presently still in two minds as to whether we should leave the subject to one side, or look into it using a different approach from the one we were using a little earlier.[75]

THEAETETUS: Of course we should look at it, Socrates, if there appears the slightest reason for thinking we should. You and Theodorus were quite rightly saying only just now that when it comes to questions like this we have all the time in the world.

SOCRATES: You're right to remind me. It probably won't be a bad moment to go back over our tracks, as it were. Better, I imagine, to accomplish a little and do it well than to get through a lot and do it badly.

b5

b10

c1

c5

d1

d10

e1

---

[73] After all, belief/believing, *doxa/doxazein*, has been agreed to meet the conditions that perception failed to meet, if it was to be the same as knowledge; namely, that it can grasp 'being' and truth. And if it is *true* belief that's in question, it will, surely, have grasped truth, so why should it not be knowledge?

[74] 'Form': *idea* again, but now used in a more obviously technical way.

[75] See 167b, 170a–172b.

THEAETETUS: It certainly is.

e5 SOCRATES: So how to proceed? What is it we actually say? Do we claim all the time that there is such a thing as false belief, and that one of us has false beliefs while another has true ones, as if things were naturally like this?

THEAETETUS: Yes, we do.

188a SOCRATES: Well, there is this much we can certainly do, isn't there, in relation to everything and to each individual thing, namely either know it or not know it? I recognize that there's learning, and forgetting, in between these, but I'm passing over them at the moment, because now they're not to my point.

a5 THEAETETUS: There's certainly no remaining alternative, Socrates, in relation to each thing, besides knowing it and not knowing it.

SOCRATES: If so, mustn't the person who believes be believing either one of the things he knows or one of the things he doesn't know?

THEAETETUS: He must.

a10
b1 SOCRATES: And yet if he knows something, it's impossible for him not to know that same thing, or to know it if he doesn't know it.

THEAETETUS: Obviously.

SOCRATES: So is the person who believes what is false thinking the things he knows are not these but some other things he knows, so that
b5 while he knows both sets of things he is also ignorant of both?

THEAETETUS: That's impossible, Socrates.

SOCRATES: Or is he supposing, of things he doesn't know, that they are some other set of things he doesn't know? Is it a matter of someone's taking it into his head, when he doesn't know either
b10 Theaetetus or Socrates, that Socrates is Theaetetus or Theaetetus Socrates?

c1 THEAETETUS: How could that be?

SOCRATES: But I imagine it can't be the case that a person thinks things he knows are things he doesn't know, nor, again, that things he doesn't know are things he knows.

THEAETETUS: It'll be a wonder if he does.

c5 SOCRATES: In that case how can anyone believe what is false? We've presumably gone through all the possible ways of believing, if we actually do always either know a thing or we don't know it; and nowhere among these does it appear possible to believe what is false.[76]

THEAETETUS: Very true.

SOCRATES: So perhaps this isn't how we should be looking into what   c10
we're after. Instead of proceeding by reference to knowing and not   d1
knowing, should we do it by reference to being and not being?

THEAETETUS: How would we do that?

SOCRATES: Perhaps the simple fact is that anyone who believes things
that are not, about anything whatever, must believe things that are false,
whatever other aspects there may be to his thinking.   d5

THEAETETUS: That too is likely enough, Socrates.

SOCRATES: So how can it be? What are we going to say, Theaetetus,
if someone asks us 'Is what is being said actually possible for anyone?
Will anyone on earth believe what is not, no matter whether he believes
it about one of the things that are, or just believes what is not itself by   d10
itself?' We, it seems, will respond by saying 'Yes, whenever he thinks   e1
and the things he thinks are not true.' Or will we?

THEAETETUS: Yes.

SOCRATES: So does this sort of thing perhaps happen in other contexts?

THEAETETUS: What sort of thing?   e5

SOCRATES: I'm asking, for example, if someone can see something yet
see nothing.

THEAETETUS: How could he?

SOCRATES: Yet if he is seeing some *one* thing, he is seeing something
belonging to the things that are. Or do you suppose that oneness is ever
to be found among the things that are not?

THEAETETUS: I certainly don't.   e10

SOCRATES: So if he is seeing some one thing, he is seeing something
that is.

THEAETETUS: Apparently.

SOCRATES: So the person who is hearing something, too, is hearing   189a
some one thing and something that is.

THEAETETUS: Yes.

---

[76] One plausible way of treating the immediately preceding stretch of argument is as an illustration of the reasons for the 'puzzlement' Socrates admitted to, just before, over the problem of false belief (187d). It fits with this interpretation that a few pages on Socrates will in fact bring in the two items explicitly 'passed over' here as 'not to my point' (188a), namely learning (191c) and memory (191d), as part of a new approach to the problem.

SOCRATES: And again, the person who touches something is touching some one thing, and something that is, if it is one?

a5 THEAETETUS: Yes to that too.

SOCRATES: But isn't the person who believes believing some one thing?

THEAETETUS: He must do so.

SOCRATES: And isn't the person who believes some one thing believing something that is?

THEAETETUS: I grant that.

a10 SOCRATES: So the person who believes what is not is believing nothing?

THEAETETUS: Apparently so.

SOCRATES: But the person who is believing nothing is not even believing at all.

THEAETETUS: That's clear, it seems.

b1 SOCRATES: In that case it's not possible to believe what is not, whether about the things that are, or what is not itself by itself.

THEAETETUS: Apparently not.

SOCRATES: So believing what is false must be something other than

b5 believing things that are not.

THEAETETUS: It seems so.

SOCRATES: So there isn't false belief in us if we look at it like this, any more than there was when we looked at it as we were doing a little earlier.[77]

THEAETETUS: You are quite right, there isn't.

b10 SOCRATES: Or do we call it false belief if it happens like this—

THEAETETUS: Like what?

SOCRATES: We claim belief is false as a sort of 'other-believing',[78]

c1 namely when someone claims that one of the things that are is another of the things that are because he's swapped them over in his mind.[79] This way what his belief is about is still something that is, only one such thing in place of another, and because he fails to hit on what he was aiming at he'll justly be said to be believing what is false.

---

[77] Here, too, Socrates may be explaining the sorts of reasons why he has difficulties with the very notion of false belief. It is worth noting in this context that the way the main speaker in the *Sophist* proposes finally to explain false belief involves a discussion of Parmenidean ideas, which Socrates has deliberately avoided here in the *Theaetetus* (183e–184b).

[78] The point is not that we (i.e., ordinary people?) say false belief *is* this, rather that its being this might be an alternative explanation of our happily continuing to say that there is such a thing.

[79] See Further notes on the text.

THEAETETUS: The way you have put it now seems to me quite correct. c5
When a person believes a shameful thing instead of a fine one or a fine
instead of a shameful one, that's when he believes things that are
truly false.

SOCRATES: Obviously, Theaetetus, rather than standing in awe of me
you're looking down on me.

THEAETETUS: Why, exactly? c10

SOCRATES: I suppose you think I'll not pick you up on your 'truly
false', and ask whether it's possible for anything to be slowly quick, or d1
heavily light, or for anything else to turn out in accordance not with its
own nature but with that of its opposite, oppositely to itself. As reward
for your boldness, I let that go. You're happy, you say, with the proposal d5
that believing what is false is 'other-believing'?

THEAETETUS: I am.

SOCRATES: So according to what *you* believe, it's possible in one's
mind to put down one thing not as what it is but as another thing.

THEAETETUS: Indeed it is.

SOCRATES: So when someone's mind is doing this, must it not be e1
thinking either of both or of one of the two things?

THEAETETUS: It certainly must; either both at once, or one after
the other.

SOCRATES: Very fine. Do you call thinking what I call it?

THEAETETUS: What do you call it? e5

SOCRATES: Talk that the soul conducts with itself about whatever it is
investigating. That's what I'm claiming, at any rate, as someone ignorant
about the subject. The image I have of the soul as it is in thought is exactly
of it as in conversation with itself, asking itself and answering questions 190a
and saying yes to this and no to that. When it fixes on something, whether
having arrived at it quite slowly or in a quick leap, and it is now saying the
same thing consistently, without wavering, that is what we set down as
something it believes. So I for my part call forming and having a belief[80] a5
talking, and belief a talk that has been conducted, not with someone else,
or out loud, but in silence with oneself. What about you?

THEAETETUS: I agree with you.

---

[80] 'Forming and having a belief': the same makeshift translation of *doxazein* as in 187a. It is in any
case clear, from the context, that Socrates is using *doxazein* here to cover both thinking about
things and reaching conclusions about them.

SOCRATES: Then when someone believes one of two things to be the
a10 other, it seems he is also saying to himself that the one is the other.

b1 THEAETETUS: Of course.

SOCRATES: Well, try to recall if you have ever yet said to yourself
that what is actually fine is absolutely and completely shameful, or
that what is actually just is absolutely unjust. Or, to sum up the point,
b5 see if you've ever tried to persuade yourself that one thing is absolutely
and completely something else, or whether it's quite the opposite, and
you've never yet had the gall even in your sleep to say to yourself
that there's no doubt about it, odd things are really even, or anything
like that.

THEAETETUS: What you say is true.

c1 SOCRATES: And do you think anyone else, either, whether healthy or
mad, has had the gall seriously to say to himself, and hoped to persuade
himself, that the ox must be a horse or the two one?

THEAETETUS: Zeus! No, I don't.

c5 SOCRATES: Well, then, if saying something to oneself is the same as
believing it, no one who is talking and thinking about[81] *both* of two
things, and grasping both with his soul, will say and believe that the one
is the other. You must let pass the form of words here, as I did for you.[82]
d1 What I'm saying is just this, that no one thinks that what is shameful is
fine, or anything else of the sort.

THEAETETUS: I will let it pass, Socrates, and what you're saying seems
right to me.

d5 SOCRATES: It's impossible, in that case, for someone who is thinking
about both of two things to think one of them to be the other.

THEAETETUS: It seems so.

SOCRATES: And yet if he is only thinking about one of the two, and not
at all about the other, he'll never think the one is the other.

d10 THEAETETUS: True; he would have to have a hold on the one he is not
thinking about too.

---

[81] The verb is again *doxazein*, the correlate of *doxa* (see preceding note), as it is for all of the next
seven occurrences of 'thinking'/'thinking about'; keeping in these cases to 'belief' or some
cognate of it would be not only awkward but positively unhelpful. (In any case, in this whole
context *doxazein* is clearly treated as interchangeable with other verbs for 'thinking'.)

[82] Cf. 189c–d. What Socrates is asking Theaetetus to let pass cannot easily be reproduced in
English: the Greek for 'the one is the other' is 'the *heteron* is *heteron*', which might suggest,
superficially, and to the ear, precisely that the one *must* be the other.

SOCRATES: In that case there is no possibility of 'other-believing', whether a person is thinking about both things or about only one of them. So if a person tries to define false belief as believing one thing to be another, he would be talking nonsense. False belief isn't showing up in us with this approach any more than it did with the previous ones.

THEAETETUS: It seems not.

SOCRATES: And yet, Theaetetus, if this isn't going to show up as something that is, we shall be forced to make many strange concessions.

THEAETETUS: What sorts of concessions?

SOCRATES: I'm not going to tell you until I try every available way of investigating the matter. I would be ashamed for us if we were forced, even while finding ourselves puzzled, into the sorts of concessions I'm referring to. If we can free ourselves by finding what we're after, that will be the time to talk about them – as things that happen to other people, while we ourselves stand safely outside the absurd spectacle. And if our puzzlement turns out to be terminal, I suppose we'll have to accept the humiliation of surrendering ourselves to the argument, like seasick passengers on a ship, to trample over us and do to us whatever it likes. – So let me tell you where I'm still finding a way forward for our investigation.

THEAETETUS: Please do!

SOCRATES: I'm going to say that it was wrong of us to concede that it was impossible for someone to believe that things he knows are things he doesn't know, and for false belief to occur in that way. In a way it is possible.

THEAETETUS: Are you saying what I myself suspected, when we said it was like that – that sometimes, though I know Socrates, in the distance I see someone else I don't know and think[83] it is Socrates whom I do know? In a case like this the sort of thing you're talking about does occur.

SOCRATES: Didn't we distance ourselves from that, on the grounds that it made us not know what we know, when we do?

THEAETETUS: We certainly did.

SOCRATES: Because let's rather set things up in the following way – perhaps it will help us, somehow, or perhaps it will work against us, but the fact is that we are caught in such a bind that it requires us to twist

e1

e5

191a

a5

b1

b5

b10

c1

---

[83] Here *oiesthai*.

and test every line of argument till it squeaks. So see if this takes us forward. Is it possible for someone who didn't know something before to go on later to learn it?

c5   THEAETETUS: It surely is.

SOCRATES: And then another thing, and another?

THEAETETUS: Of course.

SOCRATES: I want you to suppose, for the sake of argument, that our souls contain a waxen block. It is larger in one person, smaller in another,

d1   of purer wax in one, filthier in another; in some it is too hard, in others too soft, while in still others it is as it should be.

THEAETETUS: Done.

d5   SOCRATES: Let's say, then, that it is a gift from Memory, mother of the Muses, and that we imprint on it whatever we wish to remember from among the things we see or hear or the thoughts[84] we ourselves have, holding it under our perceptions and thoughts as if we were making impressions from signet rings; whatever is imprinted on the block, we

d10   remember and know for as long as its image is in the wax, while whatever
e1   is wiped off or proves incapable of being imprinted we have forgotten and do not know.

THEAETETUS: Let's say that.

SOCRATES: Now take someone who knows the things in question, and is thinking about[85] one of the things he's seeing or hearing. Consider

e5   whether he might perhaps come to a false belief in the following way.

THEAETETUS: What sort of way?

SOCRATES: By thinking, at one moment, that things he knows are things he knows, at another moment that they are things he doesn't know – because it was not a good move on our part, earlier on, to agree that such cases were impossible.

e10   THEAETETUS: What do you want to say about them now?

192a   SOCRATES: We need to say the following. From the start we shall lay it down that if a person knows something, having acquired a record of it in his soul, but is not currently perceiving it, it is impossible for him to think it is another of the things he knows – because he has an impression

a5   of it, too – but is not currently perceiving. Also that it is impossible for anyone to think, either, that something he knows is something he doesn't

---

[84] Here *ennoein*.   [85] Here *skopein*.

know and doesn't have the seal of in his wax; or that something he doesn't know is another thing he doesn't know; or that something he doesn't know is something else he does know. It is impossible too for a person to think that something he is actually perceiving is another of the things he is actually perceiving; or that something he is perceiving is one of the things he is not perceiving; or that something he is not perceiving b1 is another of the things he is not perceiving; or that something he is not perceiving is one of the things he is perceiving. Again, it is impossible for a person to think that something he knows, is perceiving, and has the imprint of, corresponding to the perception, is another of the things he knows, is perceiving, and similarly has the imprint of, corresponding to b5 the perception – this, in fact, would be an even greater impossibility, if there could be such a thing, than the previous cases. Also impossible: to think that something one knows and is perceiving, and keeping a correct record of, is something else one knows; that something one knows and is perceiving, along with a similarly correct record of it, is something else c1 one is perceiving; or again that something one doesn't know, and isn't perceiving, is some other thing one doesn't know and isn't perceiving either; or that something one doesn't know, and isn't perceiving, is something else one doesn't know; or that what one doesn't know, and isn't perceiving, is something else one isn't perceiving. The impossibility of all these cases is more than enough to rule out finding false belief in c5 them. It remains that such a thing will come about, if anywhere, in the following sorts of case.

THEAETETUS: Which are they? If you tell me what they are, maybe I'll actually understand a bit more, because as things are I'm not following you.

SOCRATES: With things one knows – thinking that they are other things one knows and is perceiving, or things one doesn't know but is c10 perceiving; or that things one knows and is perceiving are other things d1 one knows and is perceiving.

THEAETETUS: Now I'm much further behind than I was before.

SOCRATES: Here's the same point put in a different way. I know Theodorus and have a memory in myself of what he is like, and similarly with Theaetetus. Now isn't it the case that I am sometimes seeing them, d5 sometimes not, at one moment touching them, at another not, hearing them or having some other perception of them at one moment, at another having no perception relating to you and Theodorus at all, but for all that still having a memory of you and knowing you, myself in myself?

e1   THEAETETUS: Certainly.

SOCRATES: Well, take this as the first of the points I want to illustrate for you: that it is possible either not to be perceiving things we know, or to be perceiving them.

THEAETETUS: That's true.

e5   SOCRATES: And with things we don't know too, it's possible for us often not to be perceiving them either, often to be only perceiving them.

THEAETETUS: That's also true.

193a   SOCRATES: So see if you can follow a bit more now. If Socrates knows Theodorus and Theaetetus, but isn't seeing either of them, and no other perception relating to them is currently present to him either, he will never form the belief in himself that Theaetetus is Theodorus. Am I making sense or not?

a5   THEAETETUS: Yes, what you say is true.

SOCRATES: Well, this was the first of the cases I was talking about.[86]

THEAETETUS: It was.

SOCRATES: And the second was this: if I'm acquainted with one of you a10 and not the other, and I'm not perceiving either of you, again I'd never think the one I do know to be the one I don't.

THEAETETUS: Correct.

b1   SOCRATES: And the third case was where I'm not acquainted with either, nor am I currently perceiving either; I wouldn't think a person I don't know to be another person I don't know. And assume I've gone through again the whole of my original list of cases in which b5 I shall never have a false belief about you and Theodorus, whether I'm acquainted or unacquainted with both of you, or acquainted with one of you and not with the other; similarly with perceiving, if you follow me.

THEAETETUS: I do.

SOCRATES: So there remains the possibility of having a false belief in b10 the following case. I know you and Theodorus, and I have the imprints c1 of you both, as if from signet rings, in that wax block of mine. But suppose then that I see you both at a distance, and not sufficiently well:

---

[86] I.e., in 192a.

in my eagerness to refer the imprint belonging to each of you to the corresponding visual perception, and to make the latter fit its own traces, so that recognition can take place, I fail in this, switching things like someone putting his shoes on the wrong feet, and applying my perception of each of you to the imprint belonging to the other. Or it's like what happens with sight in the context of mirrors, changing its flow from right to left – the same thing happens to me in this case, and I go wrong; that's when this 'other-believing'[87] occurs, that is, believing what is false. c5

d1

THEAETETUS: That seems right, Socrates. You describe marvellously well what happens to belief.

SOCRATES: And again, when I'm acquainted with both of you, but one of you I'm perceiving as well, the other not, and the knowledge I have of the former isn't corresponding with my perception; that was the sort of way I was putting it before, and you weren't following me. d5

THEAETETUS: Right, I wasn't.

SOCRATES: Well, what I was saying was this: that if a person is acquainted with someone and is currently perceiving him, and the knowledge he has of that person corresponds with his perception of him, he will never think he is someone else he knows and is currently perceiving, if the knowledge he has of this second person also corresponds with the perception. That was it, was it not? d10

e1

THEAETETUS: Yes. e5

SOCRATES: And what remained, I think, was the sort of case we were referring to just now, in which we definitely claim false belief occurs: namely when someone is acquainted with both of two people and is currently seeing them both, or having some other sort of perception of them both, but the imprints he has of each of them do not correspond with the perceptions he has of each, the result being that he looses off like an inferior archer, deviates from the target and misses; and this is what is in fact called a falsehood. 194a

THEAETETUS: Yes, that sounds plausible. a5

SOCRATES: Also when for one of the imprints there is a perception present but not for the other, and you fit the imprint belonging to the missing perception to the present perception, your thought is in this

---

[87] See n.78 above.

b1 case certainly false. In short, in relation to things one doesn't know, and hasn't ever yet perceived, it seems that neither falsity nor false belief is possible, if what we are presently saying is at all sound. But it is different with things that we both know and are perceiving – in these very cases belief twists and turns between false and true: true when it

b5 brings together the appropriate imprints and impressions directly and without deviation, false when it does the fitting in a skewed and sideways fashion.

THEAETETUS: So, Socrates, isn't that a fine account of the matter?

c1 SOCRATES: Well, you'll say that even more when you've heard the next bit too. Believing what is true is a fine thing, believing what is false is a cause for shame.

THEAETETUS: Yes, certainly.

c5 SOCRATES: The explanation for this divergence of outcomes, they say, is the following. The wax in some people's souls can be deep and abundant, and have the smoothness that comes from proper kneading; and when the things that come through the senses are imprinted on this 'heart' of the soul, as Homer calls it, playing in riddling fashion on the

d1 word for wax,[88] then, in these cases, the imprints they make in the wax are pure, and have sufficient depth to be lasting. People of this sort are not only quick to learn but have good memories, and instead of mis-

d5 aligning imprints with perceptions they believe what is true. Because their imprints are clear and are not crammed together, they quickly assign everything to its counterpart in the wax, 'everything' here being what are called things that are; these are the people who are called wise. Or don't you agree?

THEAETETUS: I do, most emphatically.

e1 SOCRATES: Well, it's different when a person's 'heart' is 'shaggy', a thing our all-wise poet actually praises, or when it's filthy and composed of wax that is impure, or too fluid or too hard. People whose 'heart' is fluid turn out as quick to learn but forgetful; if it is hard, they turn out

e5 the opposite. Those in whom it is 'shaggy' and rough, with a stony element, or with lots of earth or filth mixed up in it, have imprints that are unclear. So too do those with the hard wax, because it lacks depth,

195a and those with the soft wax too, because the imprints run together and

[88] Cf. Homer, *Iliad* 2.851, 16.554; *kear*, 'heart', in the Homeric lines is close enough for Socrates' purposes to *kêros*, 'wax'.

---

quickly become indistinct. If on top of all this they are all in a jumble because of lack of space, as in the case of someone with a tiny little soul, they are still more unclear. So all these people turn out to be liable to form false beliefs, since when they see or hear or think of anything they cannot quickly assign each thing to each impression; slow and liable to misalignment, they mis-see, mis-hear and mis-think the most, and they in their turn are said to be mistaken about the things that are, and ignorant.

THEAETETUS: It wouldn't be humanly possible to put it better, Socrates.

SOCRATES: Shall we say, then, that there are false beliefs in us?

THEAETETUS: Yes, very much so.

SOCRATES: And true ones too?

THEAETETUS: And true ones.

SOCRATES: So do we think we now have a satisfactory agreement that there are quite certainly both these sorts of belief?

THEAETETUS: Yes, most emphatically.

SOCRATES: Truly, Theaetetus, what a terrible and unpleasant thing a man really is when he babbles!

THEAETETUS: Why? What makes you say that?

SOCRATES: It's because I'm annoyed at my own stupidity, and what truly is babbling on my part. What else but a babbler would you call someone who keeps dragging the arguments this way and that because he's too dim-witted to be convinced, and won't be separated from any one of them?

THEAETETUS: But what exactly is annoying you?

SOCRATES: It's not just that I'm annoyed. I'm also afraid about what I'll be saying, as things stand, when someone asks me 'Socrates, so you've discovered that false belief doesn't occur either in perceptions in relation to perceptions or in our thoughts, but in the combination of perception with thought?' I think I'll actually agree, and be preening myself on our having made a fine discovery.

THEAETETUS: To me, Socrates, what has just been shown seems nothing to be ashamed of.

SOCRATES: 'Are you saying', he now asks, 'that we'd never suppose that the human being we're only thinking of and not seeing was a horse that we're similarly not seeing or touching, only thinking of, not perceiving at all?' I imagine I'll agree that I am saying that.

75

THEAETETUS: Yes, and rightly so.

e1 SOCRATES: 'What then,' he goes on, 'will it not follow on this account that no one will ever suppose that the eleven he's only thinking about are a twelve he's also only thinking about?' Come on, you answer the question.

e5 THEAETETUS: My answer will be that someone could suppose that the eleven were twelve if he was seeing or touching them, but that he could never believe that about an eleven that was only in his mind.

SOCRATES: Well then, what if someone has proposed to think about

196a five and seven to himself – and I'm not talking about seven and five human beings, just five and seven by themselves, which we're saying are memories stored in that block of wax he has there in his mind, and among which we're saying it is not possible to believe what is false. The

a5 question is whether any human being in the world ever set about discussing these in conversation with himself and asked what they came to, and if indeed anyone has, whether one person has expressed the thought to himself that they made eleven, another that they made twelve; or whether everyone says and thinks to themselves that they come to twelve?

b1 THEAETETUS: Zeus, no! There are plenty of people who make them eleven; and in fact the larger the number involved the more they go wrong; I think you're talking about numbers as a whole.

SOCRATES: You're right to think that – and see whether what we have

b5 in the case we're talking about isn't actually someone's thinking that the twelve themselves there in the waxen block are eleven.

THEAETETUS: Yes, it seems so.

SOCRATES: Doesn't this take us back to what we were saying at the beginning?[89] The person to whom this happens will be thinking that

b10 something he knows is something else he knows, which we said was impossible; and on that very basis we were forcing through the conclu-

c1 sion that there was no such thing as false belief, because otherwise the same person would be forced into knowing and not knowing the same things at the same time.

THEAETETUS: Very true.

---

[89] See 188a–c.

SOCRATES: Then we must declare believing what is false to be any-   c5
thing but the misalignment of thought with perception; because if it were
that, there would never be falsehood in our thoughts by themselves. As
things stand, either false belief is not possible,[90] or else it is possible not
to know what one knows. Which do you choose?

THEAETETUS: The choice you're offering is impossible, Socrates.

SOCRATES: Yet the argument is not likely to allow both. Still, since we   d1
must try anything, how about if we were prepared to be quite shameless?

THEAETETUS: How?

SOCRATES: By allowing ourselves to say what sort of thing knowing is.   d5

THEAETETUS: And why is that shameless?

SOCRATES: You appear not to realize that our whole discussion from
the beginning has been an investigation into knowledge, on the basis that
we didn't know what it was.

THEAETETUS: I am aware of that.   d10

SOCRATES: So doesn't it look brazen, when we don't know what
knowledge is, to state what sort of thing knowing is? In fact, Theaetetus,
for some time now our discussion has been full of impurities, since over   e1
and over again we've said 'we're acquainted with' and 'we're not
acquainted with', 'we know' and 'we don't know', as if we were somehow
understanding one another even while we are still ignorant of
knowledge. Or if you will, think of what we're doing now, using 'ignor-   e5
ant of' and 'understanding' as if that was perfectly appropriate even
when knowledge is the very thing we're lacking.

THEAETETUS: But how are you going to carry on the discussion,
Socrates, if you hold off from using them?

SOCRATES: I can't, if I'm to stay who I am, though maybe I could if   197a
I were an antilogician;[91] and if that sort of person were here now, he
would have said *he* was holding off from using them and be criticizing us
severely for not doing so. Well, given that we're not up to his standards,
do you want me to try my hand at saying what sort of thing knowing is?
It seems to me it would be of some help to us.

---

[90] Except, presumably, in the (less important?) case of the 'misalignment of thought with perception', which Socrates and Theaetetus have done nothing to discredit as an explanation of at least
one sort of false belief (and thinking).

[91] See n.37 above.

a5 THEAETETUS: Then – Zeus! – please do try your hand. I'll completely forgive you if you don't hold off.

SOCRATES: Well, have you heard what people currently say knowing is?

THEAETETUS: I may have, but I don't at the moment recall.

b1 SOCRATES: I think they say it's having knowledge.

THEAETETUS: True.

SOCRATES: Well, for our part let's make a slight change and say it's *being in possession* of knowledge.

b5 THEAETETUS: So how are you going to say this differs from the other?

SOCRATES: Perhaps it doesn't at all. But anyway hear what the difference seems to me to be, and then help me assess it.

THEAETETUS: I will if I can.

SOCRATES: Well, having doesn't seem to me to be the same thing as

b10 possessing. For example, if someone bought a cloak and had control of it but was not wearing it, we wouldn't say he had it, rather that he possessed it.

THEAETETUS: That's correct.

c1 SOCRATES: So see if it's possible similarly to be in possession of knowledge and not have it. Imagine someone catching wild birds, pigeons or whatever, and looking after them at home in an aviary he'd

c5 prepared for them: in a certain way, I suppose, we would say that he has them all the time, just because they're in his possession. Right?

THEAETETUS: Yes.

SOCRATES: But in another way we wouldn't say he had any of them; rather that he has acquired power over them, by making them subject to

d1 him in his private cage, to catch and to have whenever he wishes, after he's hunted down whichever he wants at any time, and then to let them go again; and he can do this just as often as he decides.

THEAETETUS: Right.

d5 SOCRATES: So, just as in the preceding discussion we installed some sort of contraption in souls that we'd moulded out of wax, now let's make a sort of aviary in every soul, containing birds of all different varieties, some of them in flocks separate from others, some in small groups,

d10 others flying about wherever it might be on their own in among them all.

e1 THEAETETUS: Done. What's next?

SOCRATES: We're to say that when we are little children this container is empty, and think of pieces of knowledge[92] instead of the birds. If someone comes to possess a piece of knowledge and confines it in the cage, we're to say he has learned or discovered the thing this knowledge was originally of, and that is what knowing is.   e5

THEAETETUS: Let's do it.

SOCRATES: So now when he comes back to hunt for whichever piece   198a
of knowledge he wants, and catches and has it, then lets it go again, see what names for things you think are needed here – the same ones as when he was coming to possess the knowledge in the first place, or different ones? The following example will help you understand more clearly what I'm asking. You recognize a science of arithmetic?   a5

THEAETETUS: Yes.

SOCRATES: Well, think of it as a hunt for pieces of knowledge of every even and odd number.

THEAETETUS: Done.

SOCRATES: It's through this science, I suppose, that a person both has   a10
the pieces of knowledge of the numbers as subjects under his control,   b1
and also passes them on to another, if he does.

THEAETETUS: Yes.

SOCRATES: And when someone does pass them on we say he is teaching, while taking them over is learning, and as for having them, by virtue of   b5
having come to possess them in that aviary of ours, that we call knowing.

THEAETETUS: Right.

SOCRATES: So now pay attention to the next step. If someone is a perfect arithmetician, won't he know all numbers? After all, there are   b10
pieces of knowledge of all numbers in his soul.

THEAETETUS: Obviously.

SOCRATES: So would this sort of person ever do any counting, by   c1
himself to himself, whether numbers by themselves,[93] or something else, outside himself, that has number?

THEAETETUS: Of course he would.

---

[92] 'Pieces of knowledge' renders the single word *epistêmai* in the Greek, which was translated just as 'knowledges' at 146c. The 'knowledges' of 146c will presumably be some of the parts into which the form or kind, knowledge, is in fact divided, or 'cut' (*Sophist* 257c); it will be an open question whether the 'knowledges' in question here in 197e are the result of a similar cutting of the form/kind 'at the natural joints', or of simply 'breaking [it] apart in the manner of an inexpert butcher' (*Phaedrus* 265e).
[93] Cf. 196a ('not ... seven and five human beings, just five and seven by themselves').

SOCRATES: And as for counting, we won't take that as anything but looking to see how large some number actually is.

THEAETETUS: Just so.

SOCRATES: In that case, he is plainly looking for something he knows as if he didn't know it, given that we have agreed that he knows all number. I imagine you hear disputes going on along such lines.

THEAETETUS: Indeed I have.

SOCRATES: Well, we on our side will surely compare the situation to the possession and hunting down of our pigeons, and say, no, there were two sorts of hunting: the hunting that took place before he came to possess a pigeon, and for the sake of coming to possess it, and the hunting that occurred after he'd come to possess it, for the sake of catching and having in his hands what had previously come into his possession. Just so, even if he already knew the things in question, because there were pieces of knowledge of them in him that he learned long ago, he can still be learning the very same things again, by virtue of his recovering, and so having, the knowledge of each of them that he had once come to possess but did not presently have to hand in his thought.

THEAETETUS: True.

SOCRATES: This is what I was asking just now, about what names we should use when talking about these things, that is, when the expert arithmetician sets about counting, or someone expert in reading and writing sets to reading something. Should we say in that sort of situation that someone already knowledgeable is actually going back to learn again from himself the things he knows?

THEAETETUS: That would be strange, Socrates.

SOCRATES: Or are we to say that he will be reading or counting things he doesn't know, when we've granted that he knows every letter and every number?

THEAETETUS: There would be no reason to say that either.

SOCRATES: So do you want us to say that it is of no concern to us what names are used? Let people drag 'knowing' and 'learning' around however it pleases them. Having established that it is one thing to possess knowledge, another to have it, we declare it impossible not to possess what one possesses, so that it never happens that someone does not know what he knows, but yet we declare that it is still possible for him to acquire a false belief about it. For, we say, he can fail to have the knowledge of this, and have another piece of knowledge in place of this

one; when he is hunting for some piece or other, as they all fly around, he mistakenly gets hold of one instead of another – and it's then, in fact, that he thinks the eleven to be twelve, namely when he gets hold of   b5
the piece of knowledge of the eleven that is there in himself instead of the piece of knowledge of the twelve, just as he might get hold of a ring-dove instead of a pigeon.

THEAETETUS: Now that does sound reasonable.

SOCRATES: But when he gets hold of the one he's trying to get hold of, then we'll say, shall we, that in this case he is free of falsity and believes the things that are; so that this is how belief can be true or false, and none   c1
of the things that were annoying us before[94] is standing in our way any longer? Well, perhaps you'll agree; or what will you do?

THEAETETUS: I'll agree.

SOCRATES: Yes, we are done with this not knowing what we know;   c5
we're never going to turn out in any way not to possess what we possess, whether we're misled about something or not. But we seem to me to be faced with another and more frightening situation.

THEAETETUS: What is that?

SOCRATES: If the interchange of pieces of *knowledge* is going to turn   c10
out to be false belief.

THEAETETUS: How is that frightening?

SOCRATES: First of all, that someone who has knowledge of something   d1
should be ignorant of that very thing, not by reason of ignorance but by his own knowledge! Then again, as for his thinking it to be something else, and the other thing to be it, is it not utterly against reason that, when knowledge is present, the soul should recognize nothing and be   d5
ignorant about everything involved? If this is going to be our account of the matter, there is nothing to prevent the presence of ignorance also causing us to know something, or blindness from causing us to see; why not, if knowledge actually sometimes makes a person *not* know?

THEAETETUS: Yes, Socrates, and perhaps it wasn't a good move to   e1
make the birds exclusively pieces of knowledge. Maybe we should have had pieces of ignorance in the soul too, flying about with them, so that the person hunting sometimes gets hold of a piece of knowledge, sometimes a piece of ignorance about the very same thing. Then he   e5

---

[94] See 195c.

would believe what is false by virtue of ignorance, what is true by knowledge.

SOCRATES: It's hard, Theaetetus, not to applaud your effort, but do think again about what you just said. Suppose it is as you say. The
200a person who has got hold of the piece of ignorance, you say, is going to believe things that are false; right?

THEAETETUS: Yes.

SOCRATES: He presumably won't *think* he is believing what is false.

THEAETETUS: Certainly not.

a5 SOCRATES: No, he'll think he is believing what is true, and he'll behave like someone who knows about the things he's actually misled about.

THEAETETUS: Of course.

SOCRATES: He will suppose, in that case, that he has hunted down, and has, a piece of knowledge, not a piece of ignorance.

a10 THEAETETUS: Clearly.

SOCRATES: Surely, then, we've gone a long way round only to arrive
b1 back at the puzzle we started with. That expert critic of ours[95] will laugh at us and say 'Wonderful! Friends, are you saying that someone who knows both of them, a piece of knowledge and a piece of ignorance, can suppose one of them, which he knows, actually to be another of the things he knows? Or does he know neither of them, and believe that one of them, which he doesn't know, is another of the things he doesn't
b5 know? Or does he know one of them, not the other, and believe the one he knows is the one he doesn't know; or else think the one he doesn't know is the one he does? Or will you now tell me that actually there are also pieces of knowledge *of* the pieces of knowledge and ignorance, which the person who has come to possess them keeps
c1 confined in other ridiculous aviaries or wax concoctions of some sort, and which he knows so long as he possesses them, even if he does not have them to hand in his soul? Are you going to let yourselves be forced to circle round to the same point ten thousand times over without making any progress at all?' What are we going to reply to this, Theaetetus?

c5 THEAETETUS: Zeus, Socrates! I have no idea what we should say.

---

[95] I.e., in 195c–e.

SOCRATES: Well, my boy, perhaps the argument is quite properly rebuking us, and showing that it's wrong for us to be leaving our search for knowledge to one side and looking for false belief first, when in fact it's impossible to recognize false belief until one has got a sufficient hold on what knowledge is.   d1

THEAETETUS: At the present moment one can only think, Socrates, that you are right.

SOCRATES: So, starting all over again, what is one to say knowledge is?   d5
I imagine we're not going to give up yet?

THEAETETUS: Certainly not, unless you're proposing to.

SOCRATES: Tell me, then, what would be the best thing to say it was, to give us the least chance of contradicting ourselves?

THEAETETUS: What we were trying to say before, Socrates; because   e1
I've nothing else to propose.

SOCRATES: And what was that?

THEAETETUS: That true belief was knowledge. True belief is surely   e5
free from mistakes, and everything that comes about under its guidance turns out fine and good.

SOCRATES: As the man said when he led the way across the river, Theaetetus, it will show for itself: if we go on and try our river, maybe the very thing we're looking for will show because we'll bump into it. If   201a
we stay on the bank, nothing will come clear.

THEAETETUS: You're right. Let's go on and look at it.

SOCRATES: This one surely won't need a long look; there's a whole branch of expertise indicating to you that knowledge is not what you're   a5
saying it is.

THEAETETUS: How so? What expertise is this?

SOCRATES: The one possessed by the greatest in respect of wisdom, the people they call orators and advocates. I take it these people don't use their expertise to persuade an audience by teaching it, but rather by making it believe whatever they want it to believe. Or do you suppose   a10
any of them to be such clever teachers that, in the short time allowed by   b1
the water-clock, they can successfully teach judges who were not there when people were being robbed, or subjected to violence of some other sort, the truth of what actually happened?[96]

---

[96] The sense is clear here, but the text is uncertain.

b5   THEAETETUS: I don't think it's possible; but they could certainly persuade them.

SOCRATES: And you say, do you not, that persuading is making people believe something?

THEAETETUS: Of course.

SOCRATES: So when judges are justly persuaded of things that could only be known through someone's having seen them, and not

c1   otherwise, and they make the judgement they do from hearsay, having acquired a true belief, they will be making their judgement without knowledge, merely having been correctly persuaded – that is, if they have judged well.

THEAETETUS: Yes, that's certainly right.

SOCRATES: My friend, if true belief and knowledge really were the

c5   same thing, a top judge would never have correct beliefs without knowledge; but as things stand, it seems that each must be something different.

THEAETETUS: Oh yes, Socrates, there's something I heard someone saying, but had forgotten; I remember it now. What he said was that true

d1   belief was knowledge when accompanied by an account, whereas true belief that lacked an account fell outside knowledge; the sorts of things of which no account can be given he said were not knowable – that is the name he gave them, 'not knowable'[97] – while those of which an account can be given were knowable.

SOCRATES: Very good. So tell me how he wanted to distinguish these

d5   knowables from the not knowables. I'd like to see whether what you have heard is the same as I have.

THEAETETUS: I don't know if I can work it out. But if someone else spelled it out, I could probably follow.

SOCRATES: Then let me swap with you, a dream for a dream.[98] For my

e1   part, I thought I was hearing certain people saying that the primary elements, as it were, out of which we and everything else are composed, were things one couldn't give an account of. Each of them, taken itself by itself, could only be named, and nothing else could be said of it by way of

e5   addition, either that it is or that it is not; that would be already to add

---

[97] Possibly an acknowledgement that the word used for 'knowable' is unfamiliar, or a new coinage (*epistêton*, rather than *gnôston*, which will be used in what follows, *epistêton* being preferred here simply because it is cognate with *epistêmê*, the noun used in the question 'what is knowledge?').

[98] See Introduction, Section 6.

being or not-being to it, when nothing ought to be brought in if one is 202a
going to talk about that thing itself alone. In fact, one ought not to bring
in even this 'itself', or 'that', or 'each', or 'alone', or 'this', or a whole
range of things of that sort; for these run about and get themselves a5
attached to everything, when they are different from the things they are
applied to, whereas what should happen, if it was actually possible for it
to be talked about by itself, and it had an account belonging exclusively
to itself, is that it should be talked about in isolation from all those other
things. But as it is, it is impossible for any of the primary things to be b1
expressed in an account; the only possibility for it is to be named, since
this is all it has – a name. With things that are composed from these,
however, it is a different matter: just as the primary things themselves
are woven together to form the compounds, so their names become
woven together too, and form an account, since what it is to be an b5
account is a weaving together of names.[99] So it is that the elements are
unaccountable and unknowable, though they can be perceived, whereas
the compounds are knowable, because an account can be given of them,
and one can also have true beliefs about them. So when someone gets
hold of the true belief belonging to something but without an account, c1
his soul has the truth about the thing in question, but not knowledge,
since a person who is unable to give and receive an account of a thing is
ignorant about it; but if he has got hold of an account of it too, then that
makes him capable of all these things and perfectly equipped in relation c5
to knowledge. Did the dream you heard go like that, or was it different?

THEAETETUS: Like that in every respect.

SOCRATES: So are you happy to go this way, and put down true belief
with an account as knowledge?

THEAETETUS: I certainly am. c10

SOCRATES: Theaetetus, have we really now grasped, just like that, on d1
this very day, what so many wise people have sought for so long and
gone grey before they found it?

THEAETETUS: To me, at any rate, Socrates, what was said just now
seems a fine account of the matter. d5

SOCRATES: And very likely it *is* like that. What knowledge could there
possibly be apart from the account and a correct belief about something?

---

[99] All of this, in the Greek, is in indirect speech, as are the next two sentences; it is all part of what
Socrates claims to have dreamed that he heard.

There is, though, one aspect of what was just said that I am not happy with.

THEAETETUS: Which was what?

d10 SOCRATES: What actually seems the most subtle part of it, namely that
e1 the elements were unknowable, while the kind belonging to compounds was knowable.

THEAETETUS: Is that not correct?

SOCRATES: This is what we need to establish. We have as it were our hostages for the theory in the examples it used in laying it all out.

e5 THEAETETUS: Which were they?

SOCRATES: The elements and compounds we use in writing. Or do you think the person who said the things we're talking about had something else in mind when he was saying them?

THEAETETUS: No, this was what he had in mind.

203a SOCRATES: So let's put them to the test – or rather, let's test ourselves, to see whether we learned our letters like this or not. Here's the first question: do syllables have an account that can be given of them, whereas letters do not?

a5 THEAETETUS: Probably.

SOCRATES: It appears that way to me too, certainly. At any rate, if someone asked you about the first syllable of 'Socrates', and said 'Theaetetus, tell me: what is SO?' What will you answer?

THEAETETUS: That it's S and O.

a10 SOCRATES: And this is the account you have of the syllable?

THEAETETUS: Yes.

b1 SOCRATES: So come on, give me an account of the S along the same lines.

THEAETETUS: And how exactly is one going to give the elements of an element? Actually, Socrates, S is one of the voiceless letters, just a
b5 particular noise, as of the tongue hissing; B in its turn has neither voice nor noise, and neither do most of the letters. So it is quite correct for them to be said to be unaccountable, given that the seven most distinct among them, the seven vowels, only have voice, and it is impossible to give any sort of account even of them.[100]

---

[100] Vowels are 'voiced' insofar as they involve movement of the larynx; a consonant like S, while being unvoiced, has a sound of its own; consonants like B are unvoiced and cannot be pronounced on their own, i.e. without a vowel, at all. The vowels are 'most distinct' perhaps

SOCRATES: Here's something, then, my friend, that we've got right about knowledge.   b10

THEAETETUS: It appears so.

SOCRATES: What about the point that the syllable is knowable but   c1
the letter isn't – have we shown that to be right?

THEAETETUS: Yes, it looks like it.

SOCRATES: So come on, do we say that the syllable is both its letters,   c5
or all of its letters if there are more than two? Or do we rather say that it's
some unitary form that has come about from their being put together?

THEAETETUS: I think we say that it is all the letters.

SOCRATES: So think of a case where there are two, S and O. Both
together are the first syllable of my name. Mustn't someone who knows
the syllable know both of them?   c10
                                                                                                          d1
THEAETETUS: Obviously.

SOCRATES: In that case he knows the S and the O.

THEAETETUS: Yes.

SOCRATES: What then – does he actually not know either of them
individually, and know both while knowing neither?   d5

THEAETETUS: That would be strange and unaccountable, Socrates.

SOCRATES: And yet if it is necessary to know each if one is going to
know both, then it is absolutely necessary, if a person is going to know a
syllable, that he should know the letters first; in which case our beautiful   d10
account of knowledge will make its getaway and vanish from the scene.

THEAETETUS: Yes, and pretty sharply too.   e1

SOCRATES: That's because we're not watching over it closely enough.
Maybe we should have supposed the syllable not to be the letters, but
rather some unitary form that has come to be from them, one that has a
single identity[101] of its own and is different from the letters.   e5

THEAETETUS: You're quite right, and perhaps that's the way it is, not
the other.

SOCRATES: We must look and see; we should not give up on an
important and respectable account in so feeble a fashion.

THEAETETUS: No, we certainly should not.   e10

---

because they are, as it were, the most substantial, the easiest to make out on their own (but even
they are 'unaccountable').

[101] Or 'form' (*idea*); earlier in the sentence 'form' is *eidos*.

204a SOCRATES: Then let it be as we are now saying: let the compound be a unitary form that comes to be from the elements as they fit together in each case, whether in the context of writing or in any other context.

THEAETETUS: Certainly.

a5 SOCRATES: Then surely it must not have parts.

THEAETETUS: Why so?

SOCRATES: Because whenever a thing has parts, the whole of it must necessarily be all the parts. Or do you also claim that the whole has come to be out of the parts as some unitary form that is different from all the parts?

a10 THEAETETUS: I do.

b1 SOCRATES: Well, do you call all of it the same as the whole, or are these two different things?

THEAETETUS: I have no clear view of the matter, but since you tell me to be ready and willing with my answers, I shall take my chances and say they are different.

SOCRATES: Your willingness, Theaetetus, is thoroughly in order; let's

b5 see if your answer is likewise.

THEAETETUS: Yes, let's.

SOCRATES: We're presently saying the whole will be different from all of it?

THEAETETUS: Yes.

b10 SOCRATES: So, what if I ask you whether there is any difference between all of them and all of it?[102] For example, when we say 'one,

c1 two, three, four, five, six', or if we say 'two times three' or 'three times two' or 'four plus two' or 'three plus two plus one', are we talking of the same thing in all these cases, or something different?

THEAETETUS: The same thing.

SOCRATES: Six, or something else?

c5 THEAETETUS: Six.

SOCRATES: So whichever expression we use, we will have talked of all six?

THEAETETUS: Yes.

SOCRATES: But again, when we talk of all of it, are we talking of nothing?

---

[102] The renderings 'all of it' and 'all of them', representing respectively the singular, *to pan*, and plural, *ta panta*, of the same noun-phrase, are borrowed from Nicholas Denyer.

THEAETETUS: We must be talking of something.

SOCRATES: Six, or something else? c10

THEAETETUS: Six.

SOCRATES: At least in everything composed out of a number of things, d1
then, it's the same thing we're talking of when we say 'all of it' and when
we say 'all of them'?

THEAETETUS: Apparently.

SOCRATES: So let's say the following about such cases. The number of
a *plethron*[103] and the *plethron* are the same thing; right? d5

THEAETETUS: Yes.

SOCRATES: And similarly with a stade?

THEAETETUS: Yes.

SOCRATES: And the number of an army is the same as the army, and so d10
on with everything like that; all of the number, in each case, is all of what
each of them is.

THEAETETUS: Yes.

SOCRATES: But the number of each surely isn't anything other than e1
its parts?

THEAETETUS: No.

SOCRATES: So anything that has parts will be composed out of parts?

THEAETETUS: Apparently.

SOCRATES: And yet it is agreed that all the parts are all of it, given that e5
all of the number is all of it.

THEAETETUS: That is so.

SOCRATES: The whole, in that case, is not composed out of parts;[104]
since if it were, it would be all the parts, and so all of it.

THEAETETUS: It seems you're right. e10

SOCRATES: But is there anything a part is of, as a part, other than
the whole?

THEAETETUS: Yes – of all of it.

SOCRATES: You're certainly fighting your corner manfully, Theaete- 205a
tus. But isn't all of it what it is, namely all, when nothing is absent
from it?

THEAETETUS: It must be.

---

[103] See 174e, with n.55 (but a *plethron* can refer to a distance as well as an area: one-sixth of a stade).
[104] That is, if it is going to be different from 'all of it'.

SOCRATES: And won't a whole be this same thing, namely something from which nothing is missing in any way? Whereas what does have a5 something missing from it is neither a whole nor all of it, the same thing having come about from the same cause at the same time?

THEAETETUS: It seems to me now that there is no difference between all of it and a whole.

SOCRATES: So were we not saying that whenever a thing has parts, the whole and all of it will be all the parts?[105]

a10 THEAETETUS: We certainly were.

SOCRATES: Now let us go back to what I was attempting to say just b1 now.[106] If the compound is really not the elements that compose it, is it not necessary that it not have the elements as parts of itself – since otherwise it would be the same thing as them and so knowable in a similar way?

THEAETETUS: Just so.

b5 SOCRATES: And surely it was to avoid this consequence that we set it down as something different from them?

THEAETETUS: Yes.

SOCRATES: Well, if the elements are not parts of a compound, can you suggest any other things that *are* parts of a compound but at the same b10 time not elements of that compound?

THEAETETUS: I certainly can't. If I were to concede that it had parts of some sort, Socrates, I imagine it would be ridiculous to leave aside its elements and go looking for other candidates.

c1 SOCRATES: Without any question, then, Theaetetus, according to our present argument, a compound will be a unitary, partless form of some sort.

THEAETETUS: It seems so.

c5 SOCRATES: So, my friend, do you remember that a little earlier we were inclined to think it right to say that there was no account to be given of the primary elements from which other things are composed, on the grounds that each of them was, taken in and by itself, incomposite, and that it would be incorrect even to apply 'being' to them when we talk about them, or even 'this', on the grounds that it would be to refer to

---

[105] See 204a; Socrates now quietly adds 'and all of it' to what was actually said there.
[106] See 203e.

different things not belonging to them; and that this very reason made them unaccountable and unknowable? c10

THEAETETUS: I remember.

SOCRATES: And is there any other reason than this[107] for their being unitary in form and indivisible into parts? I don't see any. d1

THEAETETUS: There certainly doesn't appear to be.

SOCRATES: So does the compound not now find itself belonging to the same form as the primary element, if it really is a partless, unitary form?[108] d5

THEAETETUS: Most certainly it does.

SOCRATES: So then if, on the one hand, the compound is many elements, and some sort of whole, and these are its parts, both compounds and elements are knowable and accountable in a similar fashion, given that all the parts turned out to be the same thing as the whole. d10

THEAETETUS: Quite so. e1

SOCRATES: But if, on the other hand, the compound is something unitary and partless, it is not just an element that will be unaccountable and unknowable, but a compound will be too, in exactly the same way; the same reason will make them such.

THEAETETUS: I can't disagree. e5

SOCRATES: In that case, let us not accept it if someone says a compound is something knowable and accountable, an element the opposite.

THEAETETUS: No, not if we listen to the argument.

SOCRATES: And what if I said you'd actually be more inclined to accept someone's putting it the other way round, from your own personal experience of learning to read and write? 206a

THEAETETUS: The other way round?

SOCRATES: That when you were learning you were continually trying precisely to distinguish each letter in and by itself, whether by sight or by ear, in order that their arrangement wouldn't confuse you when they were spoken or written. a5

THEAETETUS: Very true.

SOCRATES: And at the cithara teacher's, wasn't the learning process complete precisely when you were able to follow each note and say which a10 / b1 string it belonged to – notes being what can be called the elements of music, as everybody would agree.

[107] I.e., being incomposite.   [108] 'Form' in this sentence is first *eidos*, then *idea*.

THEAETETUS: Exactly right.

b5   SOCRATES: So if we're to go by the elements and compounds we ourselves are familiar with, and use them as evidence for others, we'll say that the kind belonging to the elements is much more clearly knowable than the compound, and of much greater importance when it comes to the completion of learning in each context, and if someone

b10   claims that a compound is by nature knowable, an element by nature unknowable, we'll suppose him to be merely playing around, whether deliberately or despite himself.

THEAETETUS: Quite right!

c1   SOCRATES: Anyway, I think there would turn out to be other ways of proving this point; and none of it should allow us to forget the business in hand, which is to look and see what exactly was intended by the claim that when accompanied by true belief the addition of an *account* makes

c5   for the most perfect knowledge.[109]

THEAETETUS: Yes, we need to see that.

SOCRATES: So come on, what precisely does the author of the claim intend 'account' to signify for us? He seems to me to be saying one of three things.

THEAETETUS: What are they?

d1   SOCRATES: The first will be 'account' as making one's thought evident through speech with verbal expressions and names, imprinting the belief on the stream issuing through the mouth like a reflection in a

d5   mirror or in water. Does that sort of thing not seem to you to be an account?

THEAETETUS: Yes, given what we say of someone doing it.[110]

SOCRATES: Doesn't that surely make it something anyone can do, either off the cuff or in a more leisurely fashion? Anyone can indicate what seems to him about whatever it may be, provided that he is not dumb or deaf from the beginning, so that if we take 'account' in this way

e1   anyone who has a correct belief about anything will turn out to have it

---

[109] See 201c–d, where Theaetetus reported hearing from someone that 'true belief was knowledge when accompanied by a reasoned account'. The slightly garbled Greek perhaps results from the adaptation of the original claim to its new context.

[110] I.e., that he *legei* ('is talking', 'is speaking'); *logos*, which is 'account' in the account of knowledge currently being considered, is a noun cognate with *legein*, so that any and every occurrence of *legein* (or of 'making one's thought evident', etc.) can be understood as offering a *logos* or account – of some sort.

'with an account', and there will no longer be any correct belief any-where that's separable from knowledge.

THEAETETUS: True.

SOCRATES: Well, we shouldn't too easily convict this person of having talked nonsense when he declared knowledge to be what we're currently considering. Maybe the speaker wasn't saying that, but rather that an 'account' was a matter of being able when asked what anything is to give the questioner the answer by listing its elements.

THEAETETUS: What would be an example, Socrates?

SOCRATES: One example would be from Hesiod, when he says 'And one hundred are the timbers of a wagon.'[111] I would not myself be capable of describing these, nor, I imagine, would you; we'd be content, if someone asked us what a wagon is, if we were able to reply 'Wheels, axle, frame, rails, yoke.'

THEAETETUS: We certainly would.

SOCRATES: But he'd probably think such a reply made us just as ridiculous as if we were asked for your name and gave its syllables – because then, though we'd be correct in our belief and our expression of it, we'd be fancying that we were experts in reading and writing, and had an expert's control of the account of Theaetetus' name and his ability to express it; when in fact, the questioner would say, it is not possible to talk knowledgeably about anything until as well as having true belief one has finished going through it by way of its elements – something that was surely said earlier on in our discussion.

THEAETETUS: Yes, it was.

SOCRATES: Well, in the case of the wagon too he would say that we have correct belief about it, but that it is only by getting a hold on those 'hundred timbers', and being able to express through these what it is, that one will have added an account to one's true belief and so instead of having a mere belief, become expert and knowledgeable about what a wagon is by having gone through the whole by way of the elements.

THEAETETUS: And doesn't that seem right to you, Socrates?

SOCRATES: If it does to you, my friend, and if you accept that describing each thing element by element is an account of it, whereas

---

[111] *Works and Days* 456.

describing it according to 'syllables', or some larger unit still, is no
d1 account of it at all, do tell me, so that we can look into it.

THEAETETUS: I certainly do accept it.

SOCRATES: Is that because you think anyone is knowledgeable about
anything, no matter what, when the same thing seems to him now to
d5 belong to one thing, now to another? Or when he believes that what
belongs to the same thing is now one thing, now something else?

THEAETETUS: Zeus, no! I don't think that.

SOCRATES: Then are you forgetting that when you and the others were
learning to read and write, to start with you did just that?

d10 THEAETETUS: Are you talking about the way we would now think one
e1 letter belonged to the same syllable, now another, and would put the
same letter now into the proper syllable, now into a different one?

SOCRATES: I am.

e5 THEAETETUS: Zeus knows I don't forget it, and neither do I think
people in a condition to do that have yet acquired knowledge.

SOCRATES: So now suppose that someone at just such a stage is writing
208a 'Theaetetus': he thinks he should write T, H, E, and does; then he tries
to write 'Theodorus', but thinks he should write T, E, and writes that.
Are we going to say that he knows the first syllable of your names?

THEAETETUS: Hardly, when we just agreed that someone in that
a5 condition does not yet have knowledge.

SOCRATES: Well, is there anything to prevent the same individual
being in that condition in relation to the second syllable too, and the
third, and the fourth?

THEAETETUS: No, nothing.

SOCRATES: So when he writes 'Theaetetus' with the letters one after
a10 another, as he does so he'll have that description by element we were
talking about, along with correct belief?

THEAETETUS: Clearly so.

b1 SOCRATES: While still lacking knowledge, we're saying, even though
he has correct belief?

THEAETETUS: Yes.

SOCRATES: Despite, that is, possessing an account together with
correct belief. After all, he had the way through by element as he wrote,
which we agreed constituted an account.

THEAETETUS: True.

SOCRATES: In that case, my friend, there is correct belief with an account that ought not yet to be called knowledge.

THEAETETUS: That's probably so. b10

SOCRATES: It was only a dream of gold, then, when we thought we had in our hands the truest account of knowledge. Or shall we not draw a line under it just yet? Perhaps instead of defining 'account' this way, some- c1 one will choose the remaining way of taking it among the three we said would be available to anyone defining knowledge as correct belief with an account.

THEAETETUS: That is a timely reminder; there is still one of the three left. One option was to take it as an image, as it were, of thought in c5 speech, and the one we've just considered was the route to the whole by element. What are you saying was the third?

SOCRATES: What most people would say: that it's a matter of being able to identify some distinguishing mark by which the thing one has been asked about differs from everything else.

THEAETETUS: Can you give me an example of this sort of 'account' of something?

SOCRATES: Take the sun, if you like: I imagine you would be content, d1 if you asked what the sun was, to be told that it was the brightest of the things that travel through the heavens around the earth.

THEAETETUS: Certainly I would.

SOCRATES: See now what this illustrates. It's what we were just saying, d5 that when you get hold of the difference that marks off a thing from all other things, it's then – or so some people say – that you'll be getting hold of an account of that thing; whereas so long as your grasp is only on some common aspect it shares with other things, you'll find your account relates to all the things that share that aspect.

THEAETETUS: I see; and it seems to me a fine idea to call this sort of e1 thing an account.

SOCRATES: And if someone has correct belief about any one of the things that are, and then adds to that a grasp of its difference from all the rest, he will have become knowledgeable about a thing about which he e5 previously had belief.

THEAETETUS: That is just what we're saying.

SOCRATES: Well, Theaetetus, now that I've got close up to the option we're talking about, I feel exactly as if I were up close to a shadow-painting[112] – I can't make it out in the slightest, even though while I was standing back from it there appeared to me to be something in it.

THEAETETUS: How has this happened?

SOCRATES: I'll tell you, if I can. I have a correct belief about you: if I have an account of you as well, then I know you; if I do not, then I only have belief about you.

THEAETETUS: Yes.

SOCRATES: But we said an account would be a report of what makes you different.

THEAETETUS: We did.

SOCRATES: So when I only had belief about you, isn't it the case that so far as concerns any aspect that differentiates you from other people, I had no grasp in my mind on a single one of such aspects?

THEAETETUS: It seems not.

SOCRATES: In that case I had in mind one of the common aspects, none of which belongs to you any more than it does to anyone else.

THEAETETUS: That must be so.

SOCRATES: Then come on, in the name of Zeus! How on earth, in such a case, was my belief ever about you rather than anyone else whatever? Suppose that I'm thinking 'Theaetetus is the one who is a human being, and has a nose, eyes, a mouth', and I go on to include each one of the limbs. Well, is there any way that this thought will make it Theaetetus I'm thinking of rather than of Theodorus, or of the most distant of the proverbial Mysians?[113]

THEAETETUS: How could it?

SOCRATES: But then if I think not merely 'the one with a nose and eyes', but 'the one with a snub nose and protruding eyes', again my belief surely won't be about you any more than about me or anyone else like that?

THEAETETUS: Not at all.

SOCRATES: And it will not, I think, be *Theaetetus* that will be the subject of my belief until such time as this particular snub-nosedness

---

[112] 'Shadow-painting' is a technique, especially used for scenery in the theatre, which creates an illusion of depth.

[113] It appears that it was proverbially difficult to tell where the Mysians ended and the Phrygians began: see Strabo, *Geography* 12.4.4.

has left some imprint on my memory that differentiates it from the other cases of snub-nosedness I have seen; similarly with everything else that constitutes you. This is what will awaken my memory, even if I meet you tomorrow,[114] and will make me have correct beliefs about you. c10

THEAETETUS: Very true.

SOCRATES: In which case correct belief too, in relation to anything, d1 will have to do with what makes that thing different.

THEAETETUS: Yes, it appears so.

SOCRATES: So this getting hold of an account in addition to correct belief – what will it now amount to? If on the one hand we're being told d5 to add another belief, about how something differs from everything else, that's a quite ridiculous thing to tell us to do.

THEAETETUS: Why?

SOCRATES: Because it would be instructing us to add a correct belief about how a thing differs from everything else to a correct belief we already have about how it differs from everything else. That would make d10 the turning of a code-staff or a pestle[115] – or whatever example one e1 uses – nothing compared with the circularity of this injunction, which would be more justly called advice from the blind; telling us to 'get hold of in addition' what we already have, in order to get to know what we already believe, looks as if it could only be done by someone quite exceptionally in the dark. e5

THEAETETUS: But if, on the other hand . . .? What was the other thing you were going to say when you asked your question just now?

SOCRATES: This, my boy: if telling us to get hold of an account in addition is a matter of telling us to get to know the relevant difference, not form a belief about it, what a delightful thing the finest of our accounts in relation to knowledge would turn out to be! Getting to know something, I imagine, is to get hold of knowledge; right? 210a

THEAETETUS: Yes.

SOCRATES: Well, if this account of ours is asked what knowledge is, it seems its answer will be that it is correct belief accompanied by

---

[114] 'Even if': because without these extra conditions, as soon as he and Theaetetus parted today he would cease to have true belief about Theaetetus (let alone knowledge).

[115] 'A code-staff': a reference to a Spartan military coding system, in which the message cannot be read until one knows the dimensions of the staff around which the strip on which it was written was originally wrapped (slantwise). The turning of a pestle was apparently proverbial for endless labour that achieves nothing.

a5   knowledge of difference. That, after all, according to it, would be what it is to add an account.

THEAETETUS: It seems so.

SOCRATES: And it is surely quite simple-minded, when we're trying to find out what knowledge is, to claim that it is correct belief accompanied by knowledge, whether of difference or of anything else. – Neither can

b1   perception, then, Theaetetus, be knowledge, nor true belief, nor the addition of an account along with true belief.

THEAETETUS: It seems not.

SOCRATES: Well then, are we still pregnant with something on the

b5   subject of knowledge, and still in labour, or have we now given birth to everything we had in us?

THEAETETUS: Yes, and – Zeus knows! – I've already said more things than I had in me, thanks to you.

SOCRATES: And do our midwifery skills tell us that they were all a bag of wind, and not worthy of being fed and watered?

b10   THEAETETUS: Yes, undoubtedly.

c1   SOCRATES: Well, if you try to become pregnant with other things after these, Theaetetus, and you succeed, they'll be better things you're filled with thanks to our present inquiry; and if you are barren, you will be less overbearing to those who keep company with you, and gentler, because you'll have the sense not to think you know what you don't

c5   know. This is all that my expertise is capable of, nothing more. I know none of the things others know, all those important and wonderful men there are and have been; this midwifery of mine and my mother's is what

d1   has been allotted to us by god – hers for women, mine for the young and noble and for any who have beauty. – Well, now I must go to the Porch of the King Archon, to meet Meletus' indictment, the one he has brought against me; but in the morning, Theodorus, let's meet here again, you and I.

Sophist

THEODORUS: We've duly come, Socrates, in accordance with our agree- 216a
ment yesterday, also bringing with us this person here.[1] He's a visitor
from his native Elea, where he's a friend of the followers of Parmenides
and Zeno; the man is very much a philosopher.

SOCRATES: Theodorus, are you sure it's not as in Homer, and it's some a5
god you're bringing along, not a foreigner, and you've not noticed?
Homer says gods generally attend on all humans who show due respect, b1
but most of all he says it's the god of strangers and visitors that attends
on us humans and observes us as we overstep the mark or keep in line.[2]
So maybe this person with you will turn out to be some superior being b5
come to observe how bad we are at argument and find us out, a sort of
god come to put us to the test.

THEODORUS: That isn't our visitor's way, Socrates. There are people
who make it their speciality to win arguments,[3] but he's more measured
than them. Nor does the man seem to me a god at all – which is not to
say he is not divine; that's how I describe all philosophers! c1

SOCRATES: Quite right too, my friend. But I hazard that the philosophical kind[4] is not that much easier to make out, if easy is the word,
than the divine; it's certainly true that these individuals – the really
philosophical ones, not the ones that are merely pretending – take on 'all
sorts of shapes', thanks to everyone else's ignorance about them, as they c5

---

[1] 'We': Theodorus and a collection of young men, including Theaetetus (217d).
[2] See Homer, *Odyssey* 9.270–1.   [3] I.e., 'eristics': cf. 225e.
[4] Or 'the kind, philosopher', *to tou philosophou genos*: see Introduction, Section 2.

'visit cities of men',[5] looking down from above on the lives of those below, and seeming to some to be worth nothing at all while others think

d1 the world of them: they appear now as experts in statesmanship,[6] now as sophists,[7] now giving some the impression that they are totally mad. Our

217a visitor, though – I'd like to ask him, if it's alright with him, what people around the place he's from thought about these things, and what names they used for them.

THEODORUS: What things?

SOCRATES: Sophist, expert in statesmanship, philosopher.

a5 THEODORUS: Why exactly do you ask? What is the problem about them you're thinking of putting to him?

SOCRATES: The following: was their view that these were all one thing, or two – or did they distinguish three kinds, just as there are three names, and attach a kind to each of them, one for each name?

a10 THEODORUS: I don't suppose he would at all mind giving you an account of the matter. Am I right, stranger?

b1 VISITOR: You are, Theodorus – I don't mind at all, and the answer is easy enough: they thought they were three things, though they also thought it no small task, nor an easy one, to distinguish them clearly from one another and say what each of them is.

b5 THEODORUS: By chance, Socrates, you have put your finger on issues similar to ones that we happened to be asking him about before we came here – and he made the same excuses to us then as he is making to you now, even though he's admitting that he has heard the issues discussed well enough, and remembers.

c1 SOCRATES: Well, stranger, this is the first request we've made of you, so please don't turn us down. Just tell us this: when you want to demonstrate something to someone, are you usually happier going

c5 through it just by yourself, with a long speech, or by means of questions? I was there once, in my youth, when Parmenides himself used the latter method, and to quite splendid effect; he was by then very old indeed.[8]

---

[5] Cited from Homer, *Odyssey* XVII. 485–7: the gods in Homer never appear as themselves, and when they do appear, few recognize them for what they are.

[6] See, e.g., *Gorgias* 521d–e, where the apparently non-political philosopher Socrates suggests that he is perhaps the only Athenian to try his hand at true political expertise (on the grounds that he is the only one who sets out to say what is best for people, not just what it will please them to hear).

[7] The comic poet Aristophanes, for example, treated Socrates himself as the arch-sophist. See 230a–231b, with note.

[8] As (fictionally?) recorded in Plato's own *Parmenides*.

VISITOR: Doing it through conversation with someone else is the easier, Socrates, provided the person one's talking to causes no trouble and is easily led; if not, it's easier the other way.

SOCRATES: Well, you may choose whichever of those here you want, because they will all go along with you quietly; but if you take my advice, you'll choose one of the younger ones: Theaetetus here, or one of the others if you prefer.

VISITOR: Socrates, this being the first time I've been with you all, I would be a little ashamed not to conduct the encounter in small steps, exchanging word for word, instead prolonging things by stretching out a big speech by myself, even if it was addressed to someone else, as if I were giving a display speech – because the question now raised is genuinely not as slight as one might expect from the way it was put, and actually requires treatment at some considerable length. On the other hand, since I'm your guest, it seems to me it would be rude, even uncivilized, for me to refuse you and the others here, especially since you have spoken as you have. As for Theaetetus, I'm entirely happy to accept him as my interlocutor, given both my own earlier conversation with him and your present recommendation.

THEAETETUS: So please do that, stranger, and as Socrates has said, that will be a favour to everyone.

VISITOR: So there's probably no more to be said about it, Theaetetus! From now on the discussion is addressed to you. If the length of the labours involved turns out a little too much for you, don't blame me, blame your friends here.

THEAETETUS: As of now, I don't think I'll give up so easily. But if anything like that does happen, we'll enlist Socrates here to help, Socrates' namesake. He is the same age as I am and trains with me; it's not unusual for him to share the labour with me in most things.

VISITOR: Well said. You'll think about that for yourself as the discussion proceeds. But for now you need to be joining me in the investigation, starting from the sophist, or so it appears to me; you need to ask what exactly the sophist is, and give a clear account of him. As things stand at present, the only thing you and I have in common between us on the subject is the name, and we may well each have our own private view of the thing we call by that name. But the rule ought always to be, in relation to anything, to agree together about the thing itself through talking about it, rather than agreeing just about its name without any

d1

d5

e1

e5

218a

a5

b1

c1

c5

account to go with the name. But the tribe[9] we're now planning to look into, the sophist, isn't the easiest in the world to bring together, so as to say what exactly it is; and when it comes to grappling effectively with any
d1 of the big subjects, everyone has long thought it best to practise on small and easier things before moving on to the big ones themselves. So this, Theaetetus, is my advice for the two of us now: that we should treat
d5 tracking down the kind, sophist, as a hard thing to accomplish, and have some practice beforehand with the method we'll need for it – unless you have a less troublesome suggestion to make for approaching the subject.

THEAETETUS: No, I don't.

VISITOR: So are you content that we should pursue something of no consequence and try to establish it as a model for the more important subject?

e1 THEAETETUS: Yes.

VISITOR: So what can we set up for ourselves that is readily knowable and small, but no less accountable[10] than the bigger things? Angler, for example: isn't that something known to everyone, and not in the least
e5 worth being very serious about?

THEAETETUS: He is.

219a VISITOR: All the same I'm hoping he will provide us with a method and an account that will be serviceable for our purposes.

THEAETETUS: That would be good.

a5 VISITOR: So come on, let's start on him like this. Tell me, should we put him down as an expert, or as someone who lacks expertise but has some other sort of capacity?

THEAETETUS: He's hardly a non-expert!

VISITOR: But then if we take expertises as a whole, there are pretty much two forms.

THEAETETUS: How so?

a10 VISITOR: There's farming, and all the caring that relates to living bodies; then again there's what relates to things put together or fabricated, the
b1 things we call 'manufactured' items; and there's expertise in imitation – all of which it would be quite appropriate to refer to by a single name.

---

[9] The word is *phulon*, 'tribe' in ordinary Greek; used interchangeably with *genos*, 'kind', at 220b, and perhaps here too.
[10] 'Accountable': 'having a *logos*', i.e., susceptible to a *logos* or account; translation as at *Theaetetus* 202b, 205e, etc.

THEAETETUS: How, and what name?

VISITOR: In the case of everything that is brought into being when it was not before, I think we say that the person doing it is producing, while the thing being brought into being is produced. b5

THEAETETUS: Correct.

VISITOR: But now all the things we mentioned just now had their own capacity for doing this.

THEAETETUS: They did. b10

VISITOR: So let's sum them all up by calling them productive expertise.

THEAETETUS: Done. c1

VISITOR: On the other hand there is that whole form that has to do with learning and coming to know, there is the money-making one, and there are those that have to do with combat and hunting. Since none of these creates anything, but they all deal with things that are or have come c5 into being, in some cases mastering them by words or actions, in some preventing others from exercising mastery over them, perhaps it would be most appropriate, given these features, to say that all the parts together constituted a sort of acquisitive expertise.

THEAETETUS: Yes, it would.

VISITOR: Then if all the expertises taken together are either acquisitive d1 or productive, in which of the two, Theaetetus, shall we locate expertise in angling?

THEAETETUS: Clearly in the acquisitive, I suppose.

VISITOR: And aren't there two forms of acquisitive expertise, one of d5 them involving exchange between willing parties, through the giving of gifts, hiring or buying and selling, whereas the remaining one, since all of it is mastering, whether through actions or words, will be expertise in mastering?

THEAETETUS: That's how it looks, from what has been said.

VISITOR: But what about mastering? Shouldn't this be cut into two? d10

THEAETETUS: How?

VISITOR: By treating the whole section of it that takes place openly as e1 expertise in combat, all of it that is by stealth as expertise in hunting.

THEAETETUS: Yes.

VISITOR: And yet it would be unaccountable not to cut hunting expertise into two. e5

THEAETETUS: Tell me how.

VISITOR: By dividing hunting according to the kinds it hunts, the lifeless and the living.

THEAETETUS: Of course – if there really are these two kinds of hunting.

220a VISITOR: And how are there not? Actually, the hunting of lifeless things – it has no name except when it comes to some parts or other of diving expertise and other small exceptions like that – needs to be left aside, while we call the other kind of hunting, which is the hunting of living creatures, expertise in animal-hunting.

a5 THEAETETUS: Done.

VISITOR: And won't we be justified in talking about this form, animal-hunting expertise, as double, some of it relating to the kind equipped with feet, itself divided by many forms and names – land-animal-hunting, the rest all being of creatures that swim: water-animal-hunting, then?

a10 THEAETETUS: Yes, certainly.

b1 VISITOR: But of the kind that swims, we observe one tribe[11] with wings, another living under water.

THEAETETUS: Yes, certainly.

b5 VISITOR: And I think we find all hunting of the winged kind talked about as some sort of expertise in bird-catching.

THEAETETUS: We do, yes.

VISITOR: While the hunting of the underwater kind is, pretty much the whole of it, an expertise in fishing.

THEAETETUS: Yes.

b10 VISITOR: Well, won't we divide this hunting, in turn, into two main parts?

THEAETETUS: Which are they?

VISITOR: According to the way some of it carries out the hunting by means of enclosures, some by striking.

THEAETETUS: What are you saying? How are you distinguishing the two?

c1 VISITOR: The first is reasonably called enclosure because it includes any surrounding of something and enclosing it to prevent it escaping.

THEAETETUS: That is certainly reasonable.

c5 VISITOR: Well, baskets, nets, meshes, fish-traps, and so forth – should we call these anything else but enclosures?

---

[11] See n.9.

THEAETETUS: No.

VISITOR: This part of animal pursuit, then, we'll call 'enclosure-hunting' or something such.

THEAETETUS: Yes.

VISITOR: And the part that comes about through striking with hooks c10 or tridents we should now distinguish from this 'enclosure-hunting', d1 calling it by some such single name as 'strike-hunting'. Or could one suggest a better term, Theaetetus?

THEAETETUS: Let's not worry about the name; your suggestion will do as well as any.

VISITOR: Well, the part of strike-hunting that takes place at night d5 to lamplight is, as it happens, called 'lamp-fishing' by those actually involved in it.

THEAETETUS: It certainly is.

VISITOR: Whereas the daytime part is all hook-fishing, they say, because tridents too have hooks on their tips. d10
e1

THEAETETUS: Yes, they do say that.

VISITOR: Now of the hook-fishing part of strike-fishing, part involves movement downwards from above, and that I imagine is called a sort of tridenting, because that is mostly how tridents are used.

THEAETETUS: Some do say that. e5

VISITOR: But then there is only one form to speak of still remaining.

THEAETETUS: Which is that?

VISITOR: The one that involves striking in the opposite direction, with a hook, not to any part of fishes' bodies one happens to hit, as with 221a tridents, but on each occasion to the head, more precisely to the mouth, of the animal hunted, resulting in its being drawn from below up in the opposite direction with poles or rods – which we'll say, Theaetetus, should be called what?

THEAETETUS: I *think* we've now rounded off the very thing we a5 proposed just now we had to find.

VISITOR: If so, then you and I are agreed, on the subject of angling, not just about its name; we have also got a sufficient grasp on the account b1 to be given of the thing itself. Of all expertise taken together, we divided off the half that was acquisitive, of the acquisitive the half that involved mastering, of the mastering part the part that was hunting, of hunting the part that was animal-hunting, and of animal-hunting the part that b5 was water-animal-hunting; of water-animal-hunting we divided off the

underwater section as a whole, namely fishing; of fishing, the section that
was strike-fishing; of strike-fishing, hook-fishing; and of this the section
c1   involving a strike upwards from below, drawing the hunted animal up
from that angle, turned out to be the thing called 'angling' that we were
looking for, its name mimicking the action involved.[12]

c5   THEAETETUS: So that's been more than sufficiently shown!

VISITOR: Come on, then, let's try to find out what exactly the sophist
is, too, following this model.

THEAETETUS: Yes, let's!

VISITOR: So now the first thing we looked into about the angler was
c10   this: whether one should put him down as a non-expert, or as someone
with a particular expertise.

THEAETETUS: Yes, it was.

d1   VISITOR: Well, shall we put this new one down as a non-expert, or as
really and truly a 'sophist'?[13]

THEAETETUS: Certainly not as a non-expert – I get what you're saying:
someone with the name 'sophist' could least of all be said to be a non-
expert!

d5   VISITOR: It seems we have to put him down as possessing an expertise
of some sort.

THEAETETUS: So then what expertise will this be?

VISITOR: By the gods! Have we not noticed that the two individuals
are akin?[14]

d10   THEAETETUS: Who is akin to whom?

VISITOR: The angler to the sophist.

THEAETETUS: How so?

VISITOR: Both appear to me to be hunters of a sort.

e1   THEAETETUS: What hunting does the second do? We've talked about
the first.

VISITOR: Just now I think we divided animal pursuit as a whole into
two, the cut being between the parts dealing with what swims and what
goes on foot.

e5   THEAETETUS: Yes.

---

[12] The pun (angle/angling) is different from the one in the Greek, where *aspalieutikē*, 'angling',
sounds (a little) like *anaspasthai*, 'draw up'.

[13] Another play on words, as Theaetetus' response indicates, a *sophistēs* being, literally, someone
who professes *sophia*, 'wisdom' – or 'expertise'.

[14] I.e., they share the same kind (they are *sungeneis*), *genos* being both 'kind' and 'family'.

VISITOR: And one of these parts we went through, insofar as we dealt with the swimmers under water; but the footed part we left uncut, merely saying that it was multiform.[15]

THEAETETUS: Right, yes.   222a

VISITOR: Well, up to that point the sophist and the angler proceed together from our starting point, acquisitive expertise.

THEAETETUS: They certainly seem to.

VISITOR: But from animal-hunting onwards, their paths diverge. One   a5
of them, I imagine, goes off to the sea, rivers, and lakes, to hunt animals in these.

THEAETETUS: Of course.

VISITOR: Whereas the other goes off to the land, and to rivers of a rather different sort: this time, rivers of wealth and of youth in unlimited   a10
quantities, like meadows full of creatures to be mastered and exploited.

THEAETETUS: What are you saying?   b1

VISITOR: There turn out to be two main parts to hunting footed animals.

THEAETETUS: How do you divide them?

VISITOR: One is hunting tame animals, the other wild ones.   b5

THEAETETUS: So there is such a thing as hunting tame animals?

VISITOR: There is, if a human being is a tame animal. But choose as you like, whether to say that no animal is tame, or that some other animal is tame but the human animal is wild; or whether to say that human beings are tame but you think there is no hunting of them. Pick out   b10
whichever of these two claims you think you'd like to have been making.

THEAETETUS: Actually, stranger, I say both that we are a tame animal,   c1
and that there is hunting of human beings.

VISITOR: Well now, let's say that tame-animal-hunting expertise too is twofold.

THEAETETUS: Dividing it where?

VISITOR: By marking off the expertise belonging to piracy, enslave-   c5
ment, the tyrant, and each and every aspect of war-making, and treating them all as one thing, hunting by force.

THEAETETUS: Fine.

VISITOR: Whereas the expertise of speaking in court, that of addressing big audiences, and that of buttering up individuals, again treating the   c10

---

[15] I.e., divisible into many forms or kinds (*polueides*).

d1   whole together as one thing, we shall call some single sort of expertise in persuasion.

THEAETETUS: Quite right.

VISITOR: And let us say there are two kinds of persuasive expertise.

THEAETETUS: What are they?

d5   VISITOR: One kind operates in private, the other in public.

THEAETETUS: So yes, let each of these be a form.

VISITOR: And again, some of hunting in private involves the taking of fees, some the giving of gifts?

THEAETETUS: I don't understand.

d10   VISITOR: It seems you haven't paid attention to the way lovers hunt.

THEAETETUS: In what connection?

e1   VISITOR: The way they give their prey gifts on top of everything else.

THEAETETUS: Very true.

VISITOR: Well, let this be the form, amatory expertise.

THEAETETUS: Certainly.

e5   VISITOR: Whereas when it comes to the fee-taking form, some of it involves buttering people up by using gratification as its lure, and nothing but pleasure, and by way of a fee receiving enough to live off

223a   and no more: that, I imagine, we'll all agree to call flattery, or an expertise in pleasuring of some sort.

THEAETETUS: Clearly.

VISITOR: Some of it, on the other hand, involves associating with

a5   people by announcing it to be for the sake of excellence,[16] while exacting a fee in the form of hard cash; this kind we'll be justified in calling by a different name, will we not?

THEAETETUS: Clearly.

VISITOR: And what name will this be? Try and say.

THEAETETUS: It's obvious what it is! I do believe we've found

a10   the sophist. So I'll call it sophistry, and I think that will be the name that fits.

b1   VISITOR: Then according to what we are saying now, Theaetetus, it seems that if we take expertise in appropriation,[17] in hunting, in animal-hunting, in land-animal-hunting, in the hunting of humans, by

---

[16] Or 'goodness', or 'virtue' (*aretē*): a commodity in which, Plato's Socrates regularly suggests, the sophists typically claimed to specialize.

[17] 'Appropriation' (*oikeiōtikē*) here seems to be what was previously called 'acquisition'.

persuasion, in private, involving selling for hard cash, offering a seeming education, the part of it that hunts rich and reputable young men is – to go by what we are saying now – what we should call the expertise of the sophist.

THEAETETUS: Quite right.

VISITOR: But there's another way we should look at it, because the expertise that the thing we're looking for has a share in is no mean one; it's a quite thoroughly complex expertise. Indeed, it already gives the appearance, if we look back at the things we said earlier, of not being the kind we're presently saying it is but some other kind.

THEAETETUS: How so?

VISITOR: I think the form we labelled acquisitive expertise was two-fold, having one part that involved hunting, another involving exchange.

THEAETETUS: We did.

VISITOR: Well, of expertise in exchange let's say there are two forms, one of them having to do with gift-giving, the other with marketing.[18]

THEAETETUS: Let's do that.

VISITOR: And again, marketing – that too we'll say is cut into two.

THEAETETUS: In what way?

VISITOR: The marketing of things the seller himself makes divides off as own-product-selling expertise, the trading of others' products as expertise in trading.

THEAETETUS: Yes, quite.

VISITOR: So what about this expertise in trading? Isn't part of it, in fact roughly half, namely exchange in the city at large, called retailing?

THEAETETUS: Yes.

VISITOR: Whereas the part involving exchange by buying and selling from one city to another is called import and export?

THEAETETUS: Of course.

VISITOR: And of the expertise of importing and exporting we notice, do we not, that some of it deals in what the body is nourished by and uses, some of it in what the soul is nourished by and uses – in both cases selling for cash?

THEAETETUS: What are you saying here?

b5

c1

c5

c10

d1

d5

d10

e1

---

[18] 'Marketing': *agorastikon*, that is, having to do with the *agora*, the main location in a Greek city for selling and buying.

e5   VISITOR: We're maybe unfamiliar with the part concerned with the soul, since presumably we understand the other part well enough.

THEAETETUS: Yes.

224a VISITOR: Well, take music in general, whenever it is bought in from one city, and brought and sold into another, and similarly with painting, or conjuring, or any other of the many things that are brought in and

a5   sold for the sake of the soul, some of them to comfort it, some for serious purposes: we're not going to claim that the person who brings these in and sells them on is any less correctly said to be fulfilling the role of importer-exporter when he provides them than the person who deals in the sale of food and drink.

THEAETETUS: That's quite true.

b1   VISITOR: So you'll use this same name for the person who buys up things to be learned and peddles them for cash from city to city?

THEAETETUS: Very much so.

VISITOR: So, of this 'soul-related-import-export' of ours, some of it

b5   will most appropriately be called expertise in display,[19] won't it? For the rest, well, it's no less ridiculous a name than the previous one, but it's the selling of lessons, and we need to call it something that relates to what it does.

THEAETETUS: We certainly do.

VISITOR: And then we need to call the part of this lesson-selling that

c1   has to do with lessons in the other expertises by one name, the part that has to do with the learning of excellence[20] by another.

THEAETETUS: Obviously.

VISITOR: Well, 'expertise-selling' will fit the part concerned with the

c5   rest; you try your best to tell me the name that has to do with the latter things.[21]

THEAETETUS: And what other name could one utter and not strike the wrong note, than saying that it was the thing we are presently looking for, the kind *sophist*?

c10 VISITOR: None other. So now let's collect it all together, by saying that

d1   of expertise in acquisition, exchange, marketing, exporting-importing, and soul-related-import-export, the selling that is concerned with words

---

[19] The reference is to travelling rhetorical experts, like Thrasymachus in the *Republic*, who specialize in display speeches.
[20] The term is again *aretê*, as at 223a.   [21] I.e., lessons (supposedly) in excellence.

about and lessons in excellence is what, this second time round, expertise in sophistry has shown up as being.

THEAETETUS: Very much so.

VISITOR: But then, thirdly, if someone has settled here in the city, and   d5
set himself to make a living from selling lessons on these same things, some bought in, some also manufactured by himself, I think the name you use is no different from the one you used just now.

THEAETETUS: No, of course not!

VISITOR: And in that case, the part of acquisitive expertise that has to   e1
do with exchange, then with marketing, whether it's a matter of retailing or selling one's own products,[22] either way – whichever sort of lesson-selling it is, on the sort of subjects in question[23] – you're evidently going to go on calling it sophistry in any case.

THEAETETUS: I have to, since it follows from what we've said.   e5

VISITOR: Now let's go on and see whether the kind we're presently in pursuit of doesn't perhaps look like something of the following sort.

THEAETETUS: What sort is that?   225a

VISITOR: Of expertise in acquisition we found there was a part that related to combat.

THEAETETUS: Yes, we did.

VISITOR: Well, it won't be a bad thing for us to divide this part into two.

THEAETETUS: Tell me along what lines.   a5

VISITOR: By setting down some of it as relating to competition, some to fighting.

THEAETETUS: Right.

VISITOR: Then of expertise in fighting, it'll be pretty reasonable and appropriate for us to call the part that involves body against bodies   a10
something like 'forcible'.

THEAETETUS: Yes.

---

[22] Previously separated off; it is now retrieved, so that when in 231c–d Socrates and Theaetetus begin to summarize their different attempts to give an account of the sophist, 'lessons-salesman dealing in his own lessons' will turn up after 'retailer of lessons for the soul'.

[23] I.e., apparently, subjects like excellence; the plural here seems still to refer to *mathêmata* – otherwise 'lessons', but here perhaps used of the thing taught. The Visitor noticeably avoids any suggestion that the buying and selling are of excellence itself – as the sellers themselves might have claimed; and after all it has been built in to the previous definition (and so, by implication, into the present one) that what is on sale is only a 'seeming' education: 223b.

VISITOR: And what other name, Theaetetus, would anyone suggest we
b1 give to the part involving words against words but 'disputative'?

THEAETETUS: None.

VISITOR: And the part concerned with disputation must itself be
treated as twofold.

THEAETETUS: How?

b5 VISITOR: Well, insofar as it involves long speeches responding to
opposing long speeches, to do with what is just and unjust, and in
public, it's forensic.

THEAETETUS: Yes.

VISITOR: Whereas if it takes place in private situations, and is chopped
b10 up into questions and corresponding answers, it's not our habit, is it, to
call it anything but 'antilogic'?[24]

THEAETETUS: No.

VISITOR: As for the antilogical part, as much of it as consists in
c1 disputation about contractual matters, where disputes go on in a random
and inexpert fashion – these still need to be registered as a form, given
that the discussion has recognized it as something distinct, but it has
not been given a name by people before and doesn't merit our giving it
one now.[25]

c5 THEAETETUS: True; the parts into which it is divided are too small
and miscellaneous.

VISITOR: But the part of antilogic that does involve expertise, and
disputes about just things themselves, and unjust things, and about other
things in a general way, isn't it our habit to call that, in its turn, by the
name 'eristic'?[26]

c10 THEAETETUS: Of course.

d1 VISITOR: Part of eristic, though, is wealth-destroying, while part
actually produces wealth.

THEAETETUS: It certainly does.

d5 VISITOR: So let's try to say what name we ought to give each of these.

---

[24] For 'antilogic' (*antilogikê*, expertise or skill in contradiction: *antilegein*, 'speaking against'), see *Theaetetus* in this volume, n.37 – though here in the *Sophist*, the Visitor will go on to extend the term in an unexpected way.

[25] Because it involves no single expertise, as Theaetetus' response confirms – and after all, the whole process of division began from (and still is) a division of kinds of expertise.

[26] 'Eristic', in Plato, is a matter of debating, or rather wrangling, simply and solely with the purpose of winning the argument, or appearing to win it (cf. *Republic* 454a–b, and the *Euthydemus*, in which Socrates encounters two experts in the subject).

THEAETETUS: We certainly should.

VISITOR: Well, I think the part that goes on for the sheer pleasure of spending time on such a thing, to the neglect of one's proper affairs, whereas the style of it makes it less than a pleasure for most of its hearers to listen to – this, at any rate in my view, is called nothing other than the 'chattering' part. d10

THEAETETUS: That is the sort of way it is described.

VISITOR: So now you, in your turn, try to say what the part opposite to this is, namely the part to do with making money out of private eristic disputes. e1

THEAETETUS: And why would it not be quite wrong to say anything but that this amazing individual is now back with us again, for the fourth[27] time – the very sophist whose tracks we're following? e5

VISITOR: It seems he's nothing, this sophist of ours, as our discussion now reveals him, if he's not the wealth-producing kind which is part of eristic expertise, then of expertise in antilogic, in disputation, in fighting, in combat, in acquisition: that's what he is. 226a

THEAETETUS: Indeed he is. a5

VISITOR: So do you see how true it is to say that the beast is complex: not one to be caught with one hand, as they say.

THEAETETUS: Both hands are certainly needed!

VISITOR: They certainly are, and we must do our best to use both, following a trail he's left for us, which goes in this sort of direction: tell me, don't we ourselves use some of the names that house-slaves employ? b1

THEAETETUS: Lots; which of the many are you asking about?

VISITOR: The following: we talk, for example, about filtering, sifting, straining, winnowing. b5

THEAETETUS: Of course we do.

VISITOR: And as well as these we talk about carding, spinning, separating with the shuttle; and we know of tens of thousands of other similar things involved in the different expert crafts. b10

THEAETETUS: So you propose these examples – in order to show what? What's the general question you're asking about them? c1

VISITOR: All the things mentioned, I think, have to do with separating things out.

---

[27] Or the fifth, according to the summary in 231c–d, which is more precise; see n.22 above.

THEAETETUS: Yes, they do.

c5   VISITOR: Well, by my account there's a single expertise involved in all of them and covering them all, which we ought to treat as deserving a single name.

THEAETETUS: So what should we call it?

VISITOR: Expertise in discrimination.

THEAETETUS: Very well.

c10   VISITOR: So now see if we can't somehow see two forms of this.

THEAETETUS: That's a question I'd need time to think about, myself.

d1   VISITOR: But actually, among the cases of 'discrimination' mentioned, some were a matter of separating off worse from better, some of separating like from like.

THEAETETUS: It's pretty clear now you say it.

d5   VISITOR: For one of the two I can't point to a name in common use, but I can for the discrimination that leaves behind what is better and throws away what is worse.

THEAETETUS: Tell me what it is.

d10   VISITOR: All discrimination of that sort, as I understand it, is universally called a sort of cleansing.

THEAETETUS: Yes, it is.

e1   VISITOR: And anyone can see, can't they, that this form, cleansing, is itself twofold?

THEAETETUS: Yes, probably, at least if they're given time, but for the moment I'm certainly not seeing it.

e5   VISITOR: But surely it's fitting enough to include under a single name all the many forms of cleansing there are that relate to bodies.

THEAETETUS: Which forms, and what name?

VISITOR: There are those to do with the bodies of living creatures,

227a whether the cleansing is a matter of separating things correctly within them through the expertise of the gymnastic trainer or the doctor, or of doing it on their outside, as for example with the bathing-attendant, to use a humble example; and then there are cleansings of inanimate bodies, taken care of by the expertise of the fuller and all the rest of it that has to

a5 do with external polishing. It all falls into small parts and goes by all sorts of ridiculous-sounding names.

THEAETETUS: Quite so.

VISITOR: Yes indeed, Theaetetus. And yet in our pursuit of the argument, it matters not a bit less, or indeed any more, whether we're

dealing with sponging people down or administering medicines, or
whether the cleansing in question does us a little good or a lot. Our   a10
method aims at acquiring understanding, by attempting to grasp what   b1
is akin[28] and what is not akin among all the various expertises, and for
this purpose it values all of them equally; when things resemble each
other, it doesn't think of some of them as more ridiculous than others,
and it won't treat someone who illuminates hunting through generalship
rather than nit-picking as somehow more impressive, but rather, other   b5
things being equal, as empty-headed. Similarly now, with your question
about the name we're to give all the capacities concerned with cleansing   c1
living and inanimate bodies: it will make no difference to our method
what sort of name sounds the most respectable; it only needs to bind
together all the things that cleanse something else in order to keep them
separate from cleansings of the soul. What our method is currently
about – if we're properly understanding its purpose – is trying to
separate off cleansing in relation to thought from other cleansings.   c5

THEAETETUS: I do understand, and I agree that there are two forms of
cleansing, and that one has to do with the soul, being separate from the
one that has to do with the body.

VISITOR: You couldn't have put it better. Now, for the next step, listen   c10
to me and try cutting what we've just mentioned in its turn into two.   d1

THEAETETUS: I'll try to cut it with you, according to whatever criteria
you propose.

VISITOR: Do we talk of badness as something different in the soul
from goodness[29]?

THEAETETUS: Obviously.   d5

VISITOR: And we agreed that cleansing was retaining one of these and
throwing out anything that was in some way or other in poor condition?

THEAETETUS: That's what we agreed.

VISITOR: So with soul too, to the extent that we find something that's a
removal of badness of some sort, we'll be hitting the right note if we call d10
it cleansing.

THEAETETUS: Very much so.

VISITOR: There are, we should say, two forms of badness in relation
to soul.

---

[28] 'Akin': see 221d.   [29] I.e., *aretē*: cf. nn.16 and 20 above.

THEAETETUS: What are they?

228a VISITOR: One is like disease occurring in a body, the other like bodily ugliness.

THEAETETUS: I don't understand.

VISITOR: Perhaps it's not your view that disease and discord are the same thing?

a5 THEAETETUS: I don't know how I'm supposed to respond to this, either.

VISITOR: Is that because you think discord is something other than a disagreement in what is naturally akin, because of some sort of corruption?

THEAETETUS: No, it's exactly that.

a10 VISITOR: And ugliness: is this anything except that always unappealing kind, disproportion?

b1 THEAETETUS: No, there's nothing else it can be.

VISITOR: Well now, in a soul, when people are in poor condition, don't we observe beliefs disagreeing with desires, anger with pleasures, reason with pains, indeed all of these with each other?[30]

b5 THEAETETUS: Yes, we certainly do.

VISITOR: Yet necessity has made all of them akin to one another.[31]

THEAETETUS: Obviously.

VISITOR: Then we'll be correct in saying that discord and disease in the soul is badness.

b10 THEAETETUS: We certainly will.

c1 VISITOR: So what about things that are capable of movement and set themselves some sort of target: if they try to hit the target, but at every attempt wander away from it and miss it, are we going to say that this

c5 happens to them as a result of their being in proportion one to another, or rather of their being out of proportion?

THEAETETUS: Clearly the latter.

VISITOR: But we surely know that no soul is voluntarily ignorant of anything.

THEAETETUS: We certainly do.

---

[30] Such internal 'disagreement' in the soul is treated, in Book IV of the *Republic*, as the basis of an argument for dividing the soul into three forms or parts; if that argument were starting from what Socrates says here in the *Theaetetus*, would the division only apply in the case of souls 'in poor condition'?

[31] I.e., in that they are all aspects of a single soul.

VISITOR: And ignorance, surely, is nothing but the deviation[32] of a   c10
soul that is trying for the truth but wanders away from understanding.   d10

THEAETETUS: Yes, quite.

VISITOR: So we have to count a foolish soul as one that is ugly and
lacking in proportion.

THEAETETUS: It seems so.   d5

VISITOR: There are, then, apparently, these two kinds of badness in a
soul: one of them is what ordinary people call being bad, and is quite
clearly a disease of the soul.

THEAETETUS: Yes.

VISITOR: The other one, by contrast, they call by its name, ignorance,   d10
but they are unwilling to concede that it is badness, occurring as it does
only within a soul.[33]

THEAETETUS: I certainly have to agree, though I was doubtful about it   e1
when you said it just now, that there are two kinds of badness in a soul.
Cowardice, lack of moderation, injustice, all of these things taken
together, have to be considered a disease in us, while the widespread
and ever-varying phenomenon of ignorance needs to be understood as   e5
ugliness.

VISITOR: Now in the case of the body, in relation to these two
phenomena two corresponding sorts of expertise have come about.

THEAETETUS: Which are these?

VISITOR: For ugliness, the expertise of the gymnastic trainer; for   229a
disease, that of the doctor.

THEAETETUS: Clearly so.

VISITOR: Well, in the case of excess and injustice and cowardice too,
isn't corrective expertise the one that fits more than any other, and   a5
justly so?

THEAETETUS: So it seems, at any rate, if we're to go by what people
generally believe.

VISITOR: And what about ignorance taken as a whole? Surely the
correct expertise to talk about for this would have to be that of the   a10
teacher?

---

[32] Or 'derangement' (*paraphrosunê*); in the Greek there is a pun, or etymological play, on *paraphoros*
('wandering away').
[33] I.e., perhaps, when it is not immediately visible in a person's behaviour, as other 'wandering' or
derangement can be.

THEAETETUS: It would.

b1   VISITOR: Now think: should we say that there is only one kind of expertise in teaching, or more than one, two particular kinds being the most important?[34]

THEAETETUS: I'm thinking.

b5   VISITOR: It seems to me we'll find out most quickly in the following sort of way.

THEAETETUS: What way?

VISITOR: By looking to see whether ignorance somehow doesn't have a cut running through the middle of it. If ignorance turns out to be twofold, then clearly that will mean that teaching too must have two

b10   parts, one for one of the kinds of ignorance, one for the other.

THEAETETUS: So do we have any sight of what we're looking for?

c1   VISITOR: I certainly think I see one important and troublesome form of ignorance that is quite distinct, and equal in weight to all its other parts together.

THEAETETUS: Which is?

c5   VISITOR: Not knowing something but thinking one does; which is probably the origin of all the mistakes in thinking any of us makes.

THEAETETUS: True.

VISITOR: I think, moreover, that it's for this form of ignorance that the name 'stupidity' is reserved.

c10   THEAETETUS: Quite so.

VISITOR: So then what name should we give to the part of expertise in teaching that rids us of this?

d1   THEAETETUS: I think, stranger, the rest of it is called teaching of some craft expertise or other, whereas the part we're talking about, here at least, thanks to us Athenians, is called education.

d5   VISITOR: As it is, Theaetetus, pretty much everywhere in Greece. But there's something else we still need to look into, namely whether this is now an uncuttable whole, or whether it admits of some division worthy of the name.

THEAETETUS: So we need to look into it.

VISITOR: Well, it looks to me as if there's still a cut in this too.

THEAETETUS: Whereabouts?

---

[34] Or 'most extensive' (*megistō*).

VISITOR: One of the routes used by teaching expertise that employs   e1
words[35] seems to me to be tougher going, the other part of it less tough.

THEAETETUS: So how are we to describe each of these?

VISITOR: One is a venerable method our forefathers have handed
down to us. It's a method they would mostly employ with their sons,   e5
and many still use it now, when they find them going wrong in some   230a
way – telling them off, or taking the softer option and exhorting them;
either way, one would be entirely correct to call the whole thing expertise in admonition.

THEAETETUS: That's right.

VISITOR: On the other hand, some people will appear to have given   a5
themselves reason to suppose that all stupidity is involuntary,[36] and that
someone who believes he is wise will never want to learn any of the
things he thinks himself already accomplished in; they suppose that
the admonitory form of education achieves little at the cost of great
labour.

THEAETETUS: And they are right.   a10

VISITOR: So they set about getting rid of the belief in an another way.   b1

THEAETETUS: What way is that?

VISITOR: They ask questions on whatever someone thinks he's talking
sense about when in fact he is talking nonsense; and then, because the   b5
people whose beliefs they are examining are continually shifting their
position, their task is easy. They use the conversation to collect those
beliefs together and put them side by side, thereby revealing them as
contradicting one another not just on the same subjects but in relation
to the same things and in the same respects. When the people being
examined see what is happening, they are angry with themselves but
become less aggressive towards others; and it is in this way that they are   c1
liberated from those great, obstinate beliefs about themselves – the most
pleasing of all liberations for the listener to hear, and the most secure and
profound for the person who experiences it. Those who do the cleansing
in this case, my dear boy, think like doctors who deal with the body.   c5

---

[35] I.e., presumably, as opposed to teaching by example, as in that of the productive skills or crafts.

[36] The 'some' seem to include the Visitor and Theaetetus, to judge by their exchange at 228c ('But
we surely know that no soul is voluntarily ignorant of anything.' 'We certainly do'); 'stupidity'
(*amathia* = 'lack of learning', 'inability to learn'), they agreed at 229c, is one branch or kind of
ignorance, *agnoia*. The Socrates of the *Theaetetus* (and many other dialogues) is someone else that
does what the Visitor says 'some people . . . appear' to do.

Doctors of that sort will think a body incapable of benefiting from the sustenance applied to it until someone removes whatever obstructions there are in it, and those soul-cleansers of ours think the same about a

d1 soul: namely that it will not get the benefit of any lessons applied to it until someone challenges it and causes the person being challenged to be ashamed of himself, removes those beliefs of his that obstruct the lessons to be learned, and renders him clean and pure, thinking he knows only the things he does know and no more.

d5 THEAETETUS: Certainly the best and soundest condition to be in.

VISITOR: For all these reasons, Theaetetus, we have to say that this challenging of people is in fact the greatest and most authoritative of all cleansings, and one must suppose that if someone goes unchallenged,

e1 even if he happens to be the Great King of Persia, his remaining uncleansed in the most important respects already renders him uneducated and ugly in the very respects in which the person who is genuinely going to be happy ought to be at his cleanest, purest, and most beautiful.

e5 THEAETETUS: I agree completely.

VISITOR: Well then, what are we going to call those who employ this

231a expertise? For myself, I'm afraid to say that they are sophists.[37]

THEAETETUS: Why so?

VISITOR: Because to do so would be to attribute too great a status to them.

THEAETETUS: All the same, what has just been described does bear

a5 quite a resemblance to someone of that sort.

VISITOR: Yes, and a wolf has quite a resemblance to a dog – the most savage of creatures to the gentlest. To be safe, one must always be particularly on one's guard when it comes to similarities; for similarity is the most slippery of kinds. But still, let them stand as sophists; for the

b1 dividing lines on which the dispute will turn will, I think, be no minor ones, when they[38] guard their territory as they should.

THEAETETUS: It certainly seems so.

---

[37] The Visitor's reluctance is understandable, since the preceding description fits no one but Socrates. On the other hand, Socrates was for many indistinguishable from the sophists (cf. n.7 above); and this no doubt is a major part of the point of the whole passage.

[38] That is, those who are to 'stand as sophists' – for the moment. The difference between a dog and a wolf is, as the Visitor has already suggested, hardly minor, especially given that a typical role for a Greek dog would be to guard against wolves (as the people in question will defend themselves and others against sophists).

VISITOR: So let it be expertise in cleansing, belonging to discrimina-tive expertise, and let the part of cleansing that has to do with soul be marked off from other parts; of this, expertise in teaching; of teaching, expertise in education; and of educative expertise, let the challenging that takes place in relation to empty belief in one's own wisdom, in the account that came up just now, be said to be nothing other for us than a sophistry ennobled by kinship.[39]   b5

THEAETETUS: Yes, let's say that, but by now, given the number of things the sophist has appeared to be, I for one am at a loss as to what I'm supposed to put forward as true about him – if I'm to say '*this* is what he genuinely is', and stick to it.   c1

VISITOR: Yes, one can understand your being at a loss. But I tell you, by this stage he too ought to be very much at a loss as to how he's to go on eluding our argument; it's true, as the proverb[40] has it, that it's not easy to escape every hold. So now really is the time to go for him.   c5

THEAETETUS: Well said.

VISITOR: First let's stop to catch our breath, as it were, and while we're resting let's count up to ourselves – come on, just how many things has the sophist appeared to us to be? My own memory is that he was first of all found to be a hunter of young, rich individuals who takes fees.   d1

THEAETETUS: Yes.

VISITOR: But then, secondly, he was found as a sort of importer-exporter dealing in lessons for the soul?   d5

THEAETETUS: Certainly.

VISITOR: Thirdly, didn't he turn up as a retailer dealing in these same things?

THEAETETUS: Yes, and then the fourth thing we found him being was a lessons-salesman who dealt in his own lessons.   d10

VISITOR: You remember rightly.[41] The fifth I myself will try to recall: he was a sort of athlete in the expertise of verbal combat, set apart by his skill in disputation.   e1

---

[39] Or 'by kind' (*genei*): see Introduction, Section 2. There is another untranslatable pun in the Greek, *genei gennaia sophistikê*: *genei* is 'by kinship'/'by kind'/'by family', *gennaia* 'noble'/'of good family'.

[40] Presumably from wrestling.

[41] The Visitor is right to congratulate Theaetetus here, since the third and fourth accounts, on the present counting, were not clearly marked as separate at the time.

THEAETETUS: That he was.

e5 VISITOR: The sixth was controversial, but all the same we made a concession to him and put him down as a cleanser in relation to soul of beliefs that prevent it from learning.

THEAETETUS: Yes, definitely.

232a VISITOR: Well now, when people refer to someone by the name of a single expertise, yet he gives the appearance of having learned to do many different things, do you see how unhealthy this appearance is, for the investigator? Clearly, if we do have that sort of impression, in relation to some particular expertise, it's just because we can't see the one feature a5 of it that all these things learned actually relate to; and that's why we call its possessor by many names instead of one.

THEAETETUS: That's very much the sort of way it's likely to be.

b1 VISITOR: So let's not allow that to happen to us in our inquiry, out of laziness. Instead let's begin by taking up again one particular thing we said about the sophist. There was one point I found especially revealing of him.

b5 THEAETETUS: Which was that?

VISITOR: I think we said he was an expert in antilogic.[42]

THEAETETUS: Yes.

VISITOR: And didn't we also say that this made him a teacher of the subject to others?

b10 THEAETETUS: Of course.

VISITOR: So let's investigate what, then, such people actually say they make people experts in antilogic about. Let our investigation begin at the c1 beginning, with a question like this: tell me, what do they make people competent to conduct such disputes about – is it divine matters, of the sort that are obscure to ordinary people?

THEAETETUS: That's certainly what is said about them.

VISITOR: What about evident aspects of the earth and the heavens, and c5 of matters to do with things like that?

THEAETETUS: Those too, no question.

VISITOR: And furthermore, in private discussions, if ever something is treated as applying to everything, in relation to its coming into being or its being, we know, do we not, that they are not only expert at contra-c10 dicting it themselves but make others able to do the same as they do?

---

[42] 225b.

THEAETETUS: Yes, we certainly do.

VISITOR: And what about laws, and everything to do with running　d1
a city: don't they promise to make people expert at disputing about
these?

THEAETETUS: Yes, because practically nobody would want to talk to
them if they weren't promising that.

VISITOR: In fact each and every one of the things that need to be said　d5
in order to contradict the expert himself, both in relation to all expertises
together and for each separately, has been fashioned somewhere and set
out in written form for anyone who wishes to learn.

THEAETETUS: That looks to me like a reference to Protagoras' writings
about wrestling and other sorts of expertise.　e1

VISITOR: Marvellous! Protagoras', yes, and plenty of others' writings
too. But this matter of antilogical expertise – doesn't it seem to be a
capacity, for purposes of disputation, somehow competent to deal with
anything and everything?

THEAETETUS: It certainly seems to leave pretty well nothing out of its　e5
purview.

VISITOR: And – by the gods! – boy, do you really think this is possible?
Perhaps you young people are sharper-sighted on the issue than us
dullards.

THEAETETUS: What issue? What exactly are you getting at? I don't　233a
quite grasp what the question is.

VISITOR: Whether it's possible for some human being to know
everything.

THEAETETUS: It would certainly be a marvellous thing for this human
kind of ours if it were.

VISITOR: So how will someone who is not himself an expert be　a5
able to say anything sound in contradiction to the person who *is* an
expert?

THEAETETUS: He won't at all.

VISITOR: So what are we to make of this amazing thing that is the
sophist's expertise?

THEAETETUS: Amazing in what respect?　a10

VISITOR: In the way they somehow or other bring it about that the　b1
young believe that they are wiser than everybody else about everything.
For clearly, if they were neither contradicting people correctly nor
appeared to be doing so to their young audience, or if they did so appear

b5 but their disputations seemed still not to give them any claim on wisdom, then just as you said, it would be hard to imagine that anyone would be willing to pay them money to learn the things in question.

THEAETETUS: It certainly would.

VISITOR: But as things are, people are willing to pay them?

b10 THEAETETUS: Very much so.

c1 VISITOR: Because, I suppose, the people they're paying seem themselves to be experts in the subjects about which they deploy their antilogic.

THEAETETUS: Obviously.

VISITOR: But they deploy it, we say, about everything?

c5 THEAETETUS: Yes.

VISITOR: So they appear to their students to be wise in everything.

THEAETETUS: Of course.

VISITOR: Without actually being so; because that we said was impossible.

THEAETETUS: Yes – how wouldn't it be impossible?

c10 VISITOR: In that case the sophist has shown up for us as possessing a sort of belief-based 'knowledge' about all things, not as possessing truth.

d1 THEAETETUS: Yes, absolutely, and what we have now said about sophists is very probably the most correct account of them.

VISITOR: Well, let us take a particular example that will make the issues clearer here.

THEAETETUS: What sort of example?

VISITOR: The following – and please try to pay close attention as you answer my question.

d5 THEAETETUS: So what is the question?

VISITOR: If someone claimed to know, through a single expertise, not

d10 just how to speak or speak against on every subject, but how to make or do everything –

e1 THEAETETUS: What are you saying? *Everything*?

VISITOR: It seems to me you're not getting a word of what I said, if you don't understand my 'everything'!

THEAETETUS: I don't, no.

e5 VISITOR: Well, 'everything', I'm saying, includes you and me, and other living creatures in addition to us, and trees –

THEAETETUS: What are you talking about?

VISITOR: If someone claimed he would make me, and you, and everything else that is planted[43] –

THEAETETUS: So what sort of making is this? You won't be talking about a farmer of some sort, because you said the person in question was a maker of animals too.   234a

VISITOR: Yes, and of the sea, too, and the earth, the heavens, the gods, and everything else whatsoever; and what is more, he also makes all of them instantly and puts them on sale for very little.   a5

THEAETETUS: You're talking about some sort of game, surely.

VISITOR: Well, if someone tells us he knows everything and will teach it to another person at a cost of little money or time, mustn't we suppose him to be playing a game with us?   a10

THEAETETUS: We must, surely.

VISITOR: And do you know of any form of game-playing that involves more expertise, or is more charming, than the imitative?   b1

THEAETETUS: I certainly don't. Bring all its parts together into one, and what you're talking about is a really diverse form, more colourful than almost any other.

VISITOR: As for promises to be able to make everything by using a single expertise, I think we recognize this much, that someone who uses a painter's expertise to produce imitations bearing the names of the actual things[44] that they imitate will be able, if he shows his paintings from a distance, to dupe mindless young children into thinking that he is perfectly able to accomplish anything he puts his mind to.   b5

  b10

THEAETETUS: Clearly.   c1

VISITOR: So then are we surprised to find some other expertise, this time to do with words, by which it is actually possible to bewitch the young – standing, as they do, as yet far away from the truth of things – by way of their ears, and using words: an expertise that treats everything by showing its young hearers spoken images[45] so as to make them think   c5

---

[43] See *Republic* x 597c, where god is treated as the 'plantsman' of everything in nature: the word used is *phutourgos*, playing on *phusis*, 'nature', and there may be something similar going on in the present passage (cf. also *Sophist* 265b–e). In the *Timaeus* (90a) a human being is a 'heavenly plant' (*phuton*), i.e., one with its roots in the heavens.

[44] Or 'the things that are' (*ta onta*).

[45] That is, *eidōla*: often used of *insubstantial* images (cf., e.g., 260c), as perhaps here, but in what follows the term will be used more neutrally.

that true things are being said, and indeed that the person saying them is the wisest of all about all things?

d1   THEAETETUS: Yes, why wouldn't there be another expertise just like that?

VISITOR: Well, Theaetetus, once enough time has passed for the majority of those young listeners, as with increasing maturity they

d5   encounter things as they are from close up, and are compelled through their experiences to get a clear grasp of things as they are, won't they inevitably change the beliefs they formed earlier, so that what was big is

e1   now clearly small, what was easy is now clearly hard, and all the appearances contained in the words they once heard are completely overturned by the realities borne in on them as they act out their lives?

THEAETETUS: Yes, so far as someone of my age is able to judge. But I think I'm one of those still standing at a distance from things.

e5   VISITOR: That's the reason all of us here will try even now to bring you as close to them as possible without the experiences. In any case, tell

235a me this about the sophist: is it clear by now that he's a sort of magician, insofar as he's a producer merely of imitations of actual things? Or are we still uncertain whether he may not really and truly possess the relevant expertise about each and every thing on which he seems able to use his antilogic?

a5   THEAETETUS: How can we be, stranger? From what has been said, it is by now pretty well clear that he is just one of those tens of thousands that have no share in anything serious.

VISITOR: We must put him down as a magician, then; a producer of imitations.

THEAETETUS: We must, definitely.

a10 VISITOR: So come on, now it's up to us not to let the beast get away

b1   from us any longer; we have him pretty well caught in a net, as it were, thrown round him by the tools we have for this sort of thing in our discussions – so if he's escaped us before, he won't be able to escape *this*.

THEAETETUS: What, exactly?

b5   VISITOR: Our conclusion that he's just one of the kind illusionists belong to.[46]

THEAETETUS: That much about him I certainly agree.

---

[46] Or 'conjurers', as at 224a; literally 'wonder-workers' (*thaumatopoioi*).

VISITOR: So it's decided: as soon as we can we're to divide up expertise in image-making,[47] and once we've got to the bottom of it, if we immediately find the sophist standing up to us, we're to apprehend him in accordance with the orders of sovereign reason, then hand him over and show the king our catch; but if by any chance he slips away and tries to hide somewhere in the parts of expertise in imitation, we'll pursue him, always dividing the part that takes him in, until finally he is captured. I tell you, neither he nor any other kind will ever boast that they have got away from hunters who can carry out their pursuit in this way, methodically tracking each and every detail. b10 c1 c5

THEAETETUS: You're right, and we must do what you say in the way that you say.

VISITOR: Well, if we continue dividing as we did before, I have the impression even now that I can see two forms of expertise in imitation, but I don't yet seem to be able to tell in which of them we're going to find the form we're searching for. d1

THEAETETUS: You should say first which the two forms are; do the dividing for us. d5

VISITOR: One of the expertises I'm seeing in it is that of making likenesses. This is especially when someone contrives the coming into being of the imitation by keeping to the proportions of the original in terms of length and breadth and depth, and in addition to that also gives it the colours that belong to each part. e1

THEAETETUS: What? Don't all those who imitate something try to do that?

VISITOR: Certainly not those who are sculpting or painting one of those large-scale works. If they reproduced the true proportions of the various parts of the body, then as you know the upper parts would appear to us smaller than they should and the lower parts bigger, because we're seeing the upper ones from a distance and the lower ones from close up. e5 236a

THEAETETUS: Quite right.

VISITOR: So don't the artists in this case say goodbye to the truth, and instead create those proportions in their images that seem beautiful instead of the actual proportions? a5

THEAETETUS: Yes, definitely.

---

[47] I.e., imitation-making, where the imitations produced are in one way or another images (*eidōla*, as in 234c) of the things imitated.

VISITOR: The first sort of imitation, then, being like the original, can fairly be called a likeness.

a10 THEAETETUS: Yes.

b1 VISITOR: And accordingly, the part of imitative expertise that deals with this should be called by the name we introduced previously, namely likeness-making?

THEAETETUS: It should.

VISITOR: What then? What shall we call something that appears to
b5 resemble the corresponding beautiful original because it's being viewed from a non-ideal viewpoint, and if one acquired an ability to see such things properly, is actually not like what it claims to resemble? Since it appears to resemble the original but doesn't, we'll call it an 'apparition',[48] won't we?

THEAETETUS: Naturally.

VISITOR: And it's found widely, this part of expertise in imitation,
c1 across both painting and imitation generally.

THEAETETUS: Of course.

VISITOR: Wouldn't it be the most correct thing, then, to call the expertise that produces an appearance of a likeness, not actually a likeness, apparition-making rather than likeness-making?

c5 THEAETETUS: Much the most correct.

VISITOR: So these are the two forms of image-making[49] I was talking about: likeness-making and apparition-making.

THEAETETUS: You were right; there are two.

VISITOR: But on the point that was puzzling me before, about which of
c10 the two sorts of image-making we should place the sophist in, I still can't see
d1 the answer clearly, even now. The man really is a wonder, so difficult is he to make out – because even now he's slipped away very effectively and cleverly into a form where there are no clear ways through for the hunter.

THEAETETUS: It seems so.

d5 VISITOR: Are you agreeing with me because you recognize it for yourself, or do you have some sort of compulsion to say yes straightaway because the discussion has got you used to it?

THEAETETUS: Why do you say that? What point are you making?

---

[48] Or 'phantasm' (*phantasma*), to be distinguished from 'appearance' (*phantasia*), which may be either true or false (see 264a–b).

[49] I.e., *eidōlon*-making: what was called imitation-making, i.e., 'imitative expertise', at 235d.

VISITOR: My friend, the fact is that the investigation we are involved in is an extraordinarily difficult one. This whole matter of appearing, and seeming, but not being, and of saying things but not true things, has always caused puzzlement and confusion in the past, and it still does. It's extraordinarily difficult to grasp, Theaetetus, how one is to come out with the claim that it really is possible to say or believe things that are false, and express this without being caught up in contradiction. e1

e5

237a

THEAETETUS: How so?

VISITOR: Such a claim already dares to assume that what is not is; only on that assumption will a false thing said or believed turn out to be something that is. But, my boy, from the time I was a boy the great Parmenides never stopped testifying against it, whether expressing himself in prose or in verse: 'For never shall this prevail,' so his lines go, 'that the things that are not are; / keep you your thought, as you search, back from that path.' So we have his testimony, but most of all the statement itself[50] will demonstrate it if we subject it to moderate cross-examination. So let's observe just that happening first – unless you have a different idea. a5

b1

THEAETETUS: I'll go along with what you want. See how the argument will best go through, go that way yourself and take me with you. b5

VISITOR: I'll do just that. So tell me: we dare, I suppose, to utter the phrase 'what in no way is'?

THEAETETUS: Of course.

VISITOR: Well, suppose one of our listeners here had to give an answer – a seriously considered one, and not just for the sake of winning an argument, or playfully – to the question what this name, 'what is not', should be applied to, what do we think his response would be? To what purpose and for what sort of thing do we suppose he would use it? What would he point the questioner to? b10

c1

THEAETETUS: That's difficult to say, indeed pretty much completely impossible for the likes of me. c5

VISITOR: This much is clear, at any rate, that 'what is not' must not be applied to anything that is.

THEAETETUS: How could it be?

---

[50] I.e., what Parmenides ruled out, that 'the things that are not are'.

c10   VISITOR: So, given that it mustn't be applied to what is, it won't be right for anyone to apply it to a something, either.

THEAETETUS: What are you saying?

d1   VISITOR: Surely it's also clear to us that whenever we use this expression 'something', we say it of a thing that is; to say it by itself, as it were naked and isolated from anything and everything that is, is impossible – right?

d5   THEAETETUS: Right.

VISITOR: Are you agreeing because you recognize that anyone saying 'something' must be saying it of some *one* thing?

THEAETETUS: I am.

VISITOR: Because, you'll say, 'some' in the singular signals one thing,
d10   as opposed to 'some' in the dual,[51] when it signals two, or in the plural, when it signals more than two?

THEAETETUS: Obviously.

e1   VISITOR: But then it seems there will be no escape: if someone is not saying something, he must be saying absolutely nothing.

THEAETETUS: Right, there'll be no escape.

e5   VISITOR: So mustn't we even refuse to concede that such a person is 'saying' whatever words it may be, but saying nothing; mustn't we rather claim that someone who tries to utter the phrase 'what is not' is not even *saying* at all?[52]

THEAETETUS: That would certainly be a puzzle to cap it all!

238a VISITOR: It's too soon to boast! There are still puzzles to come, dear boy, and the greatest and first of them at that. It actually has to do with the very beginnings of the whole thing.

THEAETETUS: How so? Tell me, and no holding back.

a5   VISITOR: To something that is, I suppose, can be added another of the things that are.

THEAETETUS: Of course.

VISITOR: But will we say it's possible, ever, for any of the things that are to be added to what is not?

a10 THEAETETUS: How could it be?

---

[51] Greek has a special set of endings ('the dual') for cases where two things are being talked about.

[52] After all, to say that he is 'saying nothing' might still suggest that he is saying *something*; in fact, since the words he utters apply or refer to nothing, the claim is that he is actually not saying (anything) at all – merely uttering words that, in this context, are no more than noises.

VISITOR: Now we treat the whole of number among the things that are.

THEAETETUS: Indeed, if we so treat anything! b1

VISITOR: Let us then not even attempt to apply number – either plurality or one[53] – to what is not.

THEAETETUS: We certainly wouldn't be right to try, it seems, according to what the argument is saying. b5

VISITOR: Well, how could anyone put their lips round, or even begin to think of, 'things that are not', or 'what is not', *without* number?

THEAETETUS: Tell me the problem?

VISITOR: Whenever we say 'things that are not', aren't we trying to b10
apply a plurality of number? c1

THEAETETUS: Obviously.

VISITOR: And whenever we say 'what is not', aren't we similarly trying to apply oneness?

THEAETETUS: Yes, very clearly.

VISITOR: And yet we say it's neither justified nor correct to attach c5
what is to what is not.

THEAETETUS: Very true.

VISITOR: So do you see that it's impossible, correctly, to express or to say or to think what is not in and by itself; it's unthinkable, unsayable, c10
inexpressible, and unaccountable.[54]

THEAETETUS: Yes, absolutely.

VISITOR: So was it false to say just now that I was going to discuss the d1
greatest puzzle about the whole matter, when in fact we have an even greater one to talk about?

THEAETETUS: Which puzzle?

VISITOR: I wonder that you didn't notice from the very things we've d5
been saying that what is not reduces even a would-be challenger to puzzlement, to the extent that if ever he tries to challenge it he is forced to contradict himself on the subject.

THEAETETUS: How so? Make the point still clearer for me.

---

[53] The 'number' one is usually, in Plato as in Aristotle (see, e.g., *Metaphysics* X.1057a1–7), the measure of number, *arithmos*, rather than itself a number, which is – strictly speaking – a plurality of units; but (as Aristotle himself concedes) one will be fewer than two.

[54] For the last adjective, cf. n.10 above.

d10   VISITOR: You shouldn't be looking for greater clarity from me! It was
e1   I who laid it down that what is not should have no share in either oneness
or plurality, and just look at me – I've referred to it as one, by saying
'what is not', singular, and I'm doing it now. You take my point.

    THEAETETUS: Yes.

e5   VISITOR: And again, a little earlier I said that it *is* inexpressible,
unsayable, and unaccountable. Do you follow?

    THEAETETUS: I do. Obviously I do.

239a   VISITOR: So in trying to attach being to it I was contradicting what we
were saying before?

    THEAETETUS: Clearly so.

    VISITOR: What's more, in attaching it[55] as I did wasn't I talking about
it as if it were one?

    THEAETETUS: Yes.

a5   VISITOR: And what is more I addressed it as one by saying it was
'unaccountable' and 'unsayable' and 'inexpressible', all in the singular.

    THEAETETUS: Obviously.

    VISITOR: But we're saying that if one is going to speak correctly,
one mustn't mark it either as one or as many – or indeed call it 'it'
a10   at all; giving it that label too will be to address it using the form of
oneness.

    THEAETETUS: It certainly will.

b1   VISITOR: So what is anyone going to say about *me*? He'll find me
defeated now as always before in the matter of challenging what is not.
So, as I said, let us not look in what *I* say for the correct way of speaking
b5   about what is not, but – come on! – let's look for it now in what *you* say!

    THEAETETUS: What do you have in mind?

    VISITOR: Come, show us what you're made of! You're young, so strain
every muscle you have, and try to express something about what is not
b10 that follows the rules, without adding being or oneness or plurality of
number to it.

c1   THEAETETUS: It would be odd if I had much enthusiasm about trying
for myself, seeing the sorts of things that happen to you when you do!

    VISITOR: Fine, so let's forget about you and me, if you like; but until
c5   such time as we meet someone who can do this, let us say that the sophist

---

[55] Reading *touto*, with the manuscripts, rather than the OCT's *to to*.*

has displayed a complete and utter lack of scruple, slinking off into a place where it's difficult to follow him.

THEAETETUS: It certainly appears so.

VISITOR: Then if we're going to claim that he possesses some sort of expertise in apparition-making, that form of words will make it easy for   d1
him to get a lock on us, turning it back on us when we call him a maker of images and asking us what exactly we understand by an image in the first place. So, Theaetetus, we have to think what answer to give to the young   d5
man's question.

THEAETETUS: Clearly, we'll point to images in liquid surfaces and in mirrors; painted and sculpted ones too, and any others there may be of that general sort.

VISITOR: It's plain, Theaetetus, that you have never seen a sophist.   e1

THEAETETUS: Why do you say that?

VISITOR: He'll make you think he keeps his eyes shut, or has no eyes at all.

THEAETETUS: How so?

VISITOR: When you give him an answer like the one you've just given, he'll laugh at you for talking to him as if he could see, and talking about something in a mirror or a painting or sculpture. He'll pretend that he doesn't know anything about mirrors or liquids, or seeing in   240a
general, and simply ask you the question that arises from what you just said.

THEAETETUS: What is that?

VISITOR: It's about what runs through all the examples you gave, which you listed as many separate things but nevertheless saw fit to call by a single name, since after all you used the word 'image' for all of them,   a5
as if there was just one thing in question.[56] So speak up! Defend yourself, and don't give way to the man at all.

THEAETETUS: Well then, stranger, what else are we going to say an image is, if it's not what has been made to resemble the true original, another thing of the same sort?

VISITOR: Are you saying another *true* thing of the same sort? Or what are we to make of your 'of the same sort'?   b1

---

[56] The refusal to accept an answer to the question 'what exactly is an image?' framed in terms of examples sounds quite Socratic and philosophical; the sophist's motive for refusing it, however, is different, namely that words are all that he deals in.

THEAETETUS: I'm not at all saying it's true; I am saying it resembles the true.

VISITOR: Taking the true as what really is?

THEAETETUS: Just so.

b5 VISITOR: And what of the not true? Is that opposed to true?

THEAETETUS: Of course.

VISITOR: So aren't you calling what resembles the true something that really is not[57] – that is, if you're going to call it not true?

THEAETETUS: All the same it is, in a way.

b10 VISITOR: Only not truly, you say.

THEAETETUS: No indeed; except that it really is a likeness.

VISITOR: So while really something that is not, it really is what we're calling a likeness?

c1 THEAETETUS: It looks as though there is some such weaving together of what is not with what is, and very strange it is.

VISITOR: Yes, it definitely is strange. At any rate you can see how this

c5 many-headed sophist[58] of ours has used this exchange to force us even now to concede, however unwillingly, that what is not *is*, in a way.

THEAETETUS: I see it only too well.

VISITOR: What then? What are we going to mark off as his expertise, to enable us still to be in harmony with what we've said?

THEAETETUS: What makes you say that? What are you apprehensive about?

d1 VISITOR: When we say that he deceives in relation to what appears, and that his expertise is some sort of expertise in deception, will we be claiming that our soul believes what is false thanks to that expertise of his, or what will we say?

d5 THEAETETUS: Just that; what else would we say?

VISITOR: And false belief, in turn, will be believing things that are the opposite of those that are? Or what?

THEAETETUS: Yes, the opposite of those.

VISITOR: You're saying, then, that false belief is believing things that are not?

d10 THEAETETUS: It must be.

---

[57] Reading *ouk ontôs ouk on* rather than the OCT's preferred *ouk ontôs on*.*
[58] The best-known many-headed monster is the Hydra, which sprouted new heads for every one that Heracles cut off.

VISITOR: Believing that things that are not, are not, or that things that   e1
in no way are, are in a way?

THEAETETUS: It must be believing that things that are not are in a way,
at any rate if anyone is ever going to be even a little bit mistaken about
anything.

VISITOR: And what about things that completely are? Does false belief   e5
also believe that these in no way are?

THEAETETUS: Yes.

VISITOR: Falsehood includes this too, then.

THEAETETUS: This too.

VISITOR: And speech too, I imagine, will be considered false in the   e10
same way and the same sorts of cases, namely saying that things that are,   241a
are not, and that things that are not, are.

THEAETETUS: Yes, because how else will it turn out false?

VISITOR: Pretty much no other way. But the sophist won't say any of
this. Or ask yourself, what could possibly induce any sane person to
concede it, when the things we've agreed to, that got us to this point,   a5
were just the things we previously agreed to be inexpressible, unsayable,
unaccountable, and unthinkable?[59] Do we see, Theaetetus, what the man
is saying?

THEAETETUS: How can we not see that he'll say our brazen claim that
some of the things we say and believe are false contradicts what we were   b1
saying just now? That claim, he'll say, forces us again and again to attach
what is to what is not, when we've just agreed that this is the most
impossible thing of all.

VISITOR: You remember correctly. But now is the time to consider
what we're to do about the sophist; you see for yourself how many and   b5
readily available the counter-holds are that he can put on us, and leave us
no way out, if we seek him out by locating him in the area of expertise
that belongs to creators of false appearances and magicians.

THEAETETUS: Indeed I do.

VISITOR: The ones we've discussed are certainly only a small selection;   b10
there are practically unlimited numbers of them.   c1

THEAETETUS: In that case, if things are as you say, it seems catching
the sophist will actually be impossible.

---

[59] Reinstating *aphthengkta kai arrêta kai aloga kai adianoêta*, omitted by the OCT, before *prodiô-
mologêmena.**

VISITOR: What then? Shall we turn soft now, and give up?

c5　THEAETETUS: I for one say we shouldn't, if we can somehow get even a slight hold on the fellow.

VISITOR: So will you forgive me, and go along if we draw back a bit, as in effect you're suggesting, just for a while, from so intense a discussion?

c10　THEAETETUS: Of course I will.

d1　VISITOR: And there's this other thing I'd ask of you even more.

THEAETETUS: What's that?

VISITOR: That you don't take me to be turning into some sort of parricide, as it were.

THEAETETUS: How so?

d5　VISITOR: In order to defend ourselves we're going to need to cross-examine[60] what our father Parmenides says and force the claim through both that what is not in a certain way *is*, and conversely that what is also in a way is not.

THEAETETUS: We must obviously fight hard for that sort of conclusion in the coming discussion.

e1　VISITOR: Obviously! Apparent even to a blind person, as they say. So long as these things are neither stated[61] nor agreed, we will hardly be able ever to talk about things said or believed and say that they are false, whether we call them images, or likenesses, or imitations, or just appar-

e5　itions, nor will we be able to talk about any expertises relating to these, either, without being forced to contradict ourselves and make ourselves the object of ridicule.

THEAETETUS: Very true.

242a　VISITOR: For that reason we must take our courage in our hands and go for a frontal assault on the paternal claim. It's either that or leave it totally alone, should we hesitate for some reason to do the deed.

THEAETETUS: I can tell you, there's nothing whatever that is going to stop us from doing it!

a5　VISITOR: Well, there's a third small thing I have still to ask of you.

---

[60] Or 'test', *basanizein* (in its original context, of rubbing a thing against the touchstone to see if it is gold). The same term appeared in 237b, where what was to be 'tested' was the claim Parmenides prohibited, that 'the things that are not are'; the Visitor is now proposing to put Parmenides' own position to the test.

[61] Reading *mête lechthentôn* in place of the OCT's *mête elenchthentôn*.* The point is that a stand has to be made: we somehow *have* to say both that what is not is, and that what is, is not, even though both seem thus far to be ruled out.

THEAETETUS: You have only to ask.

VISITOR: When I was talking a few moments ago I think I said[62] that I've always found mounting a challenge on these matters too much for me, and never more than now.

THEAETETUS: You did say that.

VISITOR: Well, that makes me afraid I'll seem mad to you for doing an immediate about-turn. In fact it's for your sake that we'll be setting about challenging Parmenides' claim, if we actually manage it.

THEAETETUS: Well, I certainly won't think you are acting in any way inappropriately if you proceed straight to this challenge of yours, and your proof, so carry on, with confidence on this score at least.

VISITOR: So come on, how should one begin such a hazardous discussion? I think, my boy, that the road we most need to take is this.

THEAETETUS: Which?

VISITOR: We need first to examine the things that as of now seem so evident to us, in case we are somehow confused about these, and too ready to agree with one another because we assume our judgement good.

THEAETETUS: Tell me more clearly what you're saying.

VISITOR: It seems to me that Parmenides has communicated with us in a slapdash fashion, as has anyone that ever rushed to judgement in the matter of distinguishing how many the things that are, are, and of what sorts they are.

THEAETETUS: How so?

VISITOR: Each one of them appears to me to be telling us a story as if we were children. One of them tells us that the things that are amount to three, and that certain of them are sometimes waging a sort of war between them, while at other times they become reconciled, make marriages for themselves, have children and bring up their offspring. Another says there are two, wet and dry or hot and cold, settling them down together and marrying them off; while our Eleatic race, for their part, starting with Xenophanes or even earlier, talk in their stories as if what people call 'all things' are actually one. Certain Ionian Muses, and later some from Sicily, conceived the idea that it was safest to merge both sorts of stories and say that what is is both many and one, and is held together by enmity as well as friendship: 'as it is pulled apart it is brought

---

[62] See 239b.

together', say the more intense of these Muses,[63] whereas the softer ones
e5 relaxed the strict rule that things are always like that, and say that they
alternate, the whole being now one in friendship under the influence of
243a Aphrodite, now many things, and at war with itself by reason of some
sort of strife.[64] Now as to whether any of this, as said by any of them, is
true or not, it would be harsh and inappropriate to rebuke men of fame
and antiquity for failings on such a scale; but there is that one aspect that
a5 no one could begrudge our pointing out –

THEAETETUS: Which is what?

VISITOR: That they have been too inclined to look down their noses
at us ordinary mortals and treat us with contempt; each pursues his own
b1 project without caring at all whether we're following what they say or
being left behind.

THEAETETUS: How so?

VISITOR: Whenever any of them utters something to the effect that
many, or one, or two are, or have come into being, or are coming into
b5 being, or again that hot is mixed with cold, at some other point introdu-
cing things like separation and combination – by the gods, Theaetetus,
do you ever understand a single thing they're saying? As for myself,
when I was younger, if ever someone used the expression we're puzzled
by now, 'what is not', I used to think I understood exactly. But now you
b10 see just where we are now with it.

c1 THEAETETUS: I do see.

VISITOR: The trouble is, it may well be that we're no better off with
what is than with what is not. We may claim that there's no puzzle for us
about what is, and we understand when someone utters the phrase; it's
c5 just what is not that we're puzzled about. But actually we're in the same
boat about both.

THEAETETUS: Perhaps.

VISITOR: And let's suppose the same holds of other things we've said.[65]

THEAETETUS: Yes, certainly.

c10 VISITOR: Now most of them we'll look into later on as well, if you agree;
d1 but for now we must look into the most important, the chief and first.

---

[63] I.e., the 'later' Ionian Heraclitus (from Ephesus), for whom things were in permanent tension.
[64] The reference is to the Sicilian Empedocles, for whom the elemental 'things that are' included
Love and Strife alongside fire, air, water, and earth.
[65] I.e., that we are puzzled about them too.

THEAETETUS: Which is what? Or are you saying – clearly you are – that we need first to talk about what is, and track down exactly what those who use the expression think they're indicating by it?   d5

VISITOR: You catch my point exactly, Theaetetus. That's the direction I'm saying our pursuit needs to take. We should ask of them, as if they were here with us 'So come on, you people who claim that all things are hot and cold or some other such pair of things: what exactly are you   e1 saying about them both, that is, when you say both and each of them *are*? What are we to take this 'being' of yours to be? Is it a third thing alongside the two you started with, so that we're to count you as saying that everything comprises not just two things but three? After all, I don't suppose you're calling one of them being, if you say both equally are; whichever of   e5 them it was, that would pretty much make them one, not two.'

THEAETETUS: True.

VISITOR: 'So', we'll ask them, 'is it both of them together you want to label as being?'

THEAETETUS: Perhaps.

VISITOR: 'But, friends,' we'll say to them, 'in that case too you'd very   244a clearly be saying that the two are one.'

THEAETETUS: Quite correct.

VISITOR: 'So since we're quite puzzled about it all, it's for you to clarify for us what exactly you intend to indicate when you utter the   a5 word "is". Clearly you've known all along; we used to think we did, but now find ourselves puzzled. So before you do anything else please instruct us on this point, so that we don't think we're actually understanding what is being said on your side when what is happening is   b1 exactly the opposite of that.' If we say we expect this much from them, and from anyone else who says that everything is more than one thing, surely, my boy, we won't be behaving unreasonably?

THEAETETUS: Not in the least.   b5

VISITOR: And what of those who say that everything is one? Shouldn't we be inquiring from them as best we can what exactly they say being is?

THEAETETUS: Obviously.

VISITOR: So let them answer us this: 'You claim, it seems, that one is all there is?' They'll say 'We do' – right?   b10

THEAETETUS: Yes.

VISITOR: 'Well, is there something you call being?'

THEAETETUS: Yes.

CI VISITOR: 'Is it what you call one, so that you use two names for the same thing? Or what?'

THEAETETUS: Well, stranger, what answer can they give to this?

c5 VISITOR: Clearly, Theaetetus, anyone positing this hypothesis of theirs is not going to find it the easiest thing in the world to answer the question we just asked – or indeed any other question you like.

THEAETETUS: How so?

VISITOR: It's presumably absurd to allow that there are two names when you have posited just one thing –

c10 THEAETETUS: Obviously.

VISITOR: And completely absurd to accept anyone's saying there is a name if there is no account to be given of it.

THEAETETUS: Why so?

VISITOR: If he posits the name as something different from the thing it belongs to, he is presumably talking about two things.

d5 THEAETETUS: Yes.

VISITOR: And yet if he posits the name as being the same as the thing, either he'll be forced to say it is the name of nothing, or, if he's going to claim it as the name of something, the name will turn out to be merely a name of a name, not of anything else.

d10 THEAETETUS: Just so.

VISITOR: So the one, being just one, will turn out equally the name of the one and the one of the name.[66]

THEAETETUS: It must.

VISITOR: What then of the whole?[67] Will they claim it to be different

d15 from the 'one being',[68] or the same thing as it?

e1 THEAETETUS: Of course they will say, and they do say, that it's the same.

VISITOR: Well, if there is a whole, as Parmenides actually says there is,

> On all sides like a ball, its mass well-rounded,
> From centre outwards equal-weighted; for no greater

e5 > It must be, nor smaller, here than there –

[66] That is, if the name and the one are interchangeable, and the name is of something (a premise just introduced), then the one (= the name) will also be of the name.

[67] I.e., think now about the Eleatic One as the whole of things (the universe) – which it is, for the Eleatics.

[68] I.e., the one that (impossibly, as the argument has just shown) also is.

well, if what is is like that, it has a middle and extremities, and having those there is no way it can avoid having parts; you agree?

THEAETETUS: I do.

VISITOR: Now something divided up into parts is not in any way 245a prevented from having oneness as an attribute covering all its parts, and from being in this way both something that is, all of it taken together, and one as a whole.

THEAETETUS: Of course not.

VISITOR: But is it not impossible for something with these attributes a5 to be, itself, that one thing by itself we started with?[69]

THEAETETUS: How so?

VISITOR: What is *truly* one must, surely, according to the correct reasoning, be declared totally without parts.

THEAETETUS: Yes, it must. a10

VISITOR: And something of the sort we have been describing will be b1 out of tune with that whole reasoning,[70] being composed as it is from many parts.

THEAETETUS: I understand.

VISITOR: So will what is be one and whole by having oneness as an b5 attribute in this way, or shall we deny altogether that what is is a whole?

THEAETETUS: That's a hard choice you've offered me!

VISITOR: I couldn't agree more. For if what is has the attribute of oneness only in a way, it will clearly not be the same as the one, and the sum of things will be more than one.

THEAETETUS: Yes. b10

VISITOR: And yet if what is is not a whole through having acquired c1 the attribute of oneness like that, and at the same time the whole is, by itself, then what is turns out to be lacking itself.

THEAETETUS: It certainly does.

VISITOR: And by this argument, what is will turn out not to be, if it is c5 deprived of itself.

THEAETETUS: Just so.

---

[69] This is an over-translation: the Greek has simply 'to be, itself, the one [by] itself'; but in the context, and given the way the discussion has unfolded, it is reasonable to take the reference as being to the sort of one, or unitary entity (a one that is *just* one, and nothing else whatever) posited by the Eleatics, whom the Visitor has been criticizing since 243d.

[70] Reading *tôi holôi logôi* in place of the OCT's *tôi logôi*.*

VISITOR: Moreover all things once again become more than one, what is and the whole having each acquired its own separate nature.

c10 THEAETETUS: Yes.

d1 VISITOR: But if there is no whole at all, then not only do these same things[71] apply to what is, but to its not being would be added its not ever coming to be a thing that is, either.

THEAETETUS: Why is that?

VISITOR: What has come into being has always come to be as a whole;

d5 so it's not just being but coming into being too that you won't be able to talk of as being if you don't count wholeness among the things that are.

THEAETETUS: All this seems completely as you say.

VISITOR: Moreover what is not a whole must not be of any quantity, either, since if it is something that has quantity, whatever that quantity

d10 may be, it must be the whole of that quantity.

THEAETETUS: Yes, it certainly must.

VISITOR: And ten thousand other questions will arise, each involving

e1 an unlimited number of puzzles of its own, for anyone who tries to account for what is by claiming either that it is some pair of things or just one thing.

THEAETETUS: Our current problems make that pretty clear – one giving rise to another, and then another, each bringing greater and

e5 deeper confusion about whatever has been said before.

VISITOR: Well, we have not covered all those who make precise claims about what is and is not, but what we have said about them must suffice. Now we should take a look at those who talk about the subject in a

246a general way, so that we can see from all sides that what is is no less problematical than what is not when it comes to saying what exactly it is.

THEAETETUS: So yes, we need to proceed to these people too.

VISITOR: There actually seems to be some sort of battle between giants

a5 and gods going on among them because of their disputing claims about being.

THEAETETUS: How so?

VISITOR: Some of them try to drag down to earth everything from the heavens and the unseen, simply grasping 'rock and oak' in their

a10 hands.[72] Clasping everything like that to them they insist that what is is

[71] I.e., not being and being more than one.
[72] 'Rock and oak' is proverbial in Greek for what is hard, insensitive, unyielding.

constituted exclusively by what offers resistance to touch in some way, b1
treating body and being as the same thing; if anyone claims that anything
else is and it doesn't have body, they totally despise him and won't listen
to another word.

THEAETETUS: They are terrifying people – I've actually come across
lots of them myself. b5

VISITOR: The result is that those who take the opposing side in the
debate defend themselves very cautiously, emerging from the unseen
somewhere up above to enforce *their* view that true being consists of
some sort of intelligible and bodiless forms;[73] as for the bodies put
forward by the other side, and their so-called true being, they break c1
them into little pieces with their arguments and call it all a sort of moving
coming-into-being instead of being. In the middle, Theaetetus, there is
an immense battle about these things permanently joined between the
two sides.

THEAETETUS: True. c5

VISITOR: So let us get an account from both of the two kinds of
thinkers in turn, in defence of what they propose to treat as being.

THEAETETUS: And how will we do that?

VISITOR: With the kind that locates being among forms the task is
easier, because they are less aggressive; but it's more difficult, and perhaps c10
virtually impossible, with those who try to jam everything forcibly into d1
body. It seems to me that in their case we have to do the following.

THEAETETUS: What?

VISITOR: What one would most like to do, if it were at all possible,
would be actually to make them better people. But if that can't be done, d5
let's imagine they are better than they are, and suppose that they would
be willing to respond to us more politely than they currently do;
concessions made by better people carry more weight, presumably, than
those made by worse ones. Our own concern, though, is not with them,
only with searching out what is true.

THEAETETUS: Quite right. e1

VISITOR: So tell these improved characters of ours to answer your
questions, and report back what they say.

---

[73] The Visitor's own 'forms' seem to fit the same description (see Introduction, Section 2). The
crucial difference between him and the people he is talking about (some members of the
Academy, perhaps?) is that forms, for them, are the *only* things that truly are.

THEAETETUS: I will.

e5 VISITOR: Then let them say whether they claim a mortal creature is a something.

THEAETETUS: They do, of course.

VISITOR: And they concede, don't they, that this is a body with a soul in it?

THEAETETUS: They certainly do.

VISITOR: While positing soul as one of the things that are?

247a THEAETETUS: Yes.

VISITOR: Well then, don't they say that one soul is just and another unjust, one wise and another unwise?

THEAETETUS: Of course.

a5 VISITOR: But don't they say that each soul is just or wise by virtue of the possession or presence of justice or wisdom, and that the opposite sort of soul is opposite by the possession or presence of the opposites of these?

THEAETETUS: Yes, they say that too.

a10 VISITOR: And yet they'll say that what is capable of being added to and taken away from a thing is without doubt a something.

THEAETETUS: They certainly do say that.

b1 VISITOR: So, there being justice, wisdom, and the rest of goodness, together with their opposites, and soul, too, in which these come to be present, do they say any of these is seen and touched, or do they say they are all unseen?

b5 THEAETETUS: They say pretty much none of *these* is seen.

VISITOR: What? Surely they're not saying anything like that has some sort of body?

THEAETETUS: At this point they stop answering in the same way about the unseen as a whole: they say the soul itself seems to them to possess body of a sort, whereas when it comes to wisdom and each of the other

c1 things you've asked them about, they're too ashamed to dare either to concede that such things don't figure at all among the things that are or to insist that they are all bodies.

VISITOR: Clearly, Theaetetus, these people *have* improved. Those of them born from the earth, and sown in it,[74] would not in the least be

---

[74] A reference to a type of foundation myth, according to which the original inhabitants of a place (e.g., Athens) were literally autochthonic. Here, however, the reference is to the extreme representatives of the 'giants' (246a), the thinkers who are 'earthy' through and through (the atomists?).

ashamed to say any of these things. They would strenuously maintain of   c5
anything they can't squeeze in their fists that it is actually nothing at all.

THEAETETUS: That's pretty much the way they think.

VISITOR: So let's go back to questioning them; because if they are
willing to admit that among the things that are there is even a little bit of   d1
a thing that is without body, that will suffice. What they need to tell us is
what common feature is to be found equally among these things that lack
body and those that have it, and allows them to say that both sets of
things are. Well, perhaps they'll be at a loss for an answer; if that is pretty   d5
much their situation, then see whether they'd be ready to accept an offer
from us, and agree that to be is something like the following.

THEAETETUS: Like what? Say, and we'll soon know if they'll agree.

VISITOR: I say, then, that a thing genuinely is if it has some capacity, of   e1
whatever sort, either to act on another thing, of whatever nature, or to be
acted on, even to the slightest degree and by the most trivial of things,
and even if it is just the once. That is, what marks off the things that are
as being,[75] I propose, is nothing other than *capacity*.

THEAETETUS: Well, given that they presently have nothing better of   e5
their own to offer, they accept that.

VISITOR: Fine, for perhaps something else will occur both to us and to   248a
them later on. Meanwhile so far as this group is concerned, let this stand
as agreed.

THEAETETUS: Indeed.

VISITOR: So then let's pass on to the other group, the friends of
forms.[76] You must report back to us from them too.   a5

THEAETETUS: I shall.

VISITOR: 'When you people speak of coming into being and being,
I think you distinguish between them as separate things, do you not?'

THEAETETUS: 'Yes.'

VISITOR: 'And you say that it's by bodily means that we have our   a10
dealings with coming into being, through perception, whereas the soul is
our instrument, through reasoning, for dealing with what genuinely is;
the latter, you claim, remains forever exactly as it is,[77] while what comes
to be is now like this, now like that.'

---

[75] Omitting *dein*, added in the OCT after *horizein*.*   [76] See 246b.

[77] A form of words (*aei kata tauta* [= *ta auta*] *hôsautôs echein*) commonly used by (Plato's) Socrates himself.

b1 THEAETETUS: 'Yes, that is what we say.'

VISITOR: 'And this "dealing with" – what are we to claim you paragons to be saying it is, in both cases? Isn't it what we said just now?'

THEAETETUS: 'And what was that?'

b5 VISITOR: 'Being acted on or acting on, as a result of some capacity from the things coming together one with another.' Now perhaps, Theaetetus, you're not catching their answer to this, but I hear it perhaps because I'm familiar with it.

THEAETETUS: So what account do they give of themselves?

c1 VISITOR: They don't go along with us on what we just said about being to the earth-born.

THEAETETUS: Which was what?

VISITOR: I think we proposed that it was a sufficient mark of some-

c5 thing that is that it should have the capacity either for being acted on, or for acting on, even in relation to the slightest thing?

THEAETETUS: Yes.

VISITOR: Well, their response to that proposal is that what is *coming into being* shares in a capacity for being acted on and acting on, but a capacity for either does not fit, they claim, with *being* –

c10 THEAETETUS: So is that nonsense?

d1 VISITOR: ... to which we should respond that we still need greater clarity from them as to whether they agree that the soul knows and that being is something that is known.

THEAETETUS: They certainly claim that!

VISITOR: 'Well then,' I say to them, 'do you claim that knowing or

d5 being known is acting on or being acted on or both? Or that one of them is a case of being acted on, the other of acting on? Or are you claiming that neither of them has any share whatever in either?'

THEAETETUS: It's clear that neither shares in either, for them; otherwise they would be contradicting what they said before.

d10 VISITOR: I understand this much,[78] that if knowing is going to be a

e1 case of doing something, it necessarily follows that when something is known it in turn is having something done to it; and that therefore by this argument when being is known by knowledge, insofar as it is being known, it is to that extent being changed, namely through the fact of its

---

[78] Reading *tode* in place of the OCT's *to de ge*.*

having something done to it, which is something we say could not happen in relation to what is at rest. e5

THEAETETUS: Correct.

VISITOR: But – Zeus! – what is this? Are we in any case going to be so easily persuaded that change and life and soul and wisdom are truly absent from what completely is, and that it does not live, or think, but sits 249a there in august holiness, devoid of intelligence, fixed and unchanging?

THEAETETUS: That would be a quite shocking account of things for us to accept, stranger.

VISITOR: But are we to say that it has intelligence, but not life?

THEAETETUS: How could that be? a5

VISITOR: But do we say that it has both of these in it, and deny that it has a soul in which to have them?

THEAETETUS: How else could it have them?

VISITOR: But do we then say that it is in possession of intelligence and life and soul, but nevertheless stands there, with a soul but entirely a10 unchanging?

THEAETETUS: All of this appears to me unaccountable. b1

VISITOR: Then one must accept that what changes, and change, are also things that are.

THEAETETUS: Obviously one must.

VISITOR: In any case, Theaetetus, it follows from what we have said b5 that if things are unchanging[79] no one possesses any intelligence about any of them at all.

THEAETETUS: Quite definitely.

VISITOR: And yet if on the other hand we accept that all things are in motion and changing, this account of things too will result in our removing knowability from the things that are. b10

THEAETETUS: How?

VISITOR: Does it seem to you that without *rest* anything could ever come to remain exactly as it is, and in relation to the same thing? c1

THEAETETUS: Not at all.

VISITOR: Well, do you see any way whatever that without these conditions there could be, or come to be, intelligence about anything whatever?

---

[79] Omitting the *pantôn* added in the OCT.*

c5 THEAETETUS: Hardly.

VISITOR: And we must certainly use every argument at our disposal to see off anyone who persists in eliminating knowledge or wisdom or intelligence about anything, in whatever way he does it.

THEAETETUS: Yes, we certainly must.

c10 VISITOR: For the philosopher, then, who puts the highest value on these things,[80] it seems an absolute requirement, because of them, both

d1 to refuse to accept that everything is at rest, whether from those who say everything is one or from those who say it is the plurality of forms,[81] and to refuse to give a hearing at all to people who will do anything and everything to bring change to what is. The answer they should give instead, like children when asked to choose, is both: both what is and the all are constituted by everything *both* unchanging *and* changing.

d5 THEAETETUS: Very true.

VISITOR: Well then, don't we pretty well appear to have captured what is, now, in our account?

THEAETETUS: We certainly do.

VISITOR: But wait a minute there,[82] Theaetetus! I think we're now about to realize the true difficulty of inquiring into the subject.

e1 THEAETETUS: But how? Why?

VISITOR: My dear friend, don't you see that as things stand we're in the greatest ignorance about it, even while we appear to ourselves to be making sense?

THEAETETUS: We appear so to me, and if we really are as ignorant

e5 about it as you say, I don't quite understand how we've not noticed.

VISITOR: Then think more clearly whether what we're currently

250a agreeing to won't leave us open to the very questions we were putting to the people who say that everything is hot and cold.

THEAETETUS: What questions? Remind me.

a5 VISITOR: Certainly, and I'll try to do it by asking you the same questions I asked them, so that we can make a bit of progress at the same time.

---

[80] That is, as lovers, *philoi*, of wisdom, *sophia*.

[81] In the case of the latter group, 'everything' presumably has to be read as 'everything that is', since they accept, unlike the other group, that there is change, only not in 'what is' (248a); but after all, we are still in the process of examining what both groups say about being (see 245e–246a), and that they do restrict to forms.

[82] Omitting the *ou* inserted in the OCT before *ment'ara*.*

THEAETETUS: Quite right.

VISITOR: Very good. You treat change and rest, don't you, as very much opposed to each other?

THEAETETUS: Of course. a10

VISITOR: And yet you make the same claim of both and of either of them that they are?

THEAETETUS: Yes, I do. b1

VISITOR: Is that because when you agree that they are, you're saying that both and either of them are changing?

THEAETETUS: Not at all.

VISITOR: Well then, when you say that they both are, are you indicat- b5 ing that they're at rest?

THEAETETUS: How would I be?

VISITOR: In that case in your mind you're assuming that being is a third thing over and above these, on the basis that both rest and change are embraced by it; you've taken the two of them together and noted the b10 way they both share in being, and that's why you also say they both are – right?

THEAETETUS: It's probably true that when we say change and rest are c1 we have an obscure notion of being as a third thing.

VISITOR: In which case being is not change and rest together but something other than these.

THEAETETUS: It seems so. c5

VISITOR: So then being is not by its own nature either at rest or changing.

THEAETETUS: I suppose not.

VISITOR: So where else is left for a person to direct his thought in order to establish some clarity for himself on the subject?

THEAETETUS: Where indeed!

VISITOR: I don't think there is any easy way forward. If a thing is not changing, how is it not at rest? Or if it is in no way at rest, how is it not d1 changing? Yet being has now revealed itself to us as falling outside *both* change *and* rest. Is that possible, then?

THEAETETUS: No, nothing could be more impossible!

VISITOR: Well, in this connection we should remind ourselves of d5 something.

THEAETETUS: Which is?

VISITOR: That when asked what, exactly, one should attach the name 'what is not' to, we found ourselves totally puzzled, with no way out. You remember?

THEAETETUS: How could I not?

e1 VISITOR: So is the puzzle we're now in, about what is, any less extreme?

THEAETETUS: To me, stranger, if it's possible to say it, the one we're now in is greater.

e5 VISITOR: So let this be our account of the issues that are puzzling us. And since what is and what is not have turned out to be equally puzzling, the hope now must be that in whichever way one or the other of them reveals itself to us, whether with a lesser or a greater degree of clarity,

251a so the other will too; and if we're not able to get a sight of either of them, we will at any rate put on the best show we can as we thus push our way through[83] our account of both of them simultaneously.

THEAETETUS: Fine.

a5 VISITOR: So let's discuss how exactly it is that we keep calling this very same thing[84] by many names.

THEAETETUS: Such as what? Give an example.

VISITOR: We refer to an individual human being, surely, by calling

a10 him all sorts of things, applying colours to him, shapes, sizes, and different varieties of badness and goodness; in all of which cases, and tens

b1 of thousands of others, we are not only claiming him to be a human being, but also good and an unlimited number of other things. By the same account we treat everything else similarly – positing each thing as one, then proceeding to use many names of it and thus treating it as many.

b5 THEAETETUS: True.

VISITOR: Yes, and by so doing I think we've prepared a veritable feast for the young and for old late-learners, because it makes it all too easy for anyone to latch on to the idea that it's impossible for the many to be one or the one to be many – and then, would you believe, they delight in not

c1 allowing us to say a human is good, only that the good is good and the human is a human. I imagine, Theaetetus, that you often encounter individuals who are in earnest about this sort of thing; older people,

---

[83] Retaining the manuscript reading *diôsometha* in place of the OCT's *diakribôsometha*.*

[84] 'This', presumably, is 'what is' (or being), which is still the main topic. The question now being raised is the general one about how we can say many things of one and the same thing.

sometimes, who are impressed by such things because of the poverty of
their intellectual resources, and indeed suppose this discovery of theirs c5
the very key to wisdom.[85]

THEAETETUS: I certainly do.

VISITOR: So in order to include in our discussion anyone and everyone who has expressed a view about being, whatever it might be, let what d1
we're about to say now be put as questions both to the people we've just
described and to those we've talked to before.

THEAETETUS: And what will this be?

VISITOR: 'Are we to refuse to attach either being to change and rest or d5
anything at all to anything else at all, but to treat them in our discussions
as being unmixed, regarding it as impossible for them to share in each
other, or are we to collect them all together as being capable of combining with one another? Or are we to treat some as capable of it, some as e1
not?' How exactly are we going to say they choose among these alternatives, Theaetetus?

THEAETETUS: I've no idea how to answer that question for them!

VISITOR: So why not answer bit by bit, by considering the conse- e5
quences of each alternative in turn?

THEAETETUS: A good suggestion.

VISITOR: Right, so let's suppose them to say first, if you like, that
nothing has any capacity for combining to any extent with anything at
all. 'So', we'll ask them, 'are change and rest not going to share in being e10
in any way?'

THEAETETUS: 'No, they are not.' 252a

VISITOR: 'What then? Will either of them be, if it does not combine
with being?'

THEAETETUS: 'They will not.'

VISITOR: In a single moment, then, it seems, with this admission a5
everything is turned upside down, whether for those who have everything changing, for those who bring it to a rest by making it one, or
for those who reduce the things that are to forms that remain forever
exactly as they are; for all of these people add in *being*, some of them

---

[85] Antisthenes may be one of the thinkers referred to here (see Introduction, Section 6). He is
certainly reported as having held a theory at least resembling the one just described (contradiction is impossible, he claimed, because all that can be said about anything is what 'belongs', is
oikeios, to it).

a10 saying that things really are changing, the others saying they really
are at rest.

THEAETETUS: They certainly do.

b1 VISITOR: And what about those too who put all things together at one
time and divide them at another, whether it's an unlimited number of
elements being united into one and then derived from one, or whether
it's a limited number they're dividing into and putting things together
from – no matter whether they posit the two processes as occurring

b5 alternately or going on all the time? All of this would be nonsense if
nothing is actually capable of mixing with anything else.

THEAETETUS: Quite correct.

VISITOR: And then there are those who won't allow anything to be
called something else by reason of its sharing in some attribute; for them

b10 to pursue *their* argument will be the greatest absurdity of all.

c1 THEAETETUS: How so?

VISITOR: They're forced, presumably, to use the words 'is', 'separate',
'from everything', 'by itself', and myriad others when talking about

c5 anything. Powerless as they are to hold back and not apply them in their
arguments, they don't need others to refute them; they have their own
proverbial enemy within to oppose them, muttering away inside as if
they carried the bizarre Eurycles[86] around with them.

d1 THEAETETUS: The analogy is exactly right.

VISITOR: What, then, if we allow everything to be capable of combining with everything else?

THEAETETUS: This alternative even I can dispose of.

d5 VISITOR: How?

THEAETETUS: Because change would come to a complete rest, and
conversely rest would itself change, if they could actually supervene on
each other.

VISITOR: But this, I presume you're saying, is necessarily an utter

d10 impossibility – that change should come to a rest and rest should be
found changing?

THEAETETUS: Of course.

VISITOR: The third alternative, then, is the only one left.

THEAETETUS: Yes.

---

[86] A ventriloquist, among other things, who is mentioned in Aristophanes.

VISITOR: And moreover, one of the three *must* hold: either everything must mix, or nothing can, or some things will mix and some won't.   e1

THEAETETUS: Of course.

VISITOR: And the first two of them we found to be an impossibility.

THEAETETUS: Yes.   e5

VISITOR: In that case anyone who wants to answer correctly will propose the remaining one of the three.

THEAETETUS: Yes, absolutely.

VISITOR: So, if some things will mix and some won't, it will be pretty much with them as it is with the letters of the alphabet. These too have the feature that some of them fit together in one way or another, while others don't.   253a

THEAETETUS: Of course.

VISITOR: But the vowels, now: they differ from the other letters, running through them all and serving like a bond between them, so that without a vowel it's impossible for any of the others to fit together either.   a5

THEAETETUS: Very much so.

VISITOR: So does everybody know which sorts of letters are capable of combining with others, or does it require expertise for someone to do it satisfactorily?

THEAETETUS: It requires expertise.   a10

VISITOR: What sort of expertise?

THEAETETUS: Expertise in letters.

VISITOR: What about the sounds of high and low notes in music? Isn't it the same in their case? The person with the expertise to recognize those that mix and those that do not is an expert in music, is he not, and the one who can't do it is non-musical?   b1

THEAETETUS: Just so.   b5

VISITOR: And we'll get other similar results if we look at any other case of expertise and the lack of it.

THEAETETUS: Obviously.

VISITOR: So then given that we've agreed that kinds too mix in such ways as these,[87] must a person not have some sort of expertise to progress in his arguments if he is going to show correctly which sorts of kinds are in harmony with which and which are not receptive to each   b10   c1

[87] Reading *kata ta toiauta* instead of the OCT's *kata tauta* [= *ta auta*].*

other, and further, whether there are some that hold them together, running through them in such a way as to make them capable of mixing; and again, in cases where they divide off, whether there are others similarly running through them all that cause the division?

c5   THEAETETUS: Yes! He certainly will need expertise – pretty much the most important one of all, probably.

VISITOR: So what are we going to call this expertise, Theaetetus? Or – Zeus! – have we stumbled, without noticing, on the very expertise that makes a person free? Can we possibly, in searching for the sophist, actually have found the philosopher first?

c10   THEAETETUS: What makes you say that?

d1   VISITOR: Are we not going to claim that dividing according to kinds, and not thinking either that the same form is different or, when it is different, that it is the same, belongs to expertise in dialectic?

THEAETETUS: Yes, we will claim that.

d5   VISITOR: The person who can do this is then surely well enough equipped to see when one form is spread all through many,[88] each of them standing separately, or when many forms that are different from one another are embraced from the outside by one; or again when one is connected as one through many forms, themselves wholes, or when many forms are

e1   completely divided off and separate. This is all a matter of knowing how to determine, kind by kind, how things can or cannot combine.

THEAETETUS: Absolutely right.

VISITOR: And this matter of dialectic you'll not, I think, attribute to

e5   anyone but the philosopher, with his pure and justified love of wisdom.

THEAETETUS: It surely belongs to nobody but him.

VISITOR: So it's in some such a place as this that we will find the philosopher, whether now or if we look for him at a later date; it's difficult

254a   to get a clear sight of him, too, but in a different way – the difficulty with the sophist isn't the same as the difficulty with the philosopher.

THEAETETUS: How so?

a5   VISITOR: The sophist runs off into the darkness of what is not, practised as he is at cultivating the murk; he is made difficult to spot by the obscurity of the region. Right?

---

[88] As expertise in acquisition, e.g., was 'spread through' the 'whole form that has to do with learning and coming to know, ... the money-making [form], and ... those that have to do with competing and hunting' (219c).

THEAETETUS: It seems likely.

VISITOR: Whereas with the philosopher, because he is always engaged through reasonings with the form of what is, it is rather the brightness of the landscape that makes him so very hard to discern; for the eyes of the soul, in the case of ordinary people, are unable to endure looking towards the divine.   a10
                                                                                     b1

THEAETETUS: That too is no less likely than what you last said.

VISITOR: Well, we'll look into the philosopher in more detail soon enough, if that's still our wish, but on the sophist, I think it's clear we mustn't let up until we have a proper sight of him.   b5

THEAETETUS: Quite right.

VISITOR: So then, now that we have agreed that some kinds are ready to combine with each other, others not, some a little, others a lot, and   b10
that some, even, are perfectly capable of being in combination with all   c1
and through all, the next thing is for us to follow up this part of our argument by asking the following – not about all the forms, in case we get confused by talking about too many at once, but choosing out some of those reckoned to be the greatest:[89] first, what each of them is like, and   c5
then how they stand when it comes to their capacity to combine with each other. The aim, even if we prove unable to grasp what is and is not with complete clarity, will be at least not to leave ourselves in any way short of things to say about them, so far as the mode of our present inquiry permits, and to see whether there may after all somehow be room   d1
for us to say of what is not that it really *is* what is not, and get away unscathed.

THEAETETUS: Yes, that is what we must do.

VISITOR: Greatest, certainly, of the kinds we have just been talking about are this very one, namely being itself,[90] and rest and change.   d5

THEAETETUS: Yes, much the greatest.

VISITOR: And now two of the three we say are, themselves, unmixed with each other.

THEAETETUS: We do, emphatically.

VISITOR: Whereas being is mixed with both of them, since both of   d10
them presumably are.

---

[89] 'Greatest': most important, or simply most extensive? (Cf. 229b.)
[90] I.e., 'what is, itself' (*to on*); 'being' is substituted for *to on* here and in the following exchanges, for the sake of euphony and, probably, intelligibility.

THEAETETUS: Obviously so.

VISITOR: So they make three.

THEAETETUS: Of course.

d15 VISITOR: So each of them is different from the other two, but itself the same as itself.

e1 THEAETETUS: Just so.

VISITOR: What then about the things we're speaking of now, when we talk like this – the same and the different? Are these two more kinds, other than the three we already have, yet always necessarily mixing with

e5 them; and should we inquire into them on the assumption that there are

255a five kinds, not three? Or are we referring to one of the three with this talk of 'the same' and 'the different', and just not noticing?

THEAETETUS: Possibly.

a5 VISITOR: But change and rest certainly aren't either difference or sameness.

THEAETETUS: How so?

VISITOR: If we attribute something in common to both change and rest, neither of them can actually be that thing.

THEAETETUS: Obviously.

a10 VISITOR: Change will come to a rest and rest in its turn will change, since in both cases, that is to say, whichever of them becomes difference,

b1 that will force the other to change to the opposite of its own nature, insofar as it will have come to share in that opposite.[91]

THEAETETUS: Quite so.

VISITOR: Both certainly share in sameness and difference.

THEAETETUS: Yes, they do.

b5 VISITOR: Then let us not say that change, at any rate, is sameness or difference, or that rest is, either.

THEAETETUS: No, let's not.

VISITOR: But should we be thinking of being and sameness as one thing?

b10 THEAETETUS: Possibly.

VISITOR: But again, if 'is' and 'same' don't indicate anything distinct,

c1 when we come to say that change and rest both are, we'll be talking about them both as if they were the same thing.

---

[91] Suppose change to be difference: rest, being already different from change, will then be characterized by change as well as difference.

THEAETETUS: And that is certainly impossible.

VISITOR: In which case it's impossible for sameness and being to be one.

THEAETETUS: Pretty much.   c5

VISITOR: Are we then to posit sameness as a fourth form, over and above the three we already had?

THEAETETUS: Yes, absolutely.

VISITOR: What about difference? Should we say it's a fifth form? Or should we think of this and being[92] simply as two names for one kind?   c10

THEAETETUS: Perhaps we should.

VISITOR: But I think you agree that of the things that are, some are spoken of in and by themselves, while others are always spoken of in   c15 relation to others.

THEAETETUS: Why would I not?

VISITOR: And that difference is one of the latter – right?   d1

THEAETETUS: Just so.

VISITOR: It would not be, if being and difference were not very much distinct. If difference shared in both forms[93] in the way that being does,   d5 then among the differents, too, there would be a different that was not in relation to something else, whereas as things are we find that whatever is different simply cannot fail to be what it is, namely different, in relation to something else.

THEAETETUS: Yes, as you say.

VISITOR: The nature[94] of the different, then, we're to treat as being fifth among the forms we're singling out.   e1

THEAETETUS: Yes.

VISITOR: And moreover we're going to say that it is a nature that pervades them all; for each one of them is different from the rest not through its own nature, but rather through its sharing in this other form,   e5 difference.

THEAETETUS: Yes, quite so.

VISITOR: So let us say the following, taking each of the five in turn.

THEAETETUS: What, exactly?   e10

---

[92] The Greek still has *to on* (see n.90).

[93] I.e., both the forms just mentioned of things that are: the one that is spoken of in and by itself, and the one always spoken of in relation to others.

[94] I.e., *phusis*, used alongside *eidos* ('form') later in the present sentence, and evidently interchangeable with it (see Introduction, Section 2).

157

VISITOR: Of change, first, that it is something completely different from rest – or what do we say about it?

THEAETETUS: Just that.

VISITOR: In which case it is not rest.

e15 THEAETETUS: It certainly is not.

256a VISITOR: And yet it *is*, because of its sharing in being.

THEAETETUS: Yes, it is.

VISITOR: But then again change is something different from sameness.

THEAETETUS: I suppose so.

a5 VISITOR: In which case it is not sameness.

THEAETETUS: No, it is not.

VISITOR: And yet we said this *was* the same, because, again, they all have a share in sameness.[95]

THEAETETUS: Very much so.

a10 VISITOR: One needn't get upset, then, about having to concede that change is both the same and not the same, since we are not saying it is

b1 the same in the way we're saying it is not the same. When we say it is the same, we say it because it shares in sameness in relation to itself, whereas when we say it is not the same we say it this time because of its association with difference, because of which it separates off from sameness and becomes not that but different, so that here it is correct to speak of it as not the same.

b5 THEAETETUS: Right, absolutely.

VISITOR: If even change itself, then, somehow had a share in rest, there would be nothing strange about describing it as being at rest?

THEAETETUS: It would be quite correct, given that we're going to

b10 allow that some of the kinds will mix with one another and some not.

c1 VISITOR: And actually we arrived at the proof of this earlier in our discussion – we tested it, and it's in the nature of things to be that way.

THEAETETUS: Yes, clearly.

VISITOR: So then let's continue with our account: change is a different

c5 thing from difference, just as it was something other than sameness and rest?

THEAETETUS: Necessarily.

---

[95] I.e., in being the same as themselves (as the Visitor goes on to explain). The text translated here is *hautê ... pant'autou*, as against the OCT's *hautêi ... pan tautou.**

VISITOR: According to our present account, then, it is something that is in a way not different and different.

THEAETETUS: True.

VISITOR: So what is the next step? Are we going to say that it is different from three of our kinds, and then deny it is different from the fourth – when we've agreed that the ones about which and among which we proposed to investigate are actually five?

c10

d1

THEAETETUS: How can we? It's impossible to allow their number to be smaller than it was shown to be just now.

VISITOR: Then we're going to be fearless in defending our position that change is a different thing from being?[96]

d5

THEAETETUS: Yes, quite fearless.

VISITOR: It's clear, then, that change really is something that is not – and something that is, given that it shares in being?

THEAETETUS: Very clear.

d10

VISITOR: What is not, then, must necessarily be, both in the case of change and with all the kinds, because with all of them, the nature of the different, by rendering each a different thing from being, makes it something that is not; and in fact in accordance with this same reasoning we'll be correct in talking of all of them too as things that are not – and then again, since they share in being, in saying that they are, and talking of them as things that are.

e1

THEAETETUS: Probably.

e5

VISITOR: In relation to each of the forms, then, there is a lot of what is, and an unlimited quantity of what is not.[97]

THEAETETUS: It seems so.

VISITOR: And even what is, itself, has to be said to be different from the others.

257a

THEAETETUS: Necessarily.

VISITOR: So even what is is not, as many times over as there are other forms; not being them, it is the one thing it is, itself, but conversely it is not all the unlimited number of others.

a5

---

[96] The Greek still has *to on* (see nn.90 and 92 above).

[97] 'A lot of what is': i.e., of being; here, in view of the renewed juxtaposition of *to on* with *to mê on*, 'what is not', the translation is forced to go back to the more awkward, but more literal, rendering 'what is'. (One could render 'what is not', itself, as 'not-being', but after all one of the chief purposes of the discussion has been to show that 'what is not is', which looks an impossible combination, is not only possible but necessary; 'not-being is' tends to look just odd.)

THEAETETUS: I dare say.

VISITOR: So this shouldn't upset us, either, once given that it is the nature of kinds to combine with one another. If anyone refuses to concede this, he'll need to persuade our previous arguments first before he persuades us out of what follows from them.

a10

THEAETETUS: That's perfectly fair.

b1 VISITOR: So let's look at the following point.

THEAETETUS: Which is what?

VISITOR: When we say something is not, it seems, we're not saying that it is the opposite of what is, we're just saying it is different.

b5 THEAETETUS: How so?

VISITOR: To illustrate, when we say 'not big', does our use of the expression appear to you to indicate the small any more than the equal?

THEAETETUS: Of course not.

VISITOR: So when a negation is uttered we will not concede that it

b10 signals an opposite, but only this much, that 'not' and 'not-' when

c1 prefixed tothe names that follow them point to something other than those names – or rather other than the things to which the names following the negation relate.

THEAETETUS: I completely agree.

c5 VISITOR: And let us think about the following point, if you're agreeable.

THEAETETUS: What point?

VISITOR: The nature of difference appears to me to be cut up into pieces, just like knowledge.

THEAETETUS: How so?

c10 VISITOR: Knowledge too, I suppose, is one, but each part of it relating

d1 to a particular thing is marked off and carries a particular name that is peculiar to itself; which is why there are many sorts of things called expertise and knowledge.

THEAETETUS: Quite so.

d5 VISITOR: Well, the nature[98] of difference is one, too, and has parts, and the same thing is true of them.

THEAETETUS: Perhaps so, but can we spell it out?

VISITOR: Is there a particular part of difference that is contraposed to the beautiful?

[98] For this use of 'nature', see n.94 above.

THEAETETUS: There is.

VISITOR: So shall we treat this as nameless, or as having a particular name?

THEAETETUS: As having a name, since when we utter the words 'not beautiful' in relation to something, on each occasion that something is different from the nature of the beautiful and nothing else.   d10

VISITOR: So come on, tell me this –

THEAETETUS: What?   e1

VISITOR: Is this not how the not beautiful turns out to be – as a distinct part of one particular kind from among the things that are, contraposed to some other particular item from among these?

THEAETETUS: Right.   e5

VISITOR: So the not beautiful turns out, it seems, to be a sort of contraposition of a thing that is in relation to another thing that is.

THEAETETUS: Quite right.

VISITOR: What then? By this reckoning, are we treating the beautiful as   e10 belonging more to the things that are, the not beautiful as belonging less?

THEAETETUS: Not at all.

VISITOR: In that case we're to say that the not big and the big itself   258a both are to the same degree?

THEAETETUS: Yes.

VISITOR: The not just, then, too, is to be treated in the same way as the just, if we're asked whether one of them is to any greater degree than   a5 the other?

THEAETETUS: Of course.

VISITOR: So we'll talk about the rest like this too, given that the nature of difference has shown itself to belong to the things that are, and given that, as a consequence of its own being, we must necessarily treat its parts too as being, no less than anything else.

THEAETETUS: Obviously.   a10

VISITOR: Well then, it seems that the contraposition one to another of the nature of a part of difference, on the one hand, and of the contrasting   b1 part of the nature of what is on the other, is no less a case of being, if one dare say it, than what is, itself,[99] because it does not signal something opposite to it, only something different from it.

---

[99] I.e., being itself; 'being', a few words earlier, is *ousia*, the noun.

b5   THEAETETUS: Quite clearly.

VISITOR: So what name are we to give it?

THEAETETUS: Clearly it's the very thing, 'what is not', that we were looking for in our search for the sophist.

VISITOR: So is it the case, as you said, that it does not lag behind any of the other natures in relation to being, and that by now we should have confidence about saying that what is not is securely in possession of its

c1   own nature – so that just as the big was big and the beautiful was beautiful, the not big not big and the not beautiful not beautiful, so too what is not not only was but is what is not, a single form numbered among the many things that are? Or are we still a bit hesitant to believe it,

c5   Theaetetus?

THEAETETUS: Not at all.

VISITOR: So do you realize that our disbelief of Parmenides has taken us beyond his prohibition?

THEAETETUS: How so?

c10   VISITOR: We have shown him more than he forbade us to look into, pushing still further on with our investigation.

THEAETETUS: How?

d1   VISITOR: Because he says, I think, 'For never shall this prevail, that things that are not are; / I tell you, keep back your thought from this path of inquiry.'

THEAETETUS: Yes, he does say that.

d5   VISITOR: Whereas we have not only shown that what is not is, but have declared what the form of what is not actually is; for having shown

e1   up the nature of difference as something that is, cut up into pieces over all the things that are in their relationships with each other, we took our courage in our hands and said of the part of it that is contraposed to the what is of each thing[100] that *it* was the very thing that what is not really is.

THEAETETUS: Yes, stranger, and what we have said seems to be as

e5   completely true as it could be.

VISITOR: So let no one accuse us of having the temerity to declare that what is not is the *opposite* of being and then say that it is. We have long

259a   since waved goodbye to talking about any opposite to being, no matter

---

[100] Reading *hekastou* for the OCT's *hekaston*.*

whether it is or is not, or whether an account can be given of it or it is completely unaccountable.[101] As for what we have now said that what is not is, either someone needs to challenge us and persuade us that what we're saying is not well said, or so long as he is incapable of doing that, he too will have to talk in the same terms as us, and say both that the kinds mix with one another, and that since what is a5 and difference pervade them all and one another, difference, with its share in what is, *is*, because of that sharing, while at the same time it is certainly not what it has that share in, but rather something different from it; and since it is different from what is, he'll have to say that it is in the clearest conceivable way necessary for it to be possible for b1 it to be what is not. What is, for its part, because of the share it has in difference, will be different from the other kinds, and in being different from all of them it is not each of them, nor all the rest together, only itself, so that what is, in its turn, indisputably is not myriads b5 upon myriads of things. Similarly the other kinds, whether taken one by one or all together, in many respects are and in many respects are not.

THEAETETUS: True.

VISITOR: And if anyone is not persuaded of these oppositions, he'll b10 have to investigate the matter himself and find something to say that improves on what we have now said; or if he thinks he has spotted a c1 problem, and delights in pulling the arguments now in one direction and now in the other, our own current arguments say he'll be attending to things not worth attending to much at all. What he's doing is neither subtle nor difficult to find out about; whereas the other thing – now that c5 *is* difficult, and a fine thing too.

THEAETETUS: What other thing?

VISITOR: What we talked about before: the ability, once one has conceded that these things are possible,[102] to follow up what is being said, so that every time someone claims that a thing is the same when it is different or different when it is the same one can challenge him with regard to the way and the respect in which he is claiming it to be one or d1 the other. To claim the same to be different, the different the same, the

---

[101] Cf. 238c with note.
[102] I.e., the things referred to as 'these oppositions' in the Visitor's previous contribution (reading *hôs dunata* instead of the OCT's *hôs <panti> dunata*).*

big small or the like unlike in any old way, and delight in this sort of
d5 thing, forever countering with opposites in one's arguments – that is no
sort of true challenge, and is clearly the first baby steps of someone only
just now beginning to get to grips with things as they are.[103]

THEAETETUS: Precisely so.

VISITOR: Yes, my friend, for certainly trying to separate off everything
e1 from everything not only strikes the wrong note in other respects, but
above all is the mark of a completely uncultivated and unphilosophical
person.

THEAETETUS: Why so?

VISITOR: If one separates each thing off from everything, that completely and utterly obliterates any discourse, since it is the interweaving
of forms that gives us the possibility of talking to each other in the
first place.

THEAETETUS: True.

260a VISITOR: So think how opportune it is that we are fighting it out with
people like that, and compelling them to permit one form to mix with
another.

THEAETETUS: Opportune in what way?

a5 VISITOR: So that we can have speech as one of the kinds among the
things that are. The most important consequence, if we were to be
deprived of this, is that we'd be deprived of philosophy; but also, in
the present context, one of our tasks must be to reach agreement about
what speech is, and if it had been taken from us, so as not even to be at
b1 all, I suppose we'd not be able to say anything further. But it would
indeed have been taken from us, had we conceded that there was no
mixing of anything with anything.

THEAETETUS: That much is certainly right. But I don't understand
why we now have to reach agreement about speech.

b5 VISITOR: Maybe you'll understand most easily if I take you along
this path.

THEAETETUS: Which path?

VISITOR: We found what is not showing up as one particular kind
among the rest, dispersed over all the things that are.

THEAETETUS: We did.

[103] Cf. 234d.

VISITOR: Well, the next thing is to examine whether it mixes with both belief and speech. b10

THEAETETUS: Why so?

VISITOR: If it doesn't mix with them everything is necessarily true, c1 whereas if it does, then belief can be false and so can speech, since presumably believing and saying things that are not is precisely what falsehood is when it occurs in thought and speech.

THEAETETUS: It is. c5

VISITOR: But if there is falsehood, there is deception.

THEAETETUS: Yes.

VISITOR: And then again, as soon as there is deception, then everything will inevitably be full of images and likenesses and appearance.

THEAETETUS: Obviously. c10

VISITOR: But now I think it was this region we connected with the sophist – we said he had hidden from us here, but was in denial about d1 falsehood's even being at all, for according to him a person neither thinks nor says what is not, because what is not has no share at all or in any way in being.

THEAETETUS: We did say that.

VISITOR: Whereas actually, as we have seen, what is not clearly does d5 share in what is, so perhaps he'll give up fighting this particular battle. Perhaps he'll claim that some of the forms share in what is not but some do not, and speech and belief actually belong among those that don't – so that then he would come back at us by saying that since there is no association between belief or speech and what is not, the things in which e1 we located him, likeness-making and apparition-making, themselves completely are not; for without such an association being set up, there can be no falsehood at all. So that's why there's a need to track down speech first, along with belief and appearance, and find out what they e5 are, in order that, once they've come into view, one may actually observe their association with what is not; then, having observed that, one can go 261a on to show falsehood to be something that is, and finally, having shown that, chain the sophist up in it, if he is guilty as charged, or if he is not guilty, release him and start looking for him in some other kind.

THEAETETUS: It does seem, stranger, that what we said about the a5 sophist at the outset was quite true, and it really is difficult to hunt down his kind. He appears to have a whole series of devices to shield himself with, which we have to fight our way past, one by one, before we can get to the man himself. Thus we've just struggled our way through the defence he

a10 put up to the effect that what is not, is not, only to find he's put up another,
b1 so that now we're having to show that falsehood is, both in relation to speech and in relation to belief. After this he'll probably put up another, and then another after that, and it seems there'll never be an end to it.

VISITOR: There is no need to be discouraged, Theaetetus, if one can
b5 move even a few steps forward each time. If you lose heart in these conditions, what would you do in others, where you're either making no progress at all or have even been pushed backwards? Behave like that and
c1 it would surely be hard, as the proverb says, ever to capture the city. As things are, my friend, since we've got as far as you say we have, I dare say we'll find we've already captured the main wall, and the rest will turn out to be easier and not so high.

c5 THEAETETUS: Fine.

VISITOR: Then let's first take speech and belief, as we said just now, so that we can work out more clearly whether they are touched by what is not, or whether both of them are wholly true and neither is ever false.

c10 THEAETETUS: Right.

d1 VISITOR: So come on, let's use the same approach again as we did in relation to forms and letters,[104] this time asking about names. I'm glimpsing what we're looking for somewhere in that direction.

THEAETETUS: What is it, then, that we're supposed to understand about names?

d5 VISITOR: Whether all of them fit together with each other, or none of them do, or some will and some won't.

THEAETETUS: The answer to *that* is clear enough! Some will, some won't.

VISITOR: Probably this is the sort of thing you're saying, that if they
e1 point to something when they're said one after another they fit together, and if they don't indicate anything by being put in sequence they don't fit together.

THEAETETUS: How so? What is this you're saying?

VISITOR: Only what I thought you were supposing when you agreed
e5 with me. I imagine the indicators we give voice to in relation to being[105] are a twofold kind.

THEAETETUS: How so?

262a VISITOR: Part of it is names, part what are called verbs.

---

[104] See 252–3. [105] *Ousia.*

THEAETETUS: Tell me about each of them.

VISITOR: The part that is an indicator in the case of actions I think we call a verb.

THEAETETUS: Yes.   a5

VISITOR: Whereas what our voice signals in the case of the things that actually do those actions we call a name.

THEAETETUS: Quite.

VISITOR: Well now, no speech is ever formed from names alone being   a10 uttered one after another, and neither is it if verbs have been strung together without names.

THEAETETUS: I don't understand.

VISITOR: Clearly you must have had something else in mind when you   b1 went along with me just now. The point I wanted to make was exactly this, that simply stringing names or verbs together like this doesn't constitute speech.

THEAETETUS: Like how?

VISITOR: For example, 'walks runs sleeps', and the other verbs that   b5 signal actions – even if someone says all of them in succession, it won't make them the slightest bit more into speech.

THEAETETUS: No, of course not.

VISITOR: Then again, if one says 'lion stag horse', and all the names   b10 there are of things that do the actions, that collection of words doesn't   c1 yet constitute speech either, since no more in this case than in the other does what has been voiced indicate action, or lack of action, or the being of something that is, or of something that is not, nor will it until someone starts blending the verbs with the names. Then they fit together, and   c5 their first interweaving is at once speech, almost its most elementary and smallest manifestation.

THEAETETUS: So why do you say that?

VISITOR: When people say 'human understands', do you claim this as speech, at its smallest and most elementary?   c10

THEAETETUS: Yes, I do.   d1

VISITOR: Presumably because it is now giving an indication of things that are or are coming into being, or have come into being or are going to; they are not merely naming but accomplishing something, by weaving together verbs with nouns. That is why we described them as *saying*, not   d5 just as naming, and why we used the name 'speech' for this combination.

THEAETETUS: And rightly.

VISITOR: Thus, just as we found things themselves in some cases fitting together, in others not,[106] so too in relation to the signs we voice –
e1 some of them do not fit together, but those of them that do fit together bring about speech.

THEAETETUS: Absolutely.

VISITOR: There's still this other small point.

e5 THEAETETUS: What is that?

VISITOR: Speech, when there is speech, must necessarily say something *of* something; it's impossible for it to say something of nothing.

THEAETETUS: Agreed.

VISITOR: And must it not also be of a certain sort?

e10 THEAETETUS: Obviously.

VISITOR: Then let's turn our attention to each other.

THEAETETUS: We certainly should!

VISITOR: So I'm going to say something to you, putting together a thing with an action using name and verb. You're to tell me what exactly
e15 the speech is speaking of.

263a THEAETETUS: I'll do it as best I can.

VISITOR: 'Theaetetus sits.' There, that wasn't a long speech, was it?

THEAETETUS: No, not too long!

a5 VISITOR: Your task is to tell me what it's speaking about and of what.

THEAETETUS: Clearly, it's about me and of me.

VISITOR: And what about this one?

THEAETETUS: What one?

VISITOR: 'Theaetetus, with whom I'm presently conversing, flies.'

a10 THEAETETUS: Nobody could possibly claim anything else about this one either – it's of me and about me.

VISITOR: But now we say that each and every instance of speech must necessarily be of a certain sort.

b1 THEAETETUS: Yes.

VISITOR: So of what sort must each of our two be declared to be?

THEAETETUS: The second, presumably, false, the first true.

VISITOR: And the true one says the things that are, as they are, about
b5 you.

THEAETETUS: Obviously.

---

[106] Presumably a reference to the earlier discovery that some forms fit together, some not.

VISITOR: Whereas the false one says things that are different from those that are.

THEAETETUS: Yes.

VISITOR: In which case it says the things that are not as if they are.[107]

THEAETETUS: Pretty much.   b10

VISITOR: And yet what it says are things that are, just different things that are from those that are about you; for we said, I think, that there are many things that are about each and every thing, and many that are not.

THEAETETUS: Quite so.

VISITOR: Now as for this second bit of speech I uttered about you, the   c1
first point, given what we laid down about what speech is, is that it is necessarily one of the shortest examples there could be.

THEAETETUS: Just now, certainly, we did agree about that.

VISITOR: And the second point is that it is necessarily *of* something.   c5

THEAETETUS: Agreed.

VISITOR: But if it is not of you, it is certainly not of anybody or anything else.

THEAETETUS: It could hardly be.

VISITOR: And if it was of nothing, it would not even be speech at all;
for we showed it to be an impossibility for it to be speech and speech of   c10
nothing.

THEAETETUS: And quite correctly so.

VISITOR: When things are said about *you*, then, but different things as   d1
if the same, and things that are not as if they are – that definitely seems to be the sort of combination of verbs and names that turns out really and truly to be false speech.

THEAETETUS: Yes, very true.   d5

VISITOR: So what about thought and belief and appearance? Isn't it clear by now that all these kinds come about in our souls as false as well as true?

THEAETETUS: How so?

VISITOR: You'll see the point more easily if you first grasp what these   d10
things are and what the difference is between each of them.   e1

THEAETETUS: Please show me.

---

[107] The echoes of the Protagorean 'measure' doctrine in these lines (a human being is the measure 'of the things that are, that they are, and of the things that are not, that they are not', *Theaetetus* 152a) is clear enough, as are the differences between the position they state and that of the arch-sophist Protagoras.

VISITOR: Well, thought and speech are the same thing, with just this difference, that the first is an internal dialogue of the soul with itself that occurs without vocal expression, which is why it has the name we call it by.[108]

e5

THEAETETUS: Quite.

VISITOR: Whereas the stream that passes from the soul through the mouth together with sound is called speech.

THEAETETUS: True.

e10 VISITOR: And again, we see that any sort of speech contains –

THEAETETUS: What?

VISITOR: Assertion and denial.

THEAETETUS: We do.

264a VISITOR: Well, when this occurs in the soul as thought, and in silence, do you have any name for it except belief?

THEAETETUS: How would I?

VISITOR: And what if it presents itself to someone not by itself but through perception? When that happens, can it correctly be called anything other than appearance?

a5

THEAETETUS: It can't.

VISITOR: Given, then, that we found there to be true and false speech, and of the things we're discussing thought revealed itself as a dialogue of a soul with itself, while belief was completion of thought, and what we describe as something's 'appearing' to us was a combination of perception and belief, then it follows necessarily, since these things – thoughts, beliefs, and appearance – are related by kind[109] to speech, that sometimes some of them too will be false.

b1

b5 THEAETETUS: They will, clearly.

VISITOR: So do you realize that we've found false belief and speech sooner than we were expecting to, just now, fearing as we did then that in looking for them we were taking on a completely hopeless task.

b10 THEAETETUS: I do.

VISITOR: So let us not be pessimistic about the other things we're looking for either. Now that we're clear about these matters, let's remind ourselves of our previous divisions by forms.

c1

---

[108] I.e., thought, *dianoia*, which the Visitor perhaps pretends to get from *dia*(*logos*) *an*(*eu phônês*), 'dialogue without voice'.*

[109] I.e., *sungenê*.

THEAETETUS: Which ones?

VISITOR: We distinguished[110] two forms of image-making, likeness-making and apparition-making.

THEAETETUS: Yes.

VISITOR: And we said we were puzzled as to which of the two, likeness-making or apparition-making, we were going to put the sophist in.

THEAETETUS: We did.

VISITOR: And while we were puzzling about that a still greater dizziness descended on us, with the appearance of the argument disputing whether there could be such a thing as a likeness or an image or an apparition at all, because, it said, there was no way there could ever be any falsehood anywhere.

THEAETETUS: True.

VISITOR: Now, however, since speech has clearly shown itself to be capable of being false, and so too belief, it *is* possible both for there to be imitations of the things that are, and for this to give rise to expertise in deception.[111]

THEAETETUS: It is.

VISITOR: And moreover it was previously agreed between us that the the sophist belongs to one or the other of the things in question.

THEAETETUS: Yes.

VISITOR: So let's try our hand once more. Splitting in two any kind that presents itself to us, we'll try to proceed by way of the right-hand part of what we have cut on each occasion, sticking to whatever company the sophist keeps, until we have taken away everything that he has in common with others and thus left his own peculiar nature revealed, firstly for our own benefit, but then also for the benefit of those naturally closest in kind to this sort of procedure.[112]

THEAETETUS: Right.

VISITOR: So, when we began, didn't we divide productive and acquisitive expertise from one another?

c5

c10

d1

d5

d10

e1

265a

a5

---

[110] See 235d.

[111] I.e., expertise in making false imitations – what has just been called 'apparition-making'.

[112] Presumably those to whom the Visitor attributed 'expertise in dialectic' in 253d–254a, and identified as philosophers. See Introduction, Section 7, where this passage is compared with what Socrates says at *Phaedrus* 266b–c; perhaps, then, the Visitor (or rather the author, Plato) has one particular philosopher in mind – Socrates.

THEAETETUS: Yes.

VISITOR: And in the acquisitive, we found the sophist appearing in the hunting part, the combative, the part to do with export–import, and some such forms as these?

THEAETETUS: Absolutely.

a10 VISITOR: But now that it's an expertise in *imitation* that has embraced
b1 him, we clearly need to divide productive expertise itself before we do anything else. I take it that imitation is a sort of production, but always of images, as we're saying,[113] not of the things themselves. Right?

THEAETETUS: Absolutely.

VISITOR: First of all, then, let there be two parts of productive expertise.

b5 THEAETETUS: Which are they?

VISITOR: One divine, the other human.

THEAETETUS: I don't quite understand.

VISITOR: We called productive, if you recall what was said at the
b10 beginning, any capacity that turns out to cause things to come into being that were not before.

THEAETETUS: I do recall.

c1 VISITOR: Well, all mortal creatures, plants too, all of them that grow upon the earth from seeds and roots, and all those inanimate bodies that are formed in the earth, whether fusible or not – surely we won't claim that they come into being, after not being before, through the
c5 crafting[114] of some other agency than god? Or, using what ordinary people believe and say –

THEAETETUS: Which is what?

VISITOR: That nature begets them from some cause that brings them to birth spontaneously, without thought. Or is it after all from a cause
c10 coming from god, in the company of reason and divine knowledge?

d1 THEAETETUS: Perhaps it's because of my age, but I find myself frequently switching between both views. Now, certainly, looking at your case, and assuming you think that they come into being at least in conformity with god, I take that view myself too.

---

[113] See 234c.
[114] The verb is *dêmiourgein*, which brings to mind the Divine Craftsman (*dêmiourgos*) of the *Timaeus*.

VISITOR: That's excellent, Theaetetus. If I thought you were one of those who would take some other sort of view in the future, I would now be trying to make you agree to what I'm saying with persuasion you couldn't refuse. But since I know your nature, and that even without arguments from me it will come over of its own accord to the view you say you're drawn to now, I'll let that go – it would not be time well spent. What I shall do is to assume that things said to come about by nature are produced by divine expertise, and those put together from these by human beings are produced by human expertise; by which reckoning we have two kinds of productive expertise, one human and one divine. d5

e1

e5

THEAETETUS: Right.

VISITOR: So, there being two of them, cut each again into two.

THEAETETUS: How?

VISITOR: You've cut the whole of productive expertise across its width, as it were; now do the same lengthwise. 266a

THEAETETUS: Consider it done.

VISITOR: This way there turn out to be four parts of it in all, two from our side, the human, and two divine, from the gods' side. a5

THEAETETUS: Yes.

VISITOR: And to go back now to the ones we've divided the other way,[115] one part of each of these two sections we'll say has to do with producing the things themselves, while the remaining two may perhaps best be called image-producing; and so this way productive expertise is again divided into two.[116] a10

THEAETETUS: Tell me again how each is divided. b1

VISITOR: We ourselves, presumably, the other creatures, and the constituents of things that are born and grow – fire, water, and their kin: all of them we presumably recognize as engendered by god, each his finished product. Or how would you put it? b5

THEAETETUS: Like that.

VISITOR: But then corresponding to each of these there are images that are not the things themselves, these too the product of superhuman contrivance.

---

[115] I.e., 'lengthwise'.

[116] The Visitor is still answering Theaetetus' 'How?' in 265e – not well enough, to go by the latter's immediate response.

THEAETETUS: What are these?

b10 VISITOR: Those that appear to us in dreams, and those daytime appearances that are said to be self-generated: a shadow, when a patch

c1 of darkness occurs in firelight, or a double when the light from one's own eye and the light from something else combine as one around bright, smooth surfaces and produce a shape offering a perception of the thing which is the opposite of the way it used to be seen before.

c5 THEAETETUS: So these are two outcomes of divine production, the thing itself and the image corresponding to it in each case.

VISITOR: And what of our own expertise? Won't we say we make an actual house with building expertise, while with painting we make another sort of house, a sort of man-made dream created for people in their waking hours?

d1 THEAETETUS: Absolutely.

VISITOR: And similarly there are two in every other case, the twofold outcome of our own productive activity: the thing itself, we're saying, resulting from expertise in making actual things, and its image, resulting from image-making expertise.

d5 THEAETETUS: Now I understand better. I take it there are two forms of productive expertise to be distinguished in two different ways: divine and human productive expertise according to one cut, while according to the other cut some of it is of things themselves, some a begetting of resemblances of some sort.

VISITOR: And let's remind ourselves that of image-working expertise

d10 some was going to relate to likenesses, while some was to constitute a

e1 kind to do with apparitions, if falsehood were to show itself as really being falsehood, and as being one of the things that are.

THEAETETUS: Yes, that was what we proposed.

VISITOR: Well, did it turn out like that, and shall we therefore count

e5 them as now indisputably two forms?

THEAETETUS: Yes.

267a VISITOR: So let's divide apparition-making into two again.

THEAETETUS: How?

VISITOR: By distinguishing some of it as coming about through the use of tools, some where the very maker of the apparition provides himself as the tool.

a5 THEAETETUS: What are you saying?

VISITOR: I think when someone uses his own body or voice to make your shape or voice appear much like his own, this aspect of apparition-making is what we mostly tend to call imitation.

THEAETETUS: Yes.

VISITOR: Then let's call this aspect of it 'imitative', and locate it accordingly; as for all the rest of it, let's indulge ourselves and leave it to one side for someone else to collect it together as a single whole and give it some appropriate name. a10 / b1

THEAETETUS: Consider that all done.

VISITOR: But it's worth thinking of this imitative aspect too, Theaetetus, still as twofold; see why this is so. b5

THEAETETUS: Go on.

VISITOR: Some imitators do it knowing the thing they're imitating, others without knowing it. And yet, what greater division shall we suppose there to be than that between ignorance and knowledge?

THEAETETUS: None. b10

VISITOR: Now the example just mentioned[117] was one of knowledgeable imitation, was it not? After all it's when someone knows your shape, and you, that he'll imitate you.

THEAETETUS: Obviously. c1

VISITOR: But what about the shape of justice, and of goodness taken together as a whole? Don't lots of people who are ignorant but have some sort of belief about it try hard to be eager about making it appear that they have what they believe it to be, imitating it as closely as they can in what they do and say? c5

THEAETETUS: Lots and lots.

VISITOR: And are they all unsuccessful at seeming to be just when they are not so at all? Or is it the exact opposite of this?

THEAETETUS: The exact opposite.

VISITOR: We have to say, I think, that this imitator is quite different from the other, the ignorant one from the knowing. d1

THEAETETUS: Yes.

VISITOR: So where will one find a suitable name for each of them? Or is it clearly a difficult thing to do? It seems our predecessors have shown a long-established and unconscionable slackness about dividing the kinds d5

---

[117] I.e., in 267a.

according to forms, so that none of them has even tried to divide them, and the inevitable result is that we're not tremendously well off for names. All the same, for the sake of being able to tell things apart, even

e1 if it's a rather outrageous invention, let's call imitation accompanied by belief 'belief-imitative' imitation, and imitation accompanied by knowledge a sort of scientific imitation.

THEAETETUS: Let's do that.

e5 VISITOR: So what we need to use now is the first, since the sophist, we found, was certainly not among those who know, though he was certainly among the imitators.

THEAETETUS: Very much so.

VISITOR: So let's examine the belief-imitator as if he were a piece of iron, to see whether he's sound or whether he still has a crack of some sort in him.

e10 THEAETETUS: Let's do that.

VISITOR: Well, there's an absolutely gaping one. One of the belief-
268a imitators is simple-minded, thinking the things he believes are things he knows, whereas the figure presented by the other sort, because his arguments are continually rolling him this way and that, is that of someone who strongly suspects and fears that the very things he's presented himself to everybody else as knowing he actually doesn't know.

a5 THEAETETUS: There certainly is something corresponding to each of the two kinds you describe.

VISITOR: So shall we put one of them down as a sincere sort of imitator, the other as a dissembling[118] imitator?

THEAETETUS: That certainly seems reasonable.

a10 VISITOR: And again, are we to say there is one kind of this latter, or two?

THEAETETUS: You look and see.

b1 VISITOR: I am looking, and there do appear to me to be two kinds: I see one who is able to dissemble before large numbers of people in public and with long speeches, and another who operates in private and uses short

b5 speeches to compel the person talking to him to contradict himself.

THEAETETUS: You're quite right.

---

[118] I.e., *eirônikos*: clearly related to, but only partly overlapping in sense with, our 'ironic'.

VISITOR: So what should we declare the longer-winded one to be? An expert in statesmanship, or in demagoguery?

THEAETETUS: In demagoguery.

VISITOR: And what shall we call the other one? A wise person, or an expert in sophistry?   b10

THEAETETUS: To call him wise is presumably impossible, given that we put him down as not knowing; but being an imitator of the wise   c1 person, clearly he'll get a name derived from his – and I think I've finally pretty much gathered that this is the person we must call truly the very one that is wholly genuinely a sophist.

VISITOR: So shall we tie his name together, as before, by weaving it   c5 together from start to finish?

THEAETETUS: Yes, certainly.

VISITOR: The expert in imitation, then, belonging to the contradiction-producing half of the dissembling part of belief-based expertise, the word-conjuring part of the apparition-making kind from image-making, a   d1 human sort of production marked off from its divine counterpart – if someone says that the one who is 'of this family kind, of this blood'[119] is the real sophist, it seems his account will be the truest.

THEAETETUS: Yes, definitely.

---

[119] A reference to Homer, *Iliad* 6.211. In Homer, the reference is to family only; the Visitor puns on Homer's word for family (*genea*) and 'kind', *genos*.

Further notes on the text

Theaetetus

149d The text as transmitted seems to be possible Greek (*neon on* = 'it/ the embryo [?] being new/young'), and to give a not unreasonable sense. As becomes clear from his next contribution, Socrates is talking as much about some ideal of a midwife as about actual midwives: he suggests, to Theaetetus' surprise, and probably everybody else's, that the midwife will be an expert matchmaker, 'versatile at telling which woman needs to marry which man to produce the best children possible'. A reference to 'the early stages' suggests one situation where she might perform an abortion, namely when the wrong woman has conceived with the wrong man (that would, of course, be clear to her as soon as the woman is seen to be pregnant; no need to wait). This is not unlike what the Socratic 'midwife' will try to do – that is, eliminate bad 'offspring'/ideas at the earliest opportunity (see *Republic* II.372, where Socrates may endorse abortion, to prevent overpopulation; infanticide for eugenic reasons at V.460c?).

152c The text as transmitted here has been doubted by editors, who wonder whether we should read *d'ar'* instead of *gar*. On *d'ar'*: this would probably make the sentence look forward rather than backwards: 'And actually . . .', which would be picked up in Socrates' next contribution. On *gar*: Socrates is busy claiming that perception can be substituted for appearance in 'how *x* appears to me is how *x* is for me'. Having concluded, in the last sentence, that appearance and perception are the same, at least in some cases, he now points out that in fact things are, or 'are likely to be', for us as we perceive them to be – which supports the conclusion just reached. (Some editors choose to read *g'ar'*, another option that may be offered by part of the tradition; this would, if anything, appear to make the sentence it introduces the conclusion of an argument, but it is not clear what that argument might be.) Since *gar* is also much better attested than *d'ar'*, the OCT is right to keep it.

155b The *alla* as printed by editors makes no sense. It may very well represent a corruption of an original *allo* (as proposed by Denis O'Brien); but given the difficulty of construing the sentence even with *allo*, perhaps *allo* was itself originally a gloss (i.e., supplying 'other' in order to avoid ambiguity).

156d W. F. Hicken, one of the editors of the OCT, suggested supplying – *exempli gratia* – the words *heteran tên kinêsin kinoumena* after *gennômena*; this seems roughly right.

167c The manuscript reading must be wrong, since it would give us a noun linked by 'both ... and ...' to an adjective (*aisthêseis te kai alêtheis*); but even if this difficulty could be finessed, it is scarcely possible – *pace* the editors of the OCT – that, having just firmly declared that in his view no 'appearance' is truer than any other, Protagoras could now be supposed to be saying that some 'sound and healthy' perceptions (which for him will be the same as 'appearances') are after all true – even if they are the 'perceptions' of plants. In addition to being palaeographically plausible, 'truths' (*alêtheias*), proposed in place of *alêtheis* by Schleiermacher, would suggest a thoroughly Protagorean point: all perceptions are true, so that any perception will be a truth; 'sound and healthy' truths can then be opposed to unsound and unhealthy ones.

175c Some have recently adopted Madvig's suggestion that we should read *taü chrusion* for *t'au chrusion*, giving the sense '*much* gold'. One problem with this is that the word Socrates uses for 'gold' is – at least in origin – a diminutive.

179a The text printed in the OCT – that is, keeping *mê*, and omitting the *hautôi* found in the manuscripts – gives the sense 'if he didn't try to persuade the people who came to him that ... neither a seer nor anyone else would be a better judge than he [i.e., Protagoras] was'. Both this solution to the problems presented by the sentence and the solution offered in the translation make good sense, but the reading adopted by the OCT involves a more radical change to the text, and forces the reader to pass over the *kai* in *kai to mellon*, in lines 2–3 ('in relation to what is going to be and seem, *too*').

180e   There is, admittedly, only the smallest support in the textual tradition for replacing *telethei* with *te thelei* (see the critical apparatus to the OCT), but (a) *telethein* generally functions as a substitute for *einai*, and there seems to be no parallel for its being used with an infinitive (let alone *einai*), so that it is hard to imagine Plato so using it; (b) for what it is worth, *akinêton* is followed by *te* in the Parmenidean lines he is – apparently – misquoting, or reproducing in metrical paraphrase; and (c) the text as printed in the OCT is quite possibly unconstruable.

189c   The *ti* added by the OCT in this sentence, after *hotan tis*, makes better sense, and is more palaeographically plausible, than the *anti tinos* supplied by Burnyeat to resolve the same textual problem.

Sophist

239a   The reading adopted by the OCT is an elegant emendation (by Cornford), but is not only unnecessary but unacceptable, since both before and after this line the Visitor is criticizing his own statement that what is not is 'unsayable, inexpressible and unaccountable' (238c); to read *to to* would be to suppose him to be going back to a point already made.

240b   The OCT's reading, *ouk ontôs on*, would give us 'not something that really is', which fits rather less well with the argument than *ouk ontôs ouk on* (with the first *ouk* taken as interrogative); the sequence is *alêthinon – ontôs on/mê alêthinon – ontos ouk on*. (This reading is also better attested.)

241a   What the OCT prints (omitting *aphthengkta kai arrêta kai aloga kai adianoêta*) seems barely intelligible; quite what Plato wrote remains in some doubt, but the general sense is clear enough.

241e   The OCT's *mête elenchthentôn* would give us 'neither disproved/ refuted', making 'these things' refer to Parmenides' claim; in fact, this claim will stand, if interpreted in terms of what *in no way* is (cf. 237b). So *mête lechthentôn*, which is, in any case, the better attested, is surely to be preferred.

245b   The *holôi* is well attested, and unproblematical if we take the reference to be the same as that of 'the correct argument' in the Visitor's last sentence – that 'correct argument' being, by implication, the argument he and Theaetetus have been presenting.

247e   The addition of *dein* seems to make a difficult (and perhaps corrupt) sentence more difficult rather than easier to construe.

248d The main manuscripts have *to de*, which makes little sense; *to de ge* is suggested in one manuscript, but hardly seems an improvement, given the difficulty of construing it, and *tode* seems the most economical solution.

249b The addition of *pantôn* is unnecessary, if the point is taken as a general one: anything that is completely unchanging will be completely unknowable (given what has just been said).

249d The text is clearly corrupt here, but the *ou*, supplied by an editor, does not obviously improve matters. The general sense is, in any case, clear enough.

251a The reading of the manuscripts, *diôsometha*, makes good enough sense, if understood as proposed ('we'll force our way through'), not to require emendation, and *diakribôsometha*, 'we'll examine in detail', seems actually to fit the context rather less well.

253b The reading *kata ta toiauta* is preferable insofar as the Visitor has no reason to suggest that the mode of mixing in the case of kinds is actually the same as (*kata tauta* [= *ta auta*]), rather than merely similar to (*kata ta toiauta*), that of the mixing of letters and of musical notes; indeed part of the question he is about to ask, in the continuation of the present sentence, is whether it *is* the same.

256a The reading *hautê* ... *pant'autou* is in all the manuscripts, while *hautêi* ... *pan tautou* is one of several emendations proposed by editors; none of the latter, however ingenious or palaeographically plausible, is an obvious improvement, though admittedly there is something a bit odd about the 'this'.

258e The reading *hekastou* is not only much better attested than *hekaston*, but gives a much richer sense.

259c The reading *hôs* <*panti*> *dunata* would give us the sense 'once one has said goodbye to these things as things anyone could do', which is possible, but unnecessary, given that the text transmitted by the manuscripts can be understood as proposed.

263e The printing of *dianoia* at the end of the sentence as *dia noia*, by the editors of the OCT, perhaps suggests that they have a different solution in mind.

Index

Cambridge texts in the history of philosophy

Titles published in the series thus far

Aquinas *Disputed Questions on the Virtues* (edited by E. M. Atkins and Thomas Williams)

Aquinas *Summa Theologiae, Questions on God* (edited by Brian Davies and Brian Leftow)

Aristotle *Eudemian Ethics* (edited by Brad Inwood and Raphael Woolf)

Aristotle *Nicomachean Ethics*, revised edition (edited by Roger Crisp)

Arnauld and Nicole *Logic or the Art of Thinking* (edited by Jill Vance Buroker)

Augustine *On the Free Choice of the Will, On Grace and Free Choice, and Other Writings* (edited by Peter King)

Augustine *On the Trinity* (edited by Gareth Matthews)

Bacon *The New Organon* (edited by Lisa Jardine and Michael Silverthorne)

Berkeley *Philosophical Writings* (edited by Desmond M. Clarke)

Boyle *A Free Enquiry into the Vulgarly Received Notion of Nature* (edited by Edward B. Davis and Michael Hunter)

Bruno *Cause, Principle and Unity* and *Essays on Magic* (edited by Richard Blackwell and Robert de Lucca, with an introduction by Alfonso Ingegno)

Cavendish *Observations upon Experimental Philosophy* (edited by Eileen O'Neill)

Cicero *On Moral Ends* (edited by Julia Annas, translated by Raphael Woolf)

Clarke *A Demonstration of the Being and Attributes of God and Other Writings* (edited by Ezio Vailati)

Classic and Romantic German Aesthetics (edited by J. M. Bernstein)

Condillac *Essay on the Origin of Human Knowledge* (edited by Hans Aarsleff)

Conway *The Principles of the Most Ancient and Modern Philosophy* (edited by Allison P. Coudert and Taylor Corse)

Cudworth *A Treatise Concerning Eternal and Immutable Morality* with *A Treatise of Freewill* (edited by Sarah Hutton)

Descartes *Meditations on First Philosophy, with Selections from the Objections and Replies* (edited by John Cottingham)

Descartes *The World and Other Writings* (edited by Stephen Gaukroger)

Fichte *Attempt at a Critique of All Revelation* (edited by Allen Wood, translated by Garrett Green)

Fichte *Foundations of Natural Right* (edited by Frederick Neuhouser, translated by Michael Baur)

Fichte *The System of Ethics* (edited by Daniel Breazeale and Günter Zöller)

Greek and Roman Aesthetics (edited by Oleg V. Bychkov and Anne Sheppard)

Hamann *Philosophical Writings* (edited by Kenneth Haynes)

Heine *On the History of Religion and Philosophy in Germany and Other Writings* (edited by Terry Pinkard, translated by Howard Pollack-Milgate)

Herder *Philosophical Writings* (edited by Michael Forster)

Hobbes and Bramhall on Liberty and Necessity (edited by Vere Chappell)

Nietzsche *Daybreak* (edited by Maudemarie Clark and Brian Leiter, translated by R. J. Hollingdale)

Nietzsche *The Gay Science* (edited by Bernard Williams, translated by Josefine Nauckhoff)

Nietzsche *Human, All Too Human* (translated by R. J. Hollingdale, with an introduction by Richard Schacht)

Nietzsche *Thus Spoke Zarathustra* (edited by Adrian Del Caro and Robert B. Pippin)

Nietzsche *Untimely Meditations* (edited by Daniel Breazeale, translated by R. J. Hollingdale)

Nietzsche *Writings from the Early Notebooks* (edited by Raymond Geuss and Alexander Nehamas, translated by Ladislaus Löb)

Nietzsche *Writings from the Late Notebooks* (edited by Rüdiger Bittner, translated by Kate Sturge)

Novalis *Fichte Studies* (edited by Jane Kneller)

Plato *Meno* and *Phaedo* (edited by David Sedley and Alex Long)

Plato *The Symposium* (edited by M. C. Howatson and Frisbee C. C. Sheffield)

Plato *Theaetetus* and *Sophist* (edited by Christopher Rowe)

Reinhold *Letters on the Kantian Philosophy* (edited by Karl Ameriks, translated by James Hebbeler)

Schleiermacher *Hermeneutics and Criticism* (edited by Andrew Bowie)

Schleiermacher *Lectures on Philosophical Ethics* (edited by Robert Louden, translated by Louise Adey Huish)

Schleiermacher *On Religion: Speeches to its Cultured Despisers* (edited by Richard Crouter)

Schopenhauer *Prize Essay on the Freedom of the Will* (edited by Günter Zöller)

Sextus Empiricus *Against the Logicians* (edited by Richard Bett)

Sextus Empiricus *Outlines of Scepticism* (edited by Julia Annas and Jonathan Barnes)

Shaftesbury *Characteristics of Men, Manners, Opinions, Times* (edited by Lawrence Klein)

Adam Smith *The Theory of Moral Sentiments* (edited by Knud Haakonssen)

Spinoza *Theological-Political Treatise* (edited by Jonathan Israel, translated by Michael Silverthorne and Jonathan Israel)

Voltaire *Treatise on Tolerance and Other Writings* (edited by Simon Harvey)